# THE BRITISH CENTURY

# THE
# BRITISH CENTURY

*A photographic history of the last hundred years*

## BRIAN MOYNAHAN

Photographs researched and
edited by Sarah Jackson and
Annabel Merullo

SEVEN DIALS

For Sam, Chiara and Thomas  A.M. & S.J.
For Harold Stiles  B.M.

First published in 1997 by George Weidenfeld & Nicolson

This paperback edition first published in 1999 by
Seven Dials, Cassell & Co.
The Orion Publishing Group
Wellington House, 125 Strand
London, WC2R 0BB

Copyright © Endeavour Group UK, 1997
This book was created, designed and produced by the Endeavour Group, UK,
12a Colville Mews, London, W11 2DA

A CIP catalogue record for this book is available
from the British Library

ISBN 1 84188 002 7

PROJECT MANAGER: Annabel Merrullo
PICTURE RESEARCH: Sarah Jackson & Annabel Merrullo
EDITOR: Roger Hudson
EDITORIAL ASSISTANT: Cassandra Wilson
DESIGN: Paul Welti
PRODUCTION: Robert Gray
TYPESETTING: Peter Howard
TYPESET IN: Monotype Bembo
ORIGINATION BY: Zincografica, Bologna, Italy
PRINTED BY: Nuovo Insituto Italiano d'Arti
Grafiche SpA, Bergamo, Italy

# CONTENTS

# EDITOR'S NOTE

The photographs reproduced in this book are the result of extensive research in archives, museums and private collections throughout Great Britain. The original idea for this series came from Harold Evans of Random House, Inc., and we are most grateful for his continued support and guidance. The Hulton Getty Collection has once again proved to be an inspirational source of photographs and original negatives, providing us with prints of exceptional quality. We are also greatly indebted to all those kind people who willingly offered us their expertise and advice and we would particularly like to thank:

Nicky Akehurst; Terry Barranger, Royal Commonwealth Society Library; John Benton-Harris; Lord Brabourne, and the Trustees of The Broadlands Archive; Dr Christopher Woolgar, University of Southampton Library; Jane Carmichael and Ian Carter, Imperial War Museum; Danny Chau; Zelda Cheatle and Gareth Abbott, Zelda Cheatle Gallery; Lydia Cresswell-Jones, Sotheby's, London; Hamish Crooks, Magnum; Frances Dimond, The Royal Archives, Windsor Castle; Bobby Hanvey; Debbie Ireland, Royal Photographic Society, Bath; Joanna Scadden, Royal Geographical Society; Ken Lennox, The Sun Newspaper; Hildegarde Mahoney, Photographer's Gallery; Leon Meyer and Roger Syring, Hulton Getty; Tony Money, Radley College; Alastair Morrison; Andrew Morton; Michael Nash; Vincent Page; Terence Pepper, National Portrait Gallery; Michael Rand; David Sandison, The Independent on Sunday; Michael Shaw; Annie Trehearne; Sutcliffe Gallery, Whitby; Sebastian Wormell, AlFayed Archive.

We owe a special debt of thanks to the following photographers and their families who often spent hours in attics rummaging through old boxes and filing cabinets to search out rare images:

Bruce Bernard; Jane Bown; John Chillingworth; Philip Goodman, Lady Ottoline Morrell Collection; Sheila Hardy; Nick Hedges; Paul Hill; Charles Hopkinson; Sara Jones; Michael Joseph; Jorge Lewinski; Don McCullin; Grace Robertson; Jinx Rodger; Humphrey Spender; Wolf Suschitzky; Michael Ward; David Wedgbury; Bryan Wharton.

Photographers' names, when known, are credited in the captions. The sources of the photographs are listed in the acknowledgements on page 300.

*First page: Women's pub outing, 1954.* [PHOTO: GRACE ROBERTSON]

*Preceding four pages: Panoramic view of Scarborough, Yorkshire, 1913.* [PHOTO: A. H. ROBINSON]

*The music-hall star Gracie Fields (right), whose signature tune was 'Sally', sings to building workers after laying the foundation stone of the Prince of Wales Theatre, London, in 1937.*

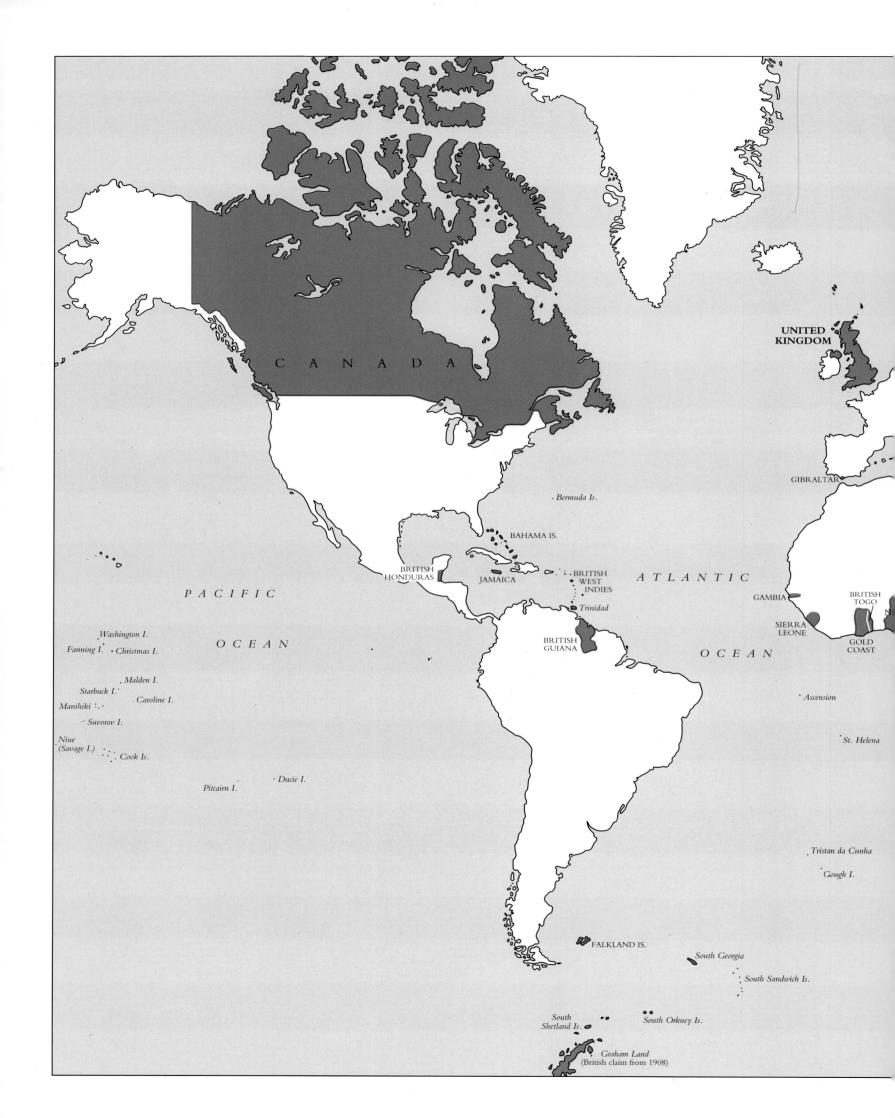

UNITED
KINGDOM

CANADA

GIBRALTAR

· Bermuda Is.

·· BAHAMA IS.

BRITISH
HONDURAS
JAMAICA

BRITISH
WEST
INDIES

*ATLANTIC*

GAMBIA

BRITISH
TOGO

SIERRA
LEONE

*Trinidad*

GOLD
COAST

*PACIFIC*

*Washington I.*

*Fanning I.* · *Christmas I.*

BRITISH
GUIANA

*OCEAN*

*OCEAN*

*Ascension*

*Malden I.*

*Starbuck I.*

*Manihiki* ·· · *Caroline I.*

· *Suvorov I.*

*St. Helena*

*Niue*
*(Savage I.)* ·· · *Cook Is.*

*Pitcairn I.* · *Ducie I.*

*Tristan da Cunha*

*Gough I.*

FALKLAND IS.

*South Georgia*

*South Sandwich Is.*

*South*
*Shetland Is.*

*South Orkney Is.*

*Graham Land*
(British claim from 1908)

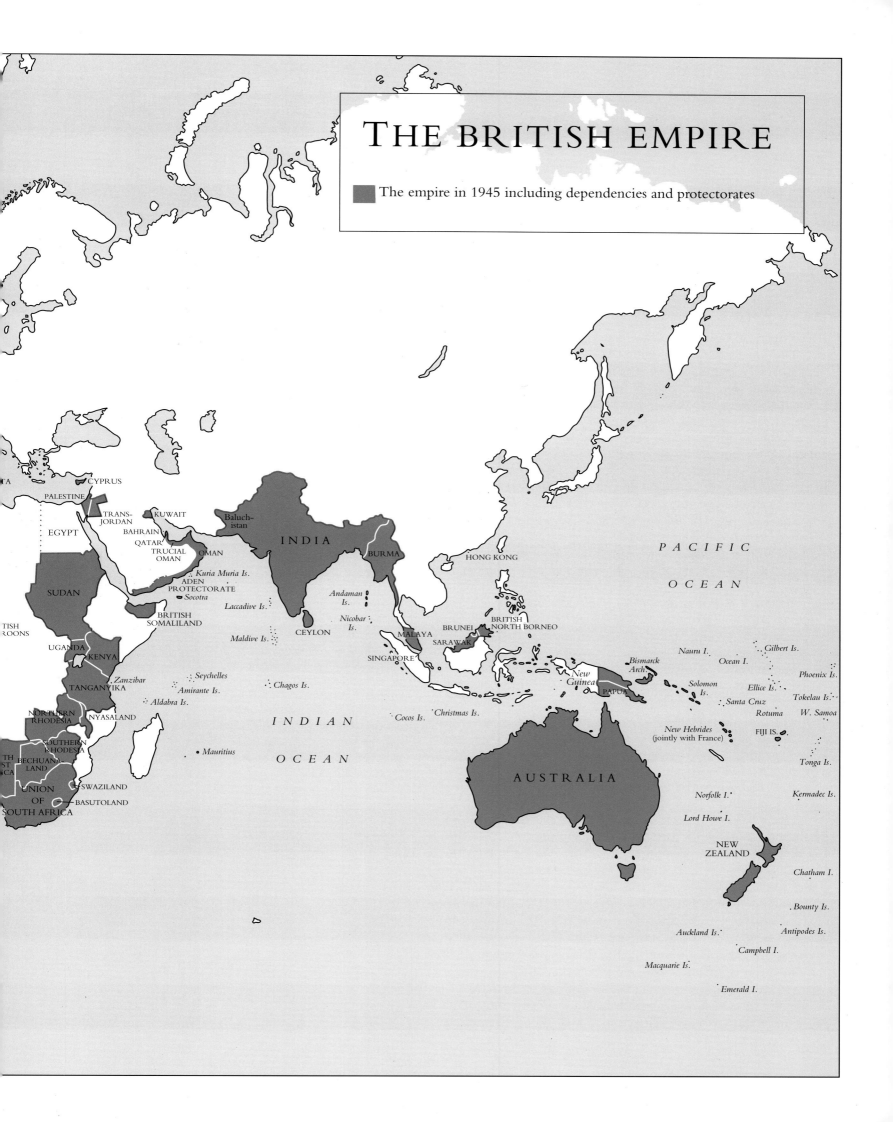

# THE BRITISH EMPIRE

The empire in 1945 including dependencies and protectorates

CYPRUS
PALESTINE
TRANS-JORDAN
KUWAIT
Baluch-istan
EGYPT
BAHRAIN
QATAR
TRUCIAL OMAN
OMAN
INDIA
BURMA
HONG KONG
PACIFIC OCEAN
Kuria Muria Is.
ADEN PROTECTORATE
Socotra
SUDAN
Andaman Is.
Laccadive Is.
BRITISH SOMALILAND
Nicobar Is.
TISH ROONS
Maldive Is.
CEYLON
MALAYA
BRUNEI
BRITISH NORTH BORNEO
UGANDA
KENYA
SINGAPORE
SARAWAK
Nauru I.
Ocean I.
Gilbert Is.
Seychelles
Chagos Is.
Bismarck Arch.
TANGANYIKA
Zanzibar
Amirante Is.
New Guinea
Solomon Is.
Phoenix Is.
Aldabra Is.
Santa Cruz
Ellice Is.
Tokelau Is.
NORTHERN RHODESIA
NYASALAND
Cocos Is.
Christmas Is.
PAPUA
Rotuma
W. Samoa
INDIAN
New Hebrides (jointly with France)
FIJI IS.
SOUTHERN RHODESIA
Mauritius
OCEAN
Tonga Is.
TH ST CA
BECHUANA-LAND
SWAZILAND
AUSTRALIA
Norfolk I.
Kermadec Is.
UNION OF SOUTH AFRICA
BASUTOLAND
Lord Howe I.
NEW ZEALAND
Chatham I.
Bounty Is.
Auckland Is.
Antipodes Is.
Campbell I.
Macquarie Is.
Emerald I.

## CHAPTER ONE

# 'GOD HELP US ALL'

I N THE DYING MONTHS OF THE OLD CENTURY, THE Queen began to founder. It is natural to think of her end as a shipwreck, for it was largely through the sea that the British projected their power, and often by means of voyages that they satisfied their abundant curiosity. It was after his travels as naturalist aboard *HMS Beagle* that Charles Darwin had laid out the evolution of man in his great work *The Origin of Species by Means of Natural Selection*. The British had little doubt that they had been naturally selected to lead.

The evidence, a grudging world admitted, appeared to support this immodest claim. The Queen and her country so dominated the age that it had come to bear her name, Victorian. She was the first monarch to undergo vaccination against smallpox, and the first to ease the pains of childbirth with chloroform, both British discoveries; the first to travel by railway, an equally home-grown invention, from Slough to Paddington in 1842; the first to send an intercontinental cable, from Windsor to Canada. She ruled one in four of all living souls, scattered over a quarter of the land surface of the globe.

She had ruled for more than sixty years, and she had not always been loved. She had worn mourning since her husband, Prince Albert, had died in 1861; his clothes still hung in the closets in his dressing room, his bed was turned down each night and his chamber pot was scrubbed in the morning as if he had used it. For twenty years, she had remained secluded in her palaces, and her remoteness from her people was deeply resented. Her empire had grown at an average rate of 100,000 square miles, an area equivalent to Britain itself, each year throughout the century; she had visited none of it. The lofty title of Empress of India, which she had taken at the prompting of her favourite prime minister, Benjamin Disraeli, was mocked by William Gladstone, the premier she most disliked, for its 'fictitious and tawdry lustre'. The *Spectator* associated it with 'parvenu personages' and said it was 'vulgarised by Muscovite and Corsican' – an icy sneer embracing Disraeli, the Tsar of Russia and the Emperor Napoleon as well as the Queen herself.

There were four attempts to kill her, the last on Windsor railway station by a lunatic who fired and missed, thanks to his arm being hit by the umbrella of a quick-thinking Eton schoolboy. By the end, though, she had earned deep affection and respect. The British loved her, as they had come to love themselves, with a fierce self-confidence that seemed to spring from the Bible itself, from Romans 8:31 – 'If God himself be with us, who can be against us?' Their mastery of coal, iron and steam had given them manufacturing pre-eminence; they clothed the world in cotton and wool, they built two thirds of the world's ships and owned and crewed half of them, and they supplied thousands of locomotives and a million tons of track for the world's railways each year.

**The Queen–Empress** *at work on her boxes in her garden-tent at Frogmore House, Windsor. She had been proclaimed Empress of India in 1876; she never visited the 'Jewel in the Crown' but from 1887 imported an Indian flavour to her court by having some Indian servants about her, like the one here. The most famous of them was Abdul Karim, the Munshi, who was soon playing a similar role in her life to the Highlander John Brown, who had died in 1883. The Queen liked subjecting herself to masterful men and the Munshi was allowed to manipulate and bully her, much to the disgust of her courtiers and children. Lord Salisbury, the Prime Minister, put his finger on it when he said, 'She really likes the emotional excitement, as being the only form of excitement she can have.'*

*She was widowed whilst young, and came to represent what the French writer Guy de Maupassant memorably described as 'those fanatical women of principle,... the sort England produces in large numbers... those straight-backed unbearable old maids who are seen in the dining-rooms of hotels throughout Europe... and wherever they go import their peculiar fads, the morals of fossilised virgins, ghastly clothes, and that faint odour of rubber which makes you suspect that at night they are put away in a box.'*

[PHOTO: HILL AND SAUNDERS]

The Industrial Revolution was undisturbed by political or social upheaval. British stability was much admired, but difficult to copy, for the strength of the system lay largely in its avoidance of the systematic. In politics, custom and precedence, open to change and compromise, acted in place of a formal written constitution. Those who pressed hard and long enough – for the extension of the vote, for better working conditions, for rights for women – had at least the prospect of eventual success. They were not made welcome, and Tory peers from the backwoods put up fierce resistance to much reform, but the door was left ajar. The British snob was so famous that the word had crossed the Channel, where a feminine version was added, 'la snobinette'. But this apparent vice was a virtue.

Snobbery served in place of a caste system; a snob might mock 'le self made man', another concept picked up by the French, but there was no rigid social hierarchy to keep him in his place. The rich man in his castle, and the poor man at his gate, could – and did – trade places.

Many made fortunes from the myriad applications of steam power, in mills, engineering works and transport, and turned their children into gentlemen by sending them to one of the mushrooming public schools where manners and the principles of muscular Christianity were caned into them. Individuals were urged, in another phrase of the age, to 'better themselves' by Sunday schools and adult literacy classes, temperance societies, boys' clubs, the Salvation Army, and a host of other

**Steam and iron** *were elemental in the rise of British power, but by the 1890s they were being challenged by electricity, internal combustion and steel. It was steel and hydraulic riveting that made possible the railway bridge over the Firth of Forth in Scotland. Massive and reassuringly solid to banish any fears left over from the collapse of the Tay Bridge a few years before, it was constructed on the cantilever principle, with upper lattice girders in tension and lower tubular members in compression. The Prince of Wales opened the bridge in 1890 by driving in the last, gilded, rivet and Gustave Eiffel watched him do so.*
[Photo: Evelyn George Carey]

institutions devoted to their improvement. As a last resort, for those whose lives were too squalid to admit hope at home, there was emigration. More than two hundred thousand were shipping out of Britain each year.

It was not an ideal situation; little was. The British prided themselves on family values and sexual probity, but thousands of child prostitutes worked their cities. They loved liberty, but blocked Home Rule for the Irish. They had been the first to abolish slavery in their colonies; after doing this, they continued for more than sixty years to transport to Australia their own political malcontents and criminals of both sexes in conditions equal to those on the slave ships that the Royal Navy was charged to hunt down. They were, in short, hypocrites, and it was in this flexibility, moral and otherwise, that their genius lay. They were known for their phlegmatic calm and the stiffness of their upper lip. They did not explode or over-heat. Steam engineers that they were, they generated great energy, but also provided themselves with safety valves.

'It is a pushing age,' a young subaltern called Winston Churchill had written in 1898 as he set off to play his part in the reconquest of the Sudan, 'and shove we must.' As the century turned, Churchill was a war correspondent in South Africa. The *Morning Post* had hired him for £250 a month, the highest fee ever paid to a journalist, to report on what was expected to be an easy victory against the Boers. But the war went badly. The Queen cancelled the autumn ghillies' ball for the staff at Balmoral, her Scottish castle. She trembled and turned pale when she opened telegrams, complaining that news of the war made her ill, but she retained her style, arranging for her troops to be sent homely Christmas parcels of knitting and chocolate, and telling a visitor, 'We are not interested in the possibilities of defeat... They do not exist'. The public was not fooled. Sir Redvers Buller, the army commander, was nicknamed 'Sir Reverse' and replaced. The world, and the German Kaiser in particular, was thrilled, rejoicing to see the lion's tail being tugged so vigorously by a few Afrikaner farmers.

**Three men,** *and some bricks, were enough to show how the 145 acres of steel in the bridge worked, the sort of practical demonstration at which the Victorians excelled.*
[Photo: Sir Benjamin Baker]

Churchill reported no British glory at Spion Kop in January 1900. Instead, he found defeat and 'the strangest and most terrible scenes I have ever witnessed'. A survivor of the battle wrote of 'men blown to atoms, joints torn asunder. Headless bodies, trunks of bodies. Awful, awful.'

A few days later, the Marquess of Queensberry died, ill-tempered, opinionated if not mad, and grand to the last, the flint-faced symbol of cruel righteousness; his only lasting achievement was to have supervised the rules of boxing which still bear his name. It was another intimation of the morality of the age. Five years before, he had presented a bouquet of cabbages to Oscar Wilde, the lover of his son Lord Alfred Douglas, with a note accusing the aesthete and playwright of 'posing as a Sodomite': the marquess's spelling was poor. Wilde sued for libel, but was prosecuted for homosexuality, imprisoned, and ruined. He was himself near death in exile, in France.

Weight of numbers began to tell in South Africa during the spring. Irish troops fought particularly well. The Queen recognised this in April by visiting Dublin for the first time in forty years, a tiny, round figure in her black widow's weeds circling the grounds of the viceregal lodge in a trap drawn by a white donkey. She created a regiment of Irish Guards, and gave them the right to wear the shamrock on St Patrick's Day. Unimpressed, Irish nationalists smashed any shop windows decorated with Union Jacks whilst the police broke up Home Rule meetings.

Mafeking was relieved in May, amid scenes of such wild rejoicing at home that a new word – 'mafficking' – was coined to describe it. Children wore buttons with the soldiers' heads on them and their parents wept to the music-hall song 'The Boers have got my Daddy'. Victoria celebrated her 81st birthday the same month. Extra staff were hired at Balmoral to cope with the flood of congratulations. Her summer holiday in Scotland, however, was spoiled by indigestion and exhaustion. Her eyesight was deteriorating; she was prescribed belladonna drops and asked for government reports to be written in larger and blacker writing.

Thousands of Boer prisoners were shipped to the remote Atlantic island of St Helena, where Napoleon had been exiled. Back on the Veldt their farms were burned and their families were held in concentration camps, filthy and overcrowded. 'A dear little chap of four, and nothing left of him but his great brown eyes and white teeth,' a British nurse wrote in shame. 'I can't describe what it is to see these children lying about in a state of collapse. It's just exactly like faded flowers thrown away…' Twenty thousand died and it caused an international scandal. The British were used to admiration for their humanity and fair play; 'Victorian' had become synonymous with morality, yet now they were vilified for their cruelty and their greed for the Boers' goldfields.

There were other signs of change. A Naval Act was passed in Berlin committing the Germans to build a fleet of thirty-eight battleships over the coming twenty years. It was the first serious challenge to British seapower since Trafalgar almost a century before. Industrial supremacy was also being challenged. More was still being manufactured than in Germany, but the

**Emotional bedrock.** *The country village – here Sansend in Yorkshire – was the national dream, the place to which the sweated labour in the cities and far-flung colonial administrators yearned to return to retire. In truth, the British were the most urbanised people on earth; English farms had been savaged by cheap imports of corn and meat from America and Australasia, Scottish crofts had been cleared to make way for sheep and sporting estates, poverty and hunger had driven the Irish from their cabins, and villages were often the sad repository of folk too old or timid to emigrate or seek their fortune in the cities. Nevertheless, the British had an intimate love for their countryside; it was one of the intangibles – love of sport and underdogs were others – that all shared and helped to create, in a country as class-riven as any, the sense of unity on which foreigners often remarked.*
[PHOTO: FRANK MEADOW SUTCLIFFE]

Americans had taken a clear lead and their inventiveness – cellophane, the caterpillar tractor and the Eastman Kodak box camera in 1900, with no comparable British advances – was increasing it. Labour relations were tense; South Wales miners came out on strike, and the British Labour Party was founded to provide a parliamentary basis for the trade union movement.

The war dragged on. The Queen's grandson, Prince Christian, had volunteered to fight and in October he died. She had other grandsons – thirty-four of them, for she was the 'Grandmother of Europe' whose descendants shared the thrones of Germany, Russia and Spain as well as England – but his death shook her badly. She could eat only arrowroot and milk. In early November, she left Balmoral, 'wretchedly gloomy and dark', for Windsor. On 18 December, she moved

on to Osborne, her great Italianate pile on the Isle of Wight. She took draughts of chloral but could not sleep. Her oldest friend, Lady Jane Churchill, died on Christmas Day. Her body was shipped across the Solent in a gale so severe the Queen feared the boat would sink.

Her 'horrible year' passed in foul westerly winds and she did not welcome 1901. 'Another year begun,' she noted, 'and I am feeling so weak and unwell that I enter upon it sadly.' On 14 January she failed to write up her diary for the first time since 1832. She gave her last command two days later; her ambassador in Berlin was respectfully to decline an honour offered by her grandson, Kaiser Wilhelm. Her children were summoned to Osborne on 18 January.

The Prince of Wales was with her on the afternoon of 22 January. She said her last word to him: 'Bertie'. Her doctor and the Kaiser supported her for two hours. She died – 'passed away' as Victorians genteelly put it – at half past six. Journalists tore down the hill into Cowes yelling in headlines: 'Queen dead! Queen dead!' She would not have been amused. She lay in state for ten days before she was carried to the mainland on the smallest of the royal yachts, *Alberta*. The gales had blown out and the smoke from the salutes of the double line of warships through which she passed – the coffin shrouded in white with the crown and sceptre on it – settled in a long festoon against a golden pink sky.

'The thought of England without Queen Victoria is dreadful even to think of,' said Princess May, the future Queen Mary. 'God help us all!'

## CHAPTER TWO

# 'WE HAPPEN TO BE THE BEST PEOPLE IN THE WORLD…'

The essence *of empire – a prodigious self-confidence, and the nerve to treat other people's houses as one's own – is captured in this photograph of a traveller camping out in the Chennakshava Temple in India in 1900. The great subcontinent and its 300 million people were administered by a mere 5000 members of the Indian Civil Service. The few British battalions were equally outnumbered by the Indian Army, British-officered but, as it had shown less than fifty years before, capable of mutiny. The arithmetic demanded that each individual should exude an unquestioned supremacy. The borderline between this 'natural authority' and outright arrogance was thin; the British Raj's reputation for fair play and justice was not a luxury, but a necessity.*

FIVE YEARS AFTER THE QUEEN'S DEATH, ANOTHER Englishwoman, Sylvia Leith-Ross, caught an essence of empire in the newly-won colony of northern Nigeria. She and a solitary white companion, riding to join her husband in Kano, came upon a line of women marching with loads on their heads. 'They walked along the grassy track in and out of the shadow and sunlight,' she wrote. 'Miles from anywhere, all alone, these women and girls walked lightly, securely, singing softly. The white man stopped his pony, looked at them, and said "Pax Britannica".'

Her husband was to die young of blackwater fever, for West Africa still lived up to its gruesome cachet of the white man's grave; a jealous sense that the British were mere exploiters would soon enough replace admiration for the British Peace, and ugly things would be said of them. But for ever after, she wrote, 'I would think of those women who, because of England, could walk safely through the bush, singing.'

'All men have foibles,' someone said of the great imperialist Cecil Rhodes, 'and Rhodes's is *size*.' It was a trait he shared with his countrymen. The British did not have one empire. In essence, they had two; one that they largely populated and worked themselves, and another, as exotic and fast-growing as a hothouse plant, where they ruled – not for the pleasure of it, or so they claimed, but because duty obliged them to take up the 'white man's burden'.

The distinction was unspoken but obvious. Emigrants to the first – Australia, Canada, New Zealand, the lost territories of the United States – went to better themselves, and they went for good. Most were poor, dispossessed Highlanders, half-starved Irish, farm labourers quitting English villages devastated by cheap food imports, Cornish miners, slum dwellers. They were the unwanted, a fact made brutally clear by the assisted passages and cheap land used as bait to tempt them to leave. Advice was offered free by the Emigrants' Information Service in Westminster, which distributed a million posters and pamphlets a year. Any local authority could provide £10 a head for its poor to emigrate. A clutch of emigration societies also provided encouragement and funds. A one-way ticket to the other side of the world, to Queensland in Australia, cost £6 for men and £3 for women. Once there, twenty thousand acres of grazing land could be had for tuppence an acre, with a half-price rail ticket to the nearest railhead; *Lebensraum* was not a problem in a state the size of Texas. Gold, silver, sapphires and opals had been found; a prospector's licence cost ten shillings a year and a miner on £6 a week was three times better off than in a British pit.

**The passage to India** *made by George V in 1911 (top) was an all-red route on which every coaling station and stopping place – Gibraltar, Malta, Suez, Aden – was garrisoned by British troops. Royal Navy officers like these controlled the Red Sea and Indian Ocean and dominated the Mediterranean. Queen Mary received fawning guests (near right) before the imperial couple travelled to the capital for the 'Delhi Durbar'. At this grand celebration, princes and maharajahs paid their respects to the King-Emperor and his consort, who appeared (main picture) on the balcony of Delhi's famous Red Fort in highly inappropriate ermine. They would have been cooler in silk, like the young princelings clustered at their feet. It was the only visit by a reigning monarch of Britain's greatest dominion; Victoria and Edward VII had appeared in India merely on postage stamps and coins, though Edward had visited as Prince of Wales.*

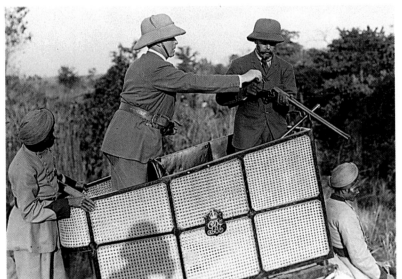

**A tiger hunt** *was mounted for George V on his Indian tour of 1911–12. Hundreds of beaters, blowing bugles and pounding drums, drove the great cats towards the elephants (left) that carried the imperial party. The howdah from which he shot his prey (above) carried the monogram GRI, confirming that in India he was not merely King (Rex) but Emperor (Imperator) too.*

*After the shoot (top), the tigers – not yet a threatened species – were laid out for him to examine his handiwork. Hunting on this scale was an integral part of the imperial image, as it had been for the Moghul Emperors, but it was not restricted to the sahibs. The memsahib Kate Martelli wrote a book with the memorably simple title* Tigers I have Shot.

the colonials had taken lack of deference to the point of ultimate sin, arguing umpires' decisions in cricket matches. The prospector in fact regretted it – 'plebianism of the rankest kind dwells in Australia and riches are now becoming the test of a man's position' – but it inspired most. One girl thought it better to be a lowly maid in a Sydney household than a governess in England. 'Servants are more considered, there is more freedom and independence here than at home,' she wrote home after a few months. 'Be sensible, undergo a little domestic change and come out here and take your chance with others with a certainty of success withal.'

That was one empire, which absorbed sixteen million people in the century after Waterloo, free and self-governing to most intents and purposes. In the other, the British were thin on the ground; there were 640 of them in Uganda, governing 2.8 million people, and twenty-three in Somaliland. They were soldiers, administrators, judges, missionaries, engineers, planters, bankers and merchant princes. The commercial group was looked down on. The others did not go to better themselves but – in theory and often in fact – to better the natives. They built, improved and ruled.

They did not go for good, unless they died in service; the annual British death rate in West Africa was 14.8 per thousand, bad enough in any circumstances, but particularly so when the victims were almost all 'men of picked physique in the prime of life'. The young men returned to Britain to marry after five years or so; after ten, the children were sent home to boarding schools; after twenty years, if they survived, husband and wife retired to a villa in Cheltenham or a West Country cottage.

Their methods were instantly recognisable. Hong Kong, one of their longest-surviving creations, is a template. Trade interested them first; the flag followed. Britain was a major importer of Chinese teas, silks and porcelain by the 1830s. British India was producing large amounts of opium. Chinese opium addicts had the potential for balancing the books. Hong Kong – then Gueng Dong, Fragrant Harbour – had one of the most splendid natural harbours in Asia. The ruthless application of seapower in the Opium Wars forced China to open ports to the opium trade, and formally to cede Hong Kong.

The flag was planted at a place still called Possession Street, and the territory claimed. Next, they named their new capital for Victoria, as they named others for other worthies, Sydney, say, or Vancouver and Auckland. The earliest buildings reflected the classic colonial trinity: God, government and – in case these failed – force. Force came first. Flagstaff House, high-ceilinged, pillared, its wooden floors gleaming with polish, housed the commander of British forces from 1844. Three years later, the Anglican cathedral of St John was opened. It was an airy and graceful place where the early taipans, the great merchants of the China trade, might, if they were so minded, seek God's pardon for the narcotic misery of the addicts from whom they extracted their fortunes. Next came the governor's mansion, followed by the other ritual fittings and fixtures, a cricket ground, a racecourse, law courts, botanical gardens, a bank guarded by stone lions, and a club with a long bar and deep armchairs. The taipans built elegant

Charities sent out orphan children – a hundred thousand to Canada alone, from Church Homes for Waifs and Strays and Dr Barnardo's – and the governors of reformatory schools were empowered to dump their delinquents in the colonies. A supply of women, essential breeding stock for these white dominions, was ensured by charities such as the British Women's Emigration Society which assembled groups of young girls, household drudges, the abandoned and the destitute, and gave them free passage and guaranteed jobs on arrival.

The voyage out, the last glimpse of the Clyde, the Mersey or the hills of western Ireland, was an ordeal; the crews thought themselves superior to emigrants, and they showed it. In earlier days, men had lined the beaches when emigrant ships arrived, 'bellowing obscenities and trying to take their pick of the women.' The stewards still did not shrink 'from shaking, pinching and pulling girls while they were in bed', but things ashore had become more genteel. 'Land of sunshine and success', an Australian advertisement promised. 'Rough pioneering is over...' The dominions were easier going and more egalitarian than Britain, with a broader franchise, better rights for women and more social reforms.

A prospector in the Victoria goldfields found 'an American type of society. All aristocratic feelings and associations of the old country are at once annihilated.' Left to their own devices,

**Escaping the slums.** *Canada was the most popular destination, and charities sent out 100,000 orphan children. Carefully chaperoned little girls (left) pose as 'Dr Barnardo's Canadian Emigration Party London to Liverpool', before sailing across the Atlantic. Dr Barnardo was an Irish doctor who had founded homes for destitute children, originally in London's East End but then across the land. They arrived in pioneer country and went barefoot in summer (below), but they had prospects beyond the dreams of the poor at home and in general they thrived.*

**Go east, go west.** *In 1913, when this advertisement ( far left) to go 'down under' appeared in the Strand in London, 300,000 were emigrating from the home islands each year. Around 70,000 of them took the proffered advice and went to Australia, tempted by cheap land and cheap tickets. Women travelled for half-price, as the empty spaces needed breeding stock.*

**Home comforts** and home-made amusements offset the rigours of the world's wild places. An easy chair (left), slotted into poles, serves as ingenious transport for Lady Curzon, wife of the Viceroy of India, on a tour of Hyderabad. Camps became travelling hotels, stoutly-made tents outfitted with uniformed servants and special furniture provided by mail order from London. Here (right) an Indian claims a reward for killing a cheetah. Venturing through the Himalayas to Tibet in 1904 (main picture), the British brought the adapted Indian game of polo with them. The flag was not to fly over Lhasa, however. The Dalai Lama fled at their approach; they set up camp, and played football and polo, until other lamas agreed to see them in the Potala palace. This was approached by a stone ramp so slippery that the British had to dismount. The talks over nuts and tea were inconclusive. As they slithered back down the ramp, in boots and spurs, they heard the lamas giggling above them. Tibet remained independent.

houses on the cool and unfevered heights of the Peak, from which they looked down on their ships, docks and warehouses.

Such senior imperialists were a distinct breed. They were physically tall – the result of healthy diets in childhood – and dressed as a caste. Ninety years on, their designs were making fortunes for the likes of Ralph Lauren. They invented the button-down collar, the polo shirt, the safari jacket, the divided skirt, chukka boots and cavalry twills; a subaltern in the Punjab, Harry Lumsden, weary of hot serge trousers, dyed his pyjama bottoms khaki, wore them in the day and created the first chinos. They dreamt up gin and tonic because the quinine in the latter warded off malaria. They dressed for dinner in the jungle. 'Always wear corsets,' Constance Larymore advised from the tropics, 'even on the warmest evenings; there is something about their absence almost as demoralising as hair in curling pins.' They played polo, fished, speared pigs from horseback and shot or hunted anything, substituting hyenas for foxes where necessary or following trails of paper scraps in paperchases. In the Indian hill stations they built to escape the heat of the plains, in an ornate style known as 'distressed Gothic', every flat surface had a tennis court. The game of bridge was created by civil servants in Calcutta, and snooker was refined by an army officer at the club in 'Ooty', Ootacamund in south India. It had been invented in Jubbalpore in 1875.

The women were as formidable as the men. 'The flesh of my left arm looks crushed into a jelly, but cold water dressings will soon bring it right, and a cut on my back bled profusely,' Isabella Bird, the first woman fellow of the Royal Geographical Society, wrote after she was thrown from her pony in a rocky canyon.

'But I really think that the rents in my riding dress will prove the most important part of the accident.' In India, they went tiger hunting perched in elephant howdahs, in garments dyed jungle green, with .450 double-express rifles. Kate Martelli, wife of a political agent, wrote in a book called *Tigers I Have Shot* of hundreds of beaters blowing bugles, pounding tom-toms and firing blanks, until the tiger at last 'advanced like an enormous cat, now crouching on the ground, now crawling forward, now turning round to try to discover the meaning of the unwonted noise behind him. When he was about 80 yards away, I fired and hit him on the shoulder…'

The explorer Mary Kingsley travelled through the Nigerian forest with three Fan cannibals. It was their habit to kill men and 'cut them into neat pieces, eat what they want and smoke the rest for future use.' She did not, she wrote, want to arrive 'in a smoked condition, even should my fragments be neat.' Adequate supplies of hippopotamus and crocodiles ensured her survival. She presented the Fans with white ladies' blouses, which they wore 'with nothing else but red paint and bunches of leopard tails', and stockings which they wore on their heads. She herself walked in a round velvet hat and thick skirts and petticoats, which saved her life when she fell into a spiked game pit. Her advice was to respect native superstitions, 'and never, never shoot too soon… because in such a situation, one white alone with no troops to back him up means a clean finish.' It was much better, she wrote, 'to walk round the obstacle than to become a mere blood splotch against it, if this can be done without losing your self-respect which is the mainspring of your power in West Africa.'

It was this self-respect that imposed the Pax Britannica which so impressed Sylvia Leith-Ross. There were just 106 Englishmen, and three women, in northern Nigeria; the achievement was astonishing, and recent. It started, as British colonies often did, with a young man's ambition and a private company. Before 1892, the country had a handful of British traders, 'counter jumpers of the worst type and biggest bounders into the bargain', who traded gin with the natives for palm oil. George Goldie created the Royal Niger Company to bring order and the flag to the huge country; 'my dream as a child was to colour the map red,' he explained. He hired Frederick Lugard, a soldier who was fighting slavers around Lake Nyasa in East Africa, to penetrate deep into northern Nigeria. Lugard, fortified by a flannel cummerbund and huge breakfasts to ward off evers, raised the West African Frontier Force and set off inland. His

officers included Sylvia Leith-Ross's husband.

He had few enough men, his strength little more than his 'assertion of superiority', and the handy back-up of the Maxim gun if that failed to impress the feuding tribesmen. A captain wrote of witnessing 'two very hot and dirty, begrimed, badly clothed Englishmen dictating to a crowd of about 600 Mohammedans, all big swells, and kicking them out.' When he set up his tripod to photograph the native chiefs, they fled for fear he was assembling a machinegun. In two years between 1902 and 1904, Lugard overran the northern Nigerian states of Sokoto and Kano. He noted that the natives had known no peace; at one moment, children played in the villages, at the next 'you may find the corpses of the men, the bodies of the children half-burnt... whilst the women are captives of the victorious raiders.' He thought the arrival of the British would prove 'the greatest blessing Africa has known since the Flood.'

A foreigner might say that the sun never set on the British empire because God would never trust an Englishman in the dark; at home, a socialist remarked tartly that there were slums in Britain on which it had never risen. It was, nevertheless, an awesome affair. At its height, as the British were fond of reminding themselves, Rome had embraced 125 million people over 2.5 million square miles. Their own empire now contained a quarter of the population of the planet and sprawled over eleven million square miles. It was still expanding. Territory fifty times larger than Britain itself had been acquired in the last decade of Victoria's reign. Huge numbers were on the move. At any one time, British ships manned by 200,000 sailors were carrying a similar number of passengers, dressing for dinner in the Red Sea aboard a P and O liner, or crammed in steerage on a rust bucket destined for Canada.

The sea was central; a perilous and alien desert to most peoples, even British landlubbers affected to think of it as a second home. No matter if it made them ill; it had done the same to Nelson. They drummed it into their children from infancy; they dressed them in little sailor's suits, and read them the sea-going stories of Robert Louis Stevenson, *Treasure Island* and *Kidnapped*, and Captain Marryat's *Mr Midshipman Easy*. The sea was synonymous with health and happiness. They swam in it for pleasure, a curious habit foreigners had only recently begun to copy; not content with building great resorts next to it, they projected amusement piers out into its waters, the lights of whose music halls and penny arcades twinkled back at the land like great liners.

By definition, since Britain was an island, the colossal enterprise was seaborne. It rested on command of the oceans; without that, even Britain itself, with a small all-volunteer army faced by the conscript masses of the Continent, was indefensible. The essence of naval power was memorably put by John Jervis, an admiral who had fought the French over the last half of the 18th century, at Quebec, Brest, in the West Indies, ultimately forestalling a French invasion with the victory over their Spanish allies off Cape St Vincent for which his earldom was named. 'I do not say the French cannot come,' he said. 'I only say they cannot come by sea.'

The man responsible for the fleet in the early 1900s, 'Jacky' Fisher, the First Sea Lord, had global reach. 'Cape Town and Singapore, Alexandria, Gibraltar and Dover are the five

**E. M. Forster,** *in his masterpiece*
A Passage to India, *caught the*
*spiritual and social clash between*
*British and Indian in a famous*
*passage centring on an alleged rape in*
*the Marabar Caves, like those near*
*Bangalore from which these two*
*earlier English* memsahibs *(above)*
*emerge unviolated.*

**Rudyard Kipling,** *seen (right)*
*with other journalists covering the*
*Boer War, was the great poet and*
*storyteller of empire and an early*
*Nobel prizewinner. His* Jungle
Stories, *based on his long experience*
*in India, are classic animal stories;*
*with* Kim, *they have inspired*
*cartoon and feature films. He caught*

*the rough romance of the far-flung army:*
'*By the old Moulmain Pagoda, lookin'*
*lazy at the sea,*
*There's a Burma girl a-settin', and I*
*know she thinks o' me;*
*The wind is in the palm-trees, and the*
*temple bells they say:*
"*Come you back, you British soldier;*
*come you back to Mandalay!*"'

**Enthusiasm for empire** *was fuelled by a stream of books. Robert Louis Stevenson revived the adventure story with* Treasure Island, *which infected many with the urge to seek a fortune in the tropics. He himself had tuberculosis and, in an attempt to escape it, ended up in Samoa (above), a South Sea island that ironically became one of the few German colonial possessions. Rider Haggard then went on to write* King Solomon's Mines, *based on his time in South Africa, specifically to outdo Stevenson's book in excitement.*
[PHOTO, ABOVE: J. DAVIS]
[PHOTO, LEFT: REINHOLD THIELE]

29

strategic keys which lock up the world,' he said. The empire controlled them all. Foreigners thought the sea bred insularity; characterised themselves as 'dagoes', 'eyeties', 'frogs' and 'huns', and aware of the feeling that 'wogs begin at Calais', they applauded the Boers and anyone else who stood up to the arrogant islanders. The British, however, spoke of 'glorious isolation'. More than half the world's ships flew the Red Duster; all used British Admiralty charts and calculated their longitude from Greenwich. Many were insured by Lloyds of London and built to the world standard, 'A1 at Lloyd's'. They steamed on Welsh coal picked up at British coaling stations. Seventy per cent of the tonnage passing through the Suez canal was British; beyond it, the Red Sea and the Persian Gulf were treated more or less as territorial waters.

A cable conference in 1898 boasted that 'the whole world is almost encircled with British wires.' Words from London travelled all-red wires to Hong Kong, passing from Gibraltar to Alexandria in Egypt, which was a colony in all but name, through the Red Sea to Aden and Bombay, across land to Madras and on to Singapore. Sydney was reached from Canada via all-red relay stations at Norfolk Island, Fiji and Fanning Island; the Overland Telegraph line in Australia ran for two thousand miles, the men in its remote relay stations raising their own cattle and sheep to survive. Its central station, Alice Springs, named for the wife of its chief engineer, was a thousand miles from the nearest towns.

It was not only white pieces who were moved over the imperial chessboard. Two million Tamils were taken from southern India to Ceylon and Malaya when the locals disdained to work on tea and rubber plantations. Indians were also shipped as indentured labourers to the West Indies and British Guiana, the only colony in South America, for the same reason; in Fiji they became a majority; in Kenya, Uganda and South Africa they built railroads and stayed on to trade. Sikhs served in the Hong Kong police. The influx of Chinese coolies into British Columbia and the Australian goldfields sparked off race riots by whites who feared for their jobs. A 'White Australia' policy followed. 'Blackbirders' took South Sea islanders to toil on the sugar estates in Queensland, and in the Peruvian guano trade, despite the Royal Navy's attempt to suppress this latter-day slaving.

The animal kingdom was not exempt : hare, trout, salmon and deer were shipped out to ensure the pleasures of rod and gun. The Maoris had no meat beyond dogs and themselves; cannibalism was the only alternative to vegetarianism. Domestic livestock was imported from Britain, so that, by the turn of the century, there were two and a half sheep, one and a half cattle and a third of a pig for each New Zealander. A less happy experiment was a consignment of twenty-four wild rabbits, shipped from England to Australia in 1859, which bred with plague-like abandon. Shot, poisoned and fenced, still they multiplied. As with livestock, so with crops. Tea was taken to Kenya, pineapples and sugar to Australia, coconuts to the Bahamas, rubber to Malaya.

Like the Australian rabbit, the empire had few natural predators. No European country could challenge it at sea, and thus no serious rival could grapple with it on land. Natives

**A 'blackbirder'** *and his human cargo in the Pacific. The captain (right) of this 'labour ship' is one of the adventurers who recruited or kidnapped islanders from the Solomons, the New Hebrides and Fiji to toil as indentured labourers, kanakas, on the cotton and sugar plantations of Queensland in Australia. Large areas of Melanesia had become seriously depopulated before 'blackbirding' became illegal in 1904, shortly after this picture was taken. Daniel Defoe, author of* Robinson Crusoe, *described the British as a 'low-born amphibious mob'; an unbroken line runs back from this ruthless seaman to the buccaneers and Elizabethan explorers.*

were no match for whites equipped with machineguns, gunboats, locomotives, and a sense of mission. At Omdurman in 1898, the Sudanese Dervishes reminded Winston Churchill of a medieval host with banners, swords and spears, and mailed cavalry. The artillery and machineguns of the Nile Expeditionary Force massacred eleven thousand in a few hours, and the British were in Khartoum the following morning.

For all that, the British had proved vulnerable to Zulus, and to properly equipped and well-led Boers, while the Afghans had shown the danger of becoming over-extended in harsh terrain. To protect India, the British had pushed into Burma in the East, and Sind and Baluchistan in the West. When they perceived a threat from the expanding Russian empire in the north-west, they made bloody and unsuccessful excursions into Afghanistan, losing the entire garrison there in 1842, the sole survivor, Dr William Brydon, escaping through the snowfields on his pony. The British nearly lost another garrison in 1880, and withdrew, a lesson the Russians ignored a century later.

Setbacks were rare, however. Even countries outside the empire, but with British blood in their veins, sometimes felt themselves a part of its inexorable progress. The Anglo-Argentine Association eagerly advertised a 'paradise for

emigration' in a popular tuppenny London magazine, *The Colonizer*. Throughout the 19th century, more had left for the United States than any other shore. Though many were Irish, who wanted to remove themselves as far from British influence as they could, and though by the 1900s more than two-thirds of all emigrants were heading for Australasia and Canada, Americans still felt an intimate bond. 'We are a part, and a great part,' the *New York Times* allowed, 'of the Greater Britain which seems so plainly destined to dominate this planet.'

To a religious people – on interminable Sundays at sea, passengers were expected to put away their cards, stub out their cigars and read hymn-books instead of the latest adventure of Sherlock Holmes – the imperial process seemed blessed by God. The feeling of the moral purpose of empire that so affected Sylvia Leith-Ross was shared by the mass of her countrymen, straddling class and politics. The social reformer Beatrice Webb railed about 'imperialism in the air, all classes drunk… with hysterical loyalty,' but her husband Sidney combined socialism with imperialism as easily as the radical young philosopher Bertrand Russell. Both would turn on it, and the Webbs' creation, the London School of Economics,

would become a hothouse of anti-imperialism; but not yet. The young Earl of Meath had brushed snow from his knees on the playing fields of Eton; a master snarled at him that if his forebears had minded a little snow, there would have been no British Canada, and if they had minded heat, no British India – 'so never let me see you shrink from heat or cold.' The earl later organised the Lads Drill Association to make sure that non-Etonians grew up equally tough, and a quarter of a million teenagers spent their evenings having Christian manliness drilled into them. From 1902 onwards, Meath had Empire Day, 24 May, celebrated in schools across the empire. No matter that a sarcastic Australian journalist dubbed it 'Vampire Day'; boys dressed up as the great figures of empire and chanted: 'Be brave, be bold, do right!'

The distillation of imperial virtue was duty, proclaimed in verse and novels, in the columns of Lord Northcliffe's mass-circulation *Daily Mail*, and in tales of imperial derring-do in the *Boys' Own Paper*. 'What should they know of England who only England know?' asked Rudyard Kipling, former journalist on the *Civil and Military Gazette* in Lahore, coiner of the phrase 'white man's burden', telling them of distant empire in a flood of highly successful poems and stories. In the adventures of

**The Viceroy of India,** *Lord Curzon, and his wife, an American heiress, pose with a victim near Hyderabad in April 1902. He was an outstanding shot, and said nothing was more exciting than tiger shooting:* *'You can hear your heart beat as he comes, unseen with the leaves crackling under his feet...'* *That autumn, he reminded himself of his Derbyshire roots by fishing in the Betwa river (left).*

Sherlock Holmes, Conan Doyle gave the stolid Dr Watson a smattering of imperial romance, making him a veteran of the Afghan wars, 'wounded by a Jezail bullet'. Dreams of wilderness were lit in books like *The Young Fur Traders*, by R. M. Ballantyne, who had worked in the Canadian backwoods for the Hudson's Bay Company; G. M. Henty awoke a thirst for glory through his books on imperial heroes in which boys could feel themselves *With Clive in India*.

A freshly-minted hero, Robert Baden-Powell, defender of Mafeking in the Boer War, founded the Boy Scouts in 1908 to instant and brilliant success. He, too, wished to give sinew to youngsters who would maintain the standards of those who had died for the empire against the Boers. 'Don't let them look down from heaven,' he admonished them, 'and see you loafing about with your hands in your pockets...' He kitted them out like his troopers in khaki shirts and shorts with broadbrimmed bush hats and bandanas. 'We'll DOB, DOB, DOB' they greeted their scoutmaster at each meeting; they would 'Do Our Best'.

That, it seemed, was exactly what adult imperialists in the field were achieving, their Best. The British had been rich, stable and energetic for so long that it seemed to them the most natural thing in the world that they should possess one quarter of its land surface, and control the intervening oceans. It was easy to mock their self-confidence. 'We happen to be the best people in the world,' said Cecil Rhodes, two thousand miles to the south of Sylvia Leith-Ross in Africa, 'with the highest ideals of decency and justice and liberty and peace, and the more of the world we inhabit, the better it is for humanity.' Five thousand miles to the east, Viscount Curzon, Viceroy of India, had not the slightest doubt that the British 'came here in obedience to what I call a decree of Providence, for the lasting benefit of millions of the human race.'

This was no bombast, however, and these were far from hollow men. Curzon felt quite at home in the Viceroy's palace in Calcutta; by happy coincidence, it was modelled on his family seat, Kedleston Hall in Derbyshire. He spoke to people, it was said, 'like a divinity addressing blackbeetles'. He was a fellow of All Souls, Oxford, one of the most brilliant men of his generation. He had journeyed through the East and written books on Persia and Asiatic Russia, and now, at thirty-nine, he was responsible for 300 million people, a figure so regal that he was honoured by thirty-one-gun salutes where a sovereign such as the King of Siam was worth but twenty-one. His wife, an

American heiress, paid with her life for the harshness of the Indian climate; Curzon was in constant pain from a curvature of the spine, but drove himself mercilessly in answer to 'the call of duty, and the means of service to mankind.'

Few men have countries named for them; Cecil Rhodes, who did, was a rare creature. The son of a Hertfordshire vicar, he was sent to South Africa for his health at seventeen. Within ten years, he had entered the Cape parliament and got himself an Oxford degree; another ten, and he was prime minister of the Cape and a multi-millionaire. His fortune came from the Kimberley diamond diggings. Fifty thousand men, 'fossickers' – an old English term for troublesome people and rummagers for gold and precious stones – with attendant whores and merchants, crowded round the 'big hole' from which diamond ore was extracted with a gigantic cat's cradle of ropes and buckets. Rhodes bought out the fossickers with what was then the largest cheque ever written, for £5,338,658 Only. Through his de Beers company, he controlled ninety per cent of the world diamond business.

He planned an all-red railway route from Cape Town to Cairo. As a first step, he set his eye on the territory ruled from a thatch-and-mud kraal in Bulawayo by the Matabele king Lobengula. White firepower won him control of the 750,000 square miles of land running from the Limpopo to the Zambesi, and Baden-Powell honed his scouting skills against the Matabele when they rebelled in 1896. From its headquarters in Kimberley, Rhodes's British South Africa Company, its house flag the Union Jack with a lion and the company logo, ran the vast new territory of Rhodesia. The company had its own police, its own railway and road gangs, its own magistrates. When the first train arrived in the new capital, Salisbury, in 1899, its locomotive bore the legend: 'Rhodes, Railroads and Imperial Expansion.'

The savaging – Baden-Powell the crypto-fascist, Curzon the insufferable patrician, Rhodes as racist megalomaniac – came later. For their contemporaries, they were the brilliant protagonists of a humane and pragmatic Greater Britain. The motto of Rhodes's company-country was 'Justice, Freedom, Commerce.' The British had come to believe that their empire meant the same.

Their greatest vice was greed. They could not pass an islet without claiming it; Rhodes wanted the whole world to be British – 'and the moon, too, I often think of that'. They acquired so many territories that the bureaucrats who drew up the Colonial Office List did not bother to tabulate them all, the list ending simply: 'Countless other smaller possessions and nearly all the rocks and isolated islands of the ocean.' Their virtues were curiosity, skill in navigation, and courage. No master plan existed for ruling the world. Colonising was done

on the hoof, often by chance – Bermuda and Honduras were acquired through shipwrecked British crews, the former inspiring Shakespeare's *The Tempest*. Some asked to be colonised; the king of Basutoland, begging for imperial protection, wrote to Victoria that 'my country is your blanket and my people the lice upon it.' Others resisted bitterly, though rarely, Americans and Afghans apart, with much success.

In the early days, the British were pirates and slavers, and Australia was used as a dumping ground for convicts. India was kept solvent by the opium trade. Yet this same empire produced missionaries who gave their lives, willingly and often, for their fellows; Mary Slessor, say, a former Dundee mill girl who walked barefoot through the forests of Nigeria – 'the Lord promised we could take up serpents so why be afraid of leopards?' – and dosed the sick with Epsom salts, quinine and laudanum. She fell so ill herself with boils and rheumatism that her hair fell out, yet felt that 'Heaven is now nearer to me than Britain,' and refused to go home – 'as long as I can nurse a motherless bairn... I'm to stick to my post and you'd cry shame if I turned tail for a bit of a fever or even a bald head.' When she died at Calabar, she was remembered as 'whirlwind, earthquake, fire and still, small voice.'

Such brutal contrasts confused and maddened outsiders. The about-face to anti-slavery and anti-piracy, when it came in the 19th century, was thought to smack of duplicity. Anti-piracy operations by the Royal Navy provided a handy fig-leaf for the expansion of the empire east from India into the South China Sea. The presence of buccaneers and other undesirables drew them into New Zealand. In West Africa, Sierra Leone, established by the British as a home for freed slaves, became a colony; Lagos was taken as a base for anti-slaving patrols. The

coast of East Africa was acquired to suppress the slave trade to Arabia, with an Anglican cathedral raised on the site of the Zanzibar slave market. Thus a side effect of the new morality was the acquisition of yet more territory; Albion seemed as *perfide* as ever.

The forms of empire were as flexible as its morals. The white colossi were still coalescing: Alberta and Saskatchewan, created from the vast lands granted to the Hudson's Bay Company, joined Canada in 1905; Newfoundland stayed out until 1949. The separate states that made up Australia only joined together in a Commonwealth in 1901. Utter confusion appeared to rule in the rest. Rajahs, emirs, khedives and kings could remain in office, provided it was understood that the decisions made by their British advisers were the ones that stuck. The empire was thus a mish-mash of paramountcies, leases, concessions, condominiums and sultanates. The top Briton could be Viceroy, Captain-General or Administrator. In Malta, Gibraltar and Bermuda, he was a military governor appointed by the War Office. In Ascension Island he was a Royal Navy captain since, for administrative purposes, the island was a ship. Tristan da Cunha, a yet more remote island, was effectively administered by a chaplain of the Society for the Propagation of the Bible.

In Egypt, he was a mere consul, for the country was a part of empire without being in it. It was ruled by a khedive, Abbas II, who had his own flag, government and army, and signed his own laws, and who in turn owed allegiance to the Sultan of Turkey. This grandeur was a sop. In practice, the country was run by the Sirdar (Commander) of the Egyptian army and the khedive's financial adviser, both British, and by Evelyn Baring, created Earl of Cromer, the British agent and consul, simply and universally known as 'the Lord'. A visitor recalled the khedive turning pale. 'Listen,' he said nervously, 'I hear the cry of the runner in front of Baring's carriage. Who knows what he is coming to tell me?'

The British brought order, but not always their own law. There were foreign countries where British law applied – consular courts in Turkey and Persia were quite outside the national legal systems – and British countries where it did not. Where local law existed at the time of imperial arrival, it was generally codified and maintained. The British were the first to tabulate and define Islamic and Hindu law in India. French Canadians in Quebec maintained pre-revolutionary French law, whilst French islands captured later, Mauritius and the Seychelles, had the Code Napoléon. Sicilian law was observed in Malta, Ottoman in Cyprus, Roman Dutch in Ceylon and the Cape.

Neither was it clear whether the empire was a private or public enterprise. Singapore, for example, was founded as a settlement by Stamford Raffles in a purely private initiative against London's wishes. The Cocos Islands, 1,700 miles from Australia in the Indian Ocean, were a nominal part of empire, but were owned and ruled by the family of a Scottish seaman, John Clunies-Ross, for 150 years until 1978. A larger example – a hundred thousand square miles – was Sarawak on the great island of Borneo. James Brooke, Benares-born and Norwich-educated, an old India hand, sailed from London to Sarawak in 1838 in a schooner, *Royalist*, he had bought himself with a £10,000 inheritance. He proved so handy to the Sultan of

**Perfidious Albion:** *the British missionaries went to China (left) to bring faith and comfort to its people, some of whom were drug addicts, their lives devastated by the British-controlled opium trade. The brave lady in Chinese dress being wheeled through Yunnan is Mary Baxter, a member of the Inland Mission to China. The tight control of* *production in India can be seen (above) in 1910, as opium is carefully weighed and registered. With the ruthless use of seapower in the 'Opium Wars', the British had seized Hong Kong in 1842 specifically to open the Chinese market to British opium traders. The trade then amounted to one seventh of British India's gross revenue.*

South Africa Company was the beneficial owner of Rhodesia.

The first decade of the new century saw huge increases in emigration to British North America (as Canada was still logged in shipping statistics), and to Australia and New Zealand. By 1912, well over a quarter of a million British subjects were leaving the Old Country for good each year. The steamer trip to Australia was thirty-eight days against the five months or more of sailing ship days; the cheapest passage on a British ship was £16, but the dirt poor could travel in 'open berth' cabins on German ships from Bremen for £6, less than a bricklayer earned in two weeks. A continent awaited them. Melbourne was already the eighth city of the empire. Sydney was noted for its town hall organ – the largest in the world – and its beaches and botanical gardens.

In Queensland, with a population of six hundred thousand scattered across almost half a billion acres, settlers could claim up to 5,120 acres of Crown Lands for a peppercorn rent, provided they cleared it of prickly pear. All land in Australia and Canada was taken by the Crown, on the grounds that the natives had not worked it; in New Zealand, it was bought from the Maoris for razors, Jew's harps, mirrors and other trinkets. In Victoria, grazing land could be leased for tuppence an acre and bought for a shilling. Twenty thousand acres could carry 6,000 sheep at an annual profit of £600 a year. Preliminary

Borneo in putting down rebel Dyak tribesmen, as well as pirates, that he was made Rajah of Sarawak in 1841. He built a castle in Kuching of Aberdeen granite and busied himself in introducing free trade and the rule of law, and ending the traditional Dyak sport of headhunting. Beating off Chinese merchants outraged at his suppression of opium-smuggling, he survived to be succeeded by his nephews; the family remained the White Rajahs of Sarawak for a century.

The Honourable East India Company continued to administer India in part, until the Mutiny of 1857 brought direct rule from London. Vast tracts of Canada were owned by the shareholders of the Hudson's Bay Company, as the British

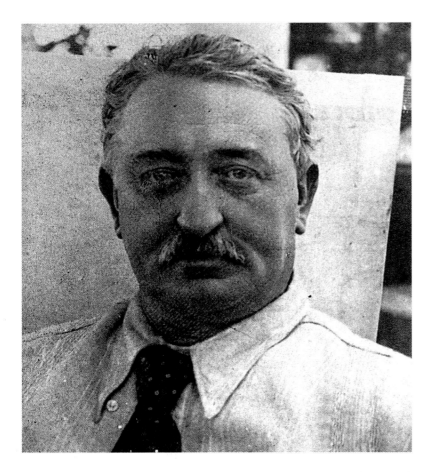

expenses were put at £3,000 – fencing £480, hut and sheepyard £75, woolpress £30 – but government aid was available for the big item, a £2,250 borehole for water. The 50,000 Maoris in New Zealand were outnumbered by just over a million whites. They were already renowned for their skill at rugby, but the largely Scottish immigrants had not taken to cricket. The average standard of living, supported by mutton, wool and butter exports, was the highest in the world.

South Africa – whose 1.2 million whites had the labour of four million natives and 619,000 coloureds and imported Asians to draw on – wanted only professional men. Southern Rhodesia, today's Zimbabwe, was still called 'The British South Africa Company's Territory'. The company's administrator was Albert Grey, a fourth earl and grandson of a prime minister, a patriot who rode a bicycle with a coronet painted on the mudguard and who wrote in address books: 'the empire is my country, England is my home'. Amongst the twenty-three thousand turbulent whites whom he governed, in addition to a million blacks, were the railway builder George Pauling, who once breakfasted with two friends on eight bottles of champagne and a thousand oysters, and Frederick Selous, an elephant hunter who wore no more than shirt, hat and belt in the bush. Northern Rhodesia, Zambia, had less than fifteen hundred whites; whilst Nyasaland, now Malawi, had seven hundred whites in 1911, paying natives four shillings a month to work on cotton and tobacco and coffee plantations.

The last spike in the Uganda railway was driven home in December 1901, to the great relief of its builders. Lions had played havoc in the railway camps, taking twenty-eight Indian

labourers, 'many more Africans', and the British superintendent; those who suffered gangrene after a mauling had their limbs amputated with a handsaw in a railway brake-van. The line ran for 582 miles through virgin territory from Mombasa on the Indian Ocean to Lake Victoria. Nairobi was a small collection of tin-roofed shacks and tents at Mile 327, plagued by mud and dust. There was a scramble to travel in the front carriages; the line was laid direct on the earth, without ballast, so the train moved in a tornado of red dust. It shook so badly that passengers were advised to remove false teeth. The chief engine driver, Sam Pike, was a hard drinker who stopped when he felt thirsty and demanded whisky from the passengers before continuing. Passengers took guns for shooting en route, using the communication cord to stop the train to bag a lion or antelope near the line; Pike blew his whistle when he spotted game. The boiler was pierced by charging rhino.

**A country was named** for Cecil Rhodes (left). Scores of Britons lent their names to far-flung cities and islands: Vancouver, Sydney, Cook, Adelaide, Wellington – but it was apt that this Hertfordshire vicar's son should have been honoured by a great spread of land in the heart of Africa. 'All men have foibles', it was said of him, 'and Rhodes's is size.' He wanted not just the whole planet to be British, but the moon as well. Sent to Africa for his health as a young man, he made his fortune in the Kimberley diamond diggings and controlled ninety per cent of the world diamond business through his de Beers company. At the end of every shift at Kimberley, the black miners (right) were stripped and searched in every orifice for concealed diamonds. Moving north, Rhodes's British South Africa Company carved out a territory of 750,000 square miles between the Limpopo and Zambesi rivers. This became Rhodesia, now Zimbabwe. Rhodes was no mere brute imperialist. He supported Home Rule for Ireland. President Clinton is among the many Rhodes Scholars at Oxford to benefit from his generosity. He died a few months after this picture was taken in 1901. 'The last photograph taken of Mr Rhodes,' the photographer Alfred Mullins noted, 'and his favourite one.'

[PHOTO, LEFT: ALFRED MULLINS]

[PHOTO, RIGHT: HORACE NICHOLLS]

The first settlers had arrived five years before. James and Mary McQueen, Scottish newlyweds, had sailed out to Mombasa because they had read that Kenya was 'a land of milk and honey'. Mombasa ran to a European club – bar in one room, billiard table in the other – and an outfitters, Boustead and Ridley, which supplied porters, head men, copper wire for currency, and beads and other trade goods to go up-country. A company, Imperial British East African, had been set up to exploit the lands stretching back from the coast to Lake Victoria. It had succeeded in navigating the lake with a steamship named after its founder, William Mackinnon, built in Scotland and carried five hundred miles by human porterage, but no minerals were found and individual pioneers opened up the region. The McQueens spent their honeymoon toiling up-country, along tracks used by slave and ivory caravans, with twenty donkeys and a tent. 'Pioneer Mary' Walsh, a redhaired Irishwoman, arrived with a pearl-handled revolver in her skirts. She had gone out to the Western Australian goldfields, leaving after her prospector husband sold the mining rights to Lake Magadi for £15; it soon proved to have an inexhaustible supply of soda. Undaunted by lack of funds, she sold handkerchiefs, mirrors and combs, and, when the drink took her, rode her mule back to front.

Ivory was fetching £1,000 a ton, sold at auction in Mombasa or to Arab traders and gunrunners in Zanzibar. Some financed themselves with it, though it was a dangerous business. The famous big game hunter Bill Pickering had his head torn off by an enraged bull elephant; it was found perfectly intact in a thorn bush, smiling. Young Hugh Cholmondeley, the third Baron Delamere, landed at Berbera on the south side of the Gulf of Aden. He left the port with a caravan of 200 camels, weighed down with beads, bolts of

American cotton, rifles and tents, a photographer and a taxidermist to stuff his hunting trophies, and A. E. Atkinson, a doctor whom his mother insisted accompany him because he was always getting into scrapes. A lion mauled Delamere in Somaliland – he was saved by a gun-bearer who dragged him from its jaws by his ankle – and thereafter walked with a limp.

He sent Atkinson off to Zanzibar to replenish supplies as they moved south. Delamere scribbled a credit note for him: 'Kindly oblige bearer with whatever he wants up to £1,000.' This was a large enough sum to buy 7,500 acres of local land, but no merchant would turn down an English peer. The pair replenished their funds shooting elephant around Lake Rudolph; Delamere is thought to have made £10,000 from ivory. When he reached the Kenya Highlands, he found glades, forest, streams, lakes and tender sweet grass, a 'perfection' for farming investment. He set up camp, surrounded by galvanised sheeting to keep lions out, and imported livestock and a Scottish shepherd, Sammy McCall, dressed always in bowler hat, tweed suit and waistcoat. Each morning, the Delamere farm woke to the strains of a gramophone record, 'All aboard for Margate'.

Atkinson stuck to trading in powder, shot and percussion caps with the African owners of Birmingham-made muzzle loaders. In 1902, negotiations with a chief who had a large pile of ivory turned sour, and he was threatened by angry tribesmen. He sat on a powder keg and, urging the chief and his retinue to come close, lit a slow fuse before strolling into the bush to urinate. He left the ensuing scene of carnage with the ivory atop the heads of his porters. The doctor was charged with murder but successfully pleaded self-defence. It was a risky and difficult business. Blacks often fled when they saw a rare white in the bush; they thought his pale colour meant that he had left the womb too early and was thus unfinished as a person.

The real riches were in the land. A huge variety of farming was on offer, from coconut plantations on the coast, through tropical and semitropical crops, to tea and coffee, and the wheatlands and cattle and sheep of the Highlands. It became the most upper-class of the colonies; effectively, it was run by the patricians of the India Office and its currency was the Indian rupee. A European had to show possession of £50 before he could come ashore, and £400 before he could apply for land; a minimum of £3,000 was needed to make a go of an estate. It was toff territory. 'A class to whom British East Africa should strongly appeal is that represented by the Public Schoolboy,' a guide for settlers reported, 'for the training which is apt to render him out of place in Colonial life in Canada or Australia will not be detrimental to him here, firstly because he will find that a large percentage of the settlers are men of his own class, and secondly because his upbringing should fit him to control the natives whose labour is essential to every undertaking.' Free from the moral constraints of home, it was a rakish place. A subaltern in the Royal Fusiliers, Richard Meinertzhagen, arrived in 1902 to find that 'everyone keeps a native girl, usually a Masai.' It became famous for its big game hunting and for its intricate adulteries. The question 'are you married or do you come from Kenya?' entered the colonial mythology.

Keeping out the plebs, however, left paradise short on whites. They fretted lest the only place in tropical Africa where

'a European people can maintain itself in congenial surroundings' find itself 'overrun by an Asiatic race, so impotent in the past to deliver it from slavery and bloodshed.' One idea was to fill it with Jews; the colonial secretary, Joseph Chamberlain, offered to set aside 5,000 square miles of eastern Uganda as a Jewish homeland. The idea was discussed by Theodore Herzl at the sixth Zionist Congress meeting in Basle. Uganda was the size of Britain. The offer was not over-generous – though Israel at its foundation was to have only 8,000 square miles of less fertile land – but it infuriated the settlers. 'Feeling here very strong against introduction of alien Jews,' Delamere telegrammed *The Times*. 'Flood of people of that class sure to lead to trouble with half-tamed natives jealous of their rights... Englishmen here appeal public opinion... against the arbitrary proceeding and consequent swamping bright future of the country.'

The cable cost him £20 but he thought it worth it. The Zionists refused Chamberlain, and the settlers returned to a pioneering whose rough edges were smoothed by sundowners served by houseboys on £2 a year, and curries prepared by Goanese cooks on £40. The settlers made a good hand of it, or so Teddy Roosevelt said when he visited Nairobi on safari in

**Spearhead of empire:** *these men are heading the drive by Rhodes's British South Africa Company into Mashonaland. The picture was taken during their armed wagon trek to the north. Two of them, Archibald Colquhoun and his secretary, acted as administrators for the new territory. With them are Frederick Selous, the most famous big-game hunter of his* *time, and Dr Leander Starr Jameson, who led the 'Jameson Raid' in 1895, a failed bid to seize Johannesburg and the Rand goldmines in the Transvaal from the Boers. Selous was later killed fighting the Germans in East Africa during the First World War. The magnificent Selous National Park in modern Tanzania is named for him.* [PHOTO: W. E. FRY]

1909. 'You young people are doing a great work of which you have every right to be proud,' the American president, and big game hunter, told them. 'You have brought freedom where there was slavery... health where there was disease... food where there was famine... peace where there was continual war. Be proud of yourselves, for the time is coming when the world will be proud of you.'

Offshore, Zanzibar had been a protectorate since 1890. It was 'Mahommedan in its religion, Arabian in its morals, a cesspool of wickedness, and a fit capital for a Dark Continent.' This was before the British came; thereafter it was naturally thought to have improved. Zanzibar town had a population of 35,000 – 'Arab, Balooch, Osmanee, Persian, Somali and at least 100 specimens of the African tribes.' It produced cloves, copra, ivory and gum. Its acquisition was a case study in the European 'scramble for Africa'; it was ceded to Britain in return for the British ceding Heligoland in the North Sea to Germany and recognising French rights in Madagascar. The Imams of Muscat in Arabia, the traditional rulers, remained as nominal Sultans. In the same year most of the East African coast was carved up between Germany and Britain; the last free fragment, the Benandir coast, became Italian Somaliland in 1904. Among the brood of colonies, British Somaliland was said to be 'the ugly duckling'. It was indisputably a colony; the flag flew – but it had a white population of twenty-three. The British cheerfully admitted that 'since our authority has never remotely approached that necessary for census-taking,' the native population figure was an estimate. It was, however, imperially precise – the uncountable numbered 344,323.

West Africa was 'suitable only for persons of strong constitution and temperate habits, and everyone should be medically examined before going there...' The British presence was again thin, with not many more than two thousand of them in Nigeria, a country as large as France and Germany combined. Twelve hundred miles out into the Atlantic was St Helena, captured from the Dutch in 1673, where Napoleon died in 1821. It was currently being used for Boer prisoners of war; its normal population was 3,477, impoverished by the opening of the Suez Canal which ruined the coaling station on the route to India. In the Indian Ocean, there were old French possessions, acquired in the revolutionary and Napoleonic wars for the most part, which still clung to their old language and Roman Catholicism. They included Mauritius, seized in 1810 together with many smaller islands such as Diego Garcia, a still surviving fragment of empire on which the United States has a major naval base; and the Seychelles, captured by a lone British ship in 1794 and formally ceded in 1810, which had 22,691 French speakers and 'fifty Britishers, nearly all officials'.

There were no openings for men without capital in the West Indies. The British islands had not recovered from the abolition of slavery across the empire in 1833. Production costs of sugar rose from 6s a hundredweight under slavery to 15s 6d under conditions of free labour. The complete ruin of the islands was only avoided by the British imposing duties on 'slave-grown sugar', notably Cuban; Spain did not ban slavery until 1886. Coffee estates in the Blue Mountains in Jamaica, without houses, sold for £2 10s an acre; sugar estates were £10 to £14 an acre.

Nassau in the Bahamas was 'one of the healthiest and most charming towns' in the empire, with a 'climate of rare perfection'. Mark Twain complained that it was so clean there was nowhere for him to throw his cigar ends. It was already a winter resort for Canadians and Americans; so was Barbados, 'Little England'. Tourists were not yet arriving in numbers in Bermuda, which survived on its Royal Navy base and the New York market for early vegetables. Deep in the South Atlantic, two thousand Britishers ignored Argentinian claims and

worked the sheep stations on the Falkland Islands or whaled in the surrounding waters.

On the American mainland, the principal interest lay far to the north, in Canada, a wilderness at once so aloof, so dehumanised in its vastness, that it struck the great Arabian traveller Freya Stark 'with awe, and an immense admiration for the courage that had tackled it'. Homesteads of 640 acres were available to any head of family or male over eighteen who was a Briton or who declared his intention of becoming one. It was the prime destination for the British, and many Americans, too, were attracted over the border. In the central wheat provinces, the *Calgary Herald* estimated that profits averaged $11.75 an acre. Ontario was advertising in London: '20 million acres of Crown land awaiting settlement. 160 acres offered free, or at 2s an acre. To the Young Man who is willing to work the Land, Employment is Guaranteed.'

In the northlands, the Klondyke gold boom of 1898 was fizzling out. Gold was a great lure of empire, and prospectors an important element in its human fuel. Rough, bearded, belted and braced, for the most part, they included the writer Jack London and noblemen seeking to restore their fortunes; Lord Avonmore, together with gentlemen partners, servants and a large reserve of champagne, made up one such party. Thousands of them had toiled over White Pass from Alaska into the Yukon, greeted at the summit by scarlet-coated Mounties, who sent back the obvious cut-throats and those with less than a year's supplies. The population of Dawson had bloated to thirty thousand; a wild place of brothels and saloons until, at two minutes to midnight on Saturday, they were closed for an imperial Sunday of sobriety and churchgoing. It was dwindling rapidly now; Avonmore had failed to arrive in time, his champagne froze and was auctioned off in Edmonton.

The romantic calling of a fur-trapper was recommended 'only for those possessed by a Wander-Geist of the most strenuous type.' Whatever London was writing in his novel *White Fang*, emigrants were assured that Canadian wolves did not hunt in great packs – 'not more than a dozen are generally met with at one time' – and that bears seldom attacked men. Traplines were up to a hundred miles long, the trapper was alone for at least ten months of the year, and Yukon winters fell to 70° below. A prime black fox skin was fetching £200, and lynx – 'much in demand for motor-coats in the States' – fetched up to £8. There were takers.

In Malaya, before 1873, the British were restricted to the Straits Settlements in the south. The discovery of tin prompted the movement north, though the official line was that tension caused by an influx of Chinese workers 'made our interference

**Gold fever.** *Wagons arrive at the Bitter Creek landing stage to collect miners and adventurers during the Yukon Gold Rush in Canada in 1910. They have come north up the coast from Vancouver and are headed for Stewart. The urge for gold was a major factor in opening up the Canadian immensity; it underlay the Boer War in South Africa; it helped populate Australia and gave Australians their nickname, 'diggers'.*

[PHOTO: DAVID MCLELLAN]

obligatory'. By 1911, there were 3,284 British in Malaya, in a population of 2.6 million, including many Chinese and Indians whom they imported. They were flourishing so mightily that no third-class tickets were on offer on the boats from England, only second-class and first. Fortunes were made from rubber as well as tin. The first seedlings of the *Hevea braziliensis* were smuggled out of the Amazon to Kew Gardens in London in 1873 and on to the botanical gardens of Ceylon and Singapore in 1877. They first fruited in 1881, and commercial-scale planting started in 1895. The British invested £90 million — enough for forty-five battleships — in rubber in the fifteen years to 1910. The market for pneumatic tyres for cars and bicycles was growing rapidly. The price peaked at twelve shillings a pound in 1910. As new plantations came on stream, the price fell rapidly to two shillings, but the business remained highly profitable.

Even this great list of colonies is not exhaustive; it omits India, where freelance settlers were unwelcome; Ceylon, where the tea plantations were among the most valuable land in the empire, at £120 an acre; Sierra Leone and the Gold Coast and other territories where individuals could not buy land. It leaves out strings of islands — Tristan da Cunha beneath its South Atlantic volcano; Pitcairn, settled by mutineers from the *Bounty*; Cyprus, which had been Phoenician, Greek, Egyptian, Persian, Roman, Byzantine, Venetian, Turkish, until, in 1878, it inevitably fell into the hands of the greatest empire of them all.

The question of how it was done was rarely asked; soul-searching was not an imperial pastime. In the white dominions, it was answered simply enough; the British were in a majority. Elsewhere, they were buckets in an ocean; one in 4,400 in Uganda, one in 800 in Malaya; recently arrived, foreign in colour, religion and upbringing, yet ruling with absolute authority in the name of a distant monarch whose head appeared on banknotes and stamps, but never in the flesh.

It was an immense aid that they were so alien, astral beings projected to earth by steamship and locomotive. Other whites, Boers and American colonists, knew with whom they were dealing and were less impressed. Asians and Africans saw only the panoply of power and invention: cockaded governors and bewigged judges, battleships, telegraph wires, plantations growing imported trees to produce rubber for the tyres of strange horseless carriages. They rarely glimpsed a poor white; when, in the First World War, colonial troops came across whites labouring in British docks and slums, it made a profound impression on them.

It helped, too, that they were so few. Small numbers were a part of the administrative genius. With the exception of India — where British rule was known simply as 'the Raj' — the colonies were the responsibility of twenty-three 'first-class clerks', as the senior mandarins of the Colonial Office modestly called themselves. They presided over five territorial departments; West Indian, North American and Australian — which for arcane reasons of history also embraced Gibraltar and Cyprus — Asian, South African and West African. The clerks were a clubby group, who called each other by their first

**Landscapes** *to suit every taste lay within the empire. The British were devoted amateur artists, and they painted them all. To draw and do watercolours was part of a young lady's accomplishments, whilst officers were encouraged to learn how to sketch so they could record the lie of the land or enemy positions. Here, the easel has been set up at the Red Bluff, a beauty spot on the Norman river in Queensland, Australia. Curiosity, natural in an island people, was a great engine of empire. With the explorer went the butterfly net, specimen bottles, sketchbooks to record new plants and animals, and theodolites and sextants to make charts and maps. After a church and a governor's mansion, a new city next acquired a botanical gardens and a zoo. The deep interest in nature — dating back to Darwin, Cook and beyond — brought commercial reward. Tea was introduced to Africa, coconuts to the Bahamas. Illegally introduced seedlings meant that by 1910, Malaya had a new and very wealthy breed of colonialist — the rubber planter.*

names, a social rarity, whose doors were left open and who rarely bothered to make appointments. Wherever possible, they left the colonies to their own devices; the resident governors generally knew best — in particular, they knew to ask sparingly for money — and many were themselves former first-class clerks. The system could be comatose but it was rarely corrupt, and it worked reasonably enough.

The men on the spot were expected to stay in the same colony throughout their working lives unless they reached the highest echelons; governors were moved every five years to ensure that they did not become too close to local bigwigs. There was no training programme. A public school boarding education — torn from home to live in a miserable dormitory, roughing it as a junior, exposed at first to cold baths, fagging, beatings, games, runs, army drilling, field days, and then a sixth-form transfer to lordly status as a prefect, responsible for

all that was surveyed – was thought enough. The classic public school product was the 'good all-rounder', spirited at games, sound in temperament and stiff of lip, loyal, not too bright and not stupid. The colonial officer was frequently a few hundred miles from the nearest railhead; he was typically in charge of the welfare of several hundred thousand people, overwhelmingly illiterate and sometimes ill-tempered, feuders or headhunters. He had to display natural authority – he was obliged, at least in extremis, to hang and flog subjects who ludicrously outnumbered him, a dangerous task for anyone of nervous or insecure disposition – whilst avoiding lapses into authoritarianism. He was expected, for a modest salary, to be 'policeman, judge, diplomat, doctor, vet, oracle and handyman.' Britain had a genius for producing people of this ilk; it was as well.

India had its own India Office, a much grander affair financed out of Indian revenues. The subcontinent – three hundred million people in half a million villages in 1901 – had been ruled since the Mutiny by five thousand civil servants recruited in Britain. Almost all were products of the public schools and the grander universities, most often Oxford and Cambridge. They sat the 'India Civil' exam in the two years after their twenty-first birthday. They were offered twenty-one papers – and what papers, the one on English Literature assuming a working knowledge of twenty-five British authors! – in subjects that ranged from German, Arabic and French to political science, logic and philosophy. No paper was compulsory and each had a different value, a maximum of 900 points in advanced mathematics, for example, or 400 for Roman History. If successful, a year's probation at an English or Scottish university was followed by a second exam.

Here, the papers in the main Indian languages, the Indian

**The dark side of the Raj:** *in the last analysis, as the imperialist Frederick Selous noted, 'chastisement' was the most effective way of dealing with insurrection. Hundreds of punitive expeditions were mounted against unwilling subjects. British troops called them 'butcher and bolt'. These pictures show dissident Burmese on the treadmill (left) and captured Burmese rebels lashed to wooden frameworks (right). Burma did not submit easily to British rule. The process began in 1824 and was not completed until Upper Burma was seized in 1885. The country was ruled as a province of India until it became a crown colony with a measure of self-government in 1937. The photographs here vividly illustrate a great moral dilemma. The empire meant British supremacy. It also claimed to represent liberty. Over the long run, it could not do both.*

penal code and contract law, and Hindu and Muslim law, were compulsory. Others were chosen from a menu that included Chinese, Sanskrit, Arabic, Persian and the history of British India. The successful candidate was also tested in horsemanship. He could fail this, and still be shipped out to India; but he would have no rise in pay until he passed, for a proconsul who could not ride a horse was unthinkable. His rules of conduct made it clear that the government was entitled to the services of its servants for twenty-four hours each day. The administrator was almost always incorruptible, and generally able, as solid and dependable as his files which, as Curzon put it, went 'round and round like the diurnal revolutions of the earth… stately, solemn, sure and slow.'

There was, of course, more to the empire than that; matters deeper, and sometimes darker. Its embrace could be fatal. The aborigines of Tasmania became extinct, hunted down by the settlers like so many rabbits, and with as little regret. The Maoris in New Zealand were decimated by alcohol and firearms, the same combination that reduced the Indians in British Columbia by more than two thirds. Measles and smallpox carried off Eskimos, and syphilis ravaged the islanders of the South Seas. Other species suffered, too; by 1911, there were no buffalo left in Canada other than a single herd preserved on an Alberta reserve.

The British were ruthless; they imposed their rules and customs on peoples who had had little notion of them, and whipped and hanged when they were broken. Kipling caught the ideal of imperial power – fair and gentle when possible,

brutal if not – and he used the instinctive imperial cliché, the rider on the horse:

*Ride with an idle whip, ride with an unused heel,*
*But, once in a way, there will come a day*
*When the colt must be taught to feel*
*The lash that falls, and the curb that galls, and the sting of the*
*    rowelled steel.*

In the Indian Mutiny in 1857, British troops forced mutineers to lick the bloodstains from a room in which they had massacred white women and children before strapping them to the mouths of cannon and blowing them to pieces. An artillery officer beat a field in which mutineers were hiding; 'pea fowl, partridges and *pandie* (mutineers) rose together,' he wrote, 'the latter giving the best sport.' The bloodlust reached home. When the gibbets were red with blood and the bayonets creaked under their burdens, when 'the ground in front of every cannon is strewn with rags, and flesh, and shattered bone', a speaker told undergraduates at the Cambridge Union, only then 'talk of mercy'. Firing squads executing Pathan mullahs were issued with .303 and .457 ammunition to see which was ballistically superior.

Only through 'chastisement', the big game hunter Frederick Selous wrote in Rhodesia, would Ndebele tribesmen learn the 'uselessness of rebelling against the white man'. A British soldier, John Rose, described the process of chastising a Ndebele village. 'All over the place it was nothing but dead or dying niggers,' he wrote. 'We burnt all the huts and a lot of niggers that could not come out were burnt to death, and we could hear them screaming, but it served them right. We took about five women prisoners but let them go again; one woman was holding a baby and someone shot the baby through the leg and through the woman's side, but it was nothing and our doctor bandaged the wounds up.'

After the battle of Omdurman, to the disgust of Winston Churchill, who witnessed it, wounded dervishes were left to die or were finished off on the orders of Major John Maxwell, who said that 'a dead fanatic is the only one to extend any sympathy to.' A group of MPs were so outraged that they opposed a parliamentary grant of £30,000 to the successful general, Kitchener. It did not prevent him from becoming Earl Kitchener of Khartoum; Maxwell, who would later command in Dublin at the time of the Easter Rising, and Selous, both became knights. It took the British thirty years to subdue the tribes of the southern Sudan, cattle rustlers with an aversion to paying taxes. Scores of punitive expeditions meted out many hangings in the Nuba mountains. 'The less attention is drawn to these matters the better,' Lord Cromer noted from Cairo.

Such forays, destroying villages and crops, were known as 'butcher and bolt'; they were endemic also on the North-West Frontier of India.

The empire was racist; if not in the modern catchall use of the word, at least in the sense of discrimination. The explorer Sir Harry Johnston said in lordly fashion that Africa south of the Zambesi should be settled by 'white and whitish' races, whilst tropical Africa should be 'ruled by whites, developed by Indians and worked by blacks.' A white engine driver in India was paid 370 rupees a month on the mainline expresses. Indian drivers were paid twenty rupees and restricted to branchlines. As late as 1915, only one in twenty senior civil service posts was held by an Indian. No Chinese were allowed to live on Hong Kong's lofty and healthy Peak. They were spoken to in pidgin, an infantile and specially constructed English, as if they were incapable of learning an adult language. The settlers guarded their privileges – the Australian pearl fisheries were a white preserve – and were quick to cry foul. In Kenya, traders complained of the 'distorted sense of fair play' which allowed

**His Excellency.** *Sir Henry Hesketh Bell's career – governor of small islands in the Caribbean sun and immense slices of Africa, author, hunter, inventor of a system of hurricane insurance, expert on sleeping sickness and witchcraft – was workaday by the standards of his time. He is seen (above) as Governor of Uganda in 1908. It had become a British Protectorate sixteen years before. Wearing dark uniform and white gloves, he is giving the opening speech at the Kampala Agricultural and Industrial Exhibition, flanked by the nominal 'rulers' of Uganda, including the Kings of Bunyoro, Ankole and Toro. The British were careful to preserve local chiefs where it helped maintain stability. But it was the Pax Britannica that provided peace and security and Bell was ruler of Uganda in all but name. He is at the opening of the railway linking Port Bell on Lake Victoria (near right), named in his honour, with Kampala.*

**Sir Henry** *was a man of many interests; he poses (centre, above) with assistants and 'an assortment' of his big game trophies. As a young administrator in West Indian colonies, as well as his system of hurricane insurance, he created irrigation schemes and an*

experimental plantation. His postings took him to Barbados, Grenada, the Gold Coast (now Ghana), the Bahamas and Dominica. After Uganda, he was promoted to be Governor of Northern Nigeria, but blighted his career by allowing missionaries into Kano against London's orders. He was demoted to Governor of the Leeward Islands, and his last post was as Governor of Mauritius in 1924. He wrote memoirs, fiction, studies of witchcraft and an award-winning study of the Dutch and French colonial systems.

them to be 'brought into commercial competition with the Asiatic, whose mode of life and code of business are on an altogether lower plane...'

There was, however, more to it than simple colour. By and large, the British thought themselves superior to anyone. In the Fashoda incident in 1898, when they encountered a party of their old cross-Channel rivals on the Upper Nile, *The Times* thundered that they were not to be robbed of fresh pickings 'by a promenade of eight or nine Frenchmen.' There was an imperial pecking order and they distinguished carefully between peoples, an essential process since they used some – most notably the troops of the Indian Army – to rule others. In Kenya, for example, they found the coastal Swahili 'an excellent agriculturalist, a good servant, generally clean in his person and altogether of a higher type than the inland tribes'.

The Wa-kamba was much in demand for his 'curious aptitude for controlling machinery'. They admired the Masai as 'essentially a fighting race', although, unfortunately from their point of view, 'tribal custom debars him from working and barter.' The Kikuyu, by contrast, was 'altogether lacking in bravery and sense of honour... but of greater intellectual capacity.' Most scorn was reserved for the imported Indians, 'coolies of a low type employed in the construction of the Uganda railway... generally regarded with disfavour by the Europeans having done much to depreciate the natives morally and physically.'

They felt akin to 'warrior races', Zulus, Pathans and Afridis, Sikhs and Gurkhas. The troops who fought the Maoris admired them enough to raise the funds for a memorial dedicated to them. Administrators respected Indian and Malay

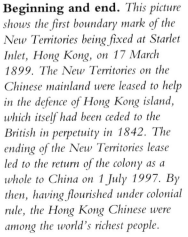

**Blood brothers.** *The flag often followed trade. Here (left), three members of the Imperial British East Africa Company, Frederick Jackson, James Martin and Dr Archibald Mackinnon, forge a treaty with the Kikuyu tribe in what would only later become Kenya colony. Pioneers like this respected local customs, such as the blood-brotherhood ceremonies insisted on by this Kikuyu chief, and had little time for the squeamish at home. 'After all, what is it?' Jackson asked. 'Simply swallowing a bit of well-cooked meat or liver of a goat, killed for the occasion, with a tiny speck of each other's blood on it…'*
[PHOTO, LEFT: ERNEST GEDGE]

**Beginning and end.** *This picture shows the first boundary mark of the New Territories being fixed at Starlet Inlet, Hong Kong, on 17 March 1899. The New Territories on the Chinese mainland were leased to help in the defence of Hong Kong island, which itself had been ceded to the British in perpetuity in 1842. The ending of the New Territories lease led to the return of the colony as a whole to China on 1 July 1997. By then, having flourished under colonial rule, the Hong Kong Chinese were among the world's richest people.*

princes and rajahs, and Nigerian emirs, and loathed white traders, making little secret of the fact; commercial men, in turn, despised the lofty civil servants and worked closely with Zoroastrian Parsees, and Jews, whose business acumen they held in high regard. The British were well aware of the sharp differences between peoples, and the imperial habit of lumping them together in single territories for no more than administrative convenience would extract a terrible toll in civil wars when the Pax Britannica broke down.

The dilemma that undermined it was already breaking surface. The empire meant British supremacy; it also claimed to represent liberty. Over the long haul, it could not do both. Allan Octavian Hume was a man who combined the moral magnificence of empire, at its quiet and humanitarian best, and the seeds of its destruction. His father, Joseph, had made a fortune in the East India Company, and devoted himself to free trade with India, and the abolition of army floggings, naval press gangs and imprisonment for debt. The son served in Bengal, doing much to improve farming and public health. A naturalist, he built a great library and museum for his collection of Oriental birds at Simla. Hume's Tawny Owl, Lesser Whitethroat and Wheatear were named in his honour. He was also the founder, and first secretary from 1885 to 1908, of the Indian National Congress. It was devoted to Indian self–government; under Mahatma Gandhi, at this time a lawyer in South Africa, it would achieve it.

Richard Meinertzhagen, the young subaltern in Kenya, sensed the end. 'I cannot see millions of educated Africans – as there will be in a hundred years' time – submitting tamely to white domination,' he wrote. 'Then blood will be spilled and I have little doubt about the outcome… sooner or later it must lead to a clash between black and white.'

**'Great God! this is an awful place...'** *Captain Scott (bottom left, in his den) wrote of Antarctica on his doomed expedition. His men expected to be the first to reach the South Pole when they sailed in the* Terra Nova *(top left). The expedition had only a few dogs (right). The going was too hard for their ponies, and Scott and his four companions had to haul their supplies themselves. They reached the Pole on 16 January 1912, to find a black flag attached to a sledge runner: the Norwegian Roald Amundsen had beaten them by a month. Crippled with frostbite on the return, Laurence Oates (centre, with ponies) left the tent to sacrifice his life to help his companions. 'He said, "I am just going outside and may be some time,"' Scott wrote. 'He went out into the blizzard and we have not seen him since.' On 29 March, blizzard-bound, Scott wrote a letter to his friend J. M. Barrie, the writer of* Peter Pan: *'We are showing that Englishmen can still die with a bold spirit, fighting it out to the end.' He made a last entry in his journal: 'It seems a pity but I do not think I can write more. For God's sake look after our people.' The bodies were found eight months later close to a food dump that would have saved them.*

[PHOTOS: HERBERT PONTING]

## CHAPTER THREE

# HIGH LIFE, LOW LIFE

**A Grenadier Guards** *officer and a peeress are eyed by less exalted subjects as he ushers her into Westminster Abbey for the coronation of George V in 1911. He was one of fifty gentlemen summoned as 'Gold Staff Officers' by the Earl Marshal to show guests to their places. The life of a Guards officer was agreeable – six months' annual leave for colonels, five for majors – though they were expected to maintain a style far beyond that possible on their army pay, and a private income was essential. There were other minor inconveniences, such as going to war, and not compromising the dignity of the Brigade of Guards by smoking Virginia cigarettes, reversing in the waltz, carrying parcels in public or wearing brown shoes east of Ascot.*

'WHAT WILL BECOME OF THE POOR COUNTRY when I die?' Queen Victoria had asked in a fit of depression over her pleasure-loving eldest son. 'If Bertie succeeds he would spend his life in one whirl of amusements.' Edward VII, 'Bertie' to the royal family and 'Tum-Tum' to others, was a genial man. He encouraged the child of one of his mistresses to run slices of hot buttered toast down the stripes of his trousers, buttered side downwards for better lubrication, and to call him 'Kingy'. He had an eye for pretty women with the hourglass, petticoated and corseted figures of late-Victorian and Edwardian society – like the 'Jersey Lily's', the actress Lillie Langtry – and a taste for the clubby, male worlds of gambling and racing. His easy nature fitted into the comfortable worlds of 'the Upper Ten Thousand', the great landowning families, and of the plutocrats, the company promoters, those who had done well in the South African mines, and other financial jugglers whose 'flash money' he helped spend at cards and on the grouse moor. The British began the Edwardian decade as the world's richest people, and national income increased by almost a fifth during it.

The richest four per cent in the country owned ninety per cent of its private wealth, and the top one per cent owned two thirds of it. Spending power was intensely concentrated, into individual ownership of land, shipyards, mines, businesses, streets of back-to-back slums and elegant London squares. There was much scope for indulgence, and Edwardian society used it to the full.

The country house and estate were under threat from the agricultural depression that had begun in the 1870s. The old deference to the landed gentry died hard, however, and those who made their pile in cities and factories still sought social respect in 'broad acres'. Thus Sir William Armstrong, who had hauled himself up from Newcastle articled clerk to engineering magnate, by way of inventing the hydraulic crane and producing engines, ships and artillery pieces, was not happy until he owned sixteen thousand acres and had added the stately Bamburgh Castle to his grandiose house, Cragside.

Money was poured into sporting estates: grouse moors, deer forests and stretches of river bank, where it was possible for men with neither the nerve nor the seat for foxhunting to shoot and fish. They might be coached by the professional ghillies and gamekeepers, stalkers, loaders and beaters, drawn from the rural poor for whom 'country sports' had long been a livelihood. It went, also, into new houses, less overwhelming than the great turreted Victorian piles, their styles influenced by the Arts and Crafts movement or the revival of interest in the Baroque. Both helped to make them look 'as old as a new house could', hinting at breeding and ancestry more than wealth.

**The Prince of Wales,** *the future Edward VII, enjoyed horseracing, gambling, sailing, café society and several mistresses. He is seen dressed as a Grand Master of the Knights Hospitallers of Malta attending the 1897 Devonshire House fancy dress ball, given in London to mark Queen Victoria's Diamond Jubilee. He had caused a scandal by being cited as a witness in a divorce suit in 1870; he appeared as a witness again, in a case involving cheating at cards, in 1891; his mother was not amused. His mistress Lillie Langtry (above right) was known as the 'Jersey Lily', since she was the daughter of the Dean of Jersey. She became an actress and one of the most noted beauties of the age, though no photograph did her justice. The press was then more circumspect, but a sporting newspaper ran a one-line story saying that there was 'nothing between the Prince of Wales and Lillie Langtry'. It followed that up a week later with the following words: 'Not even a sheet'. By the time her former lover*

*inherited the throne, she had
remarried to become Lillie de Bathe
and was a celebrated racehorse owner.
Edward VII became a well-loved and
energetic king who lent his name to a
stylish and easy-going age.*

[PHOTOS: LAFAYETTE]

**Social status** – and less importantly, food supplies – were derived from killing things. At Stonor Park near Henley-on-Thames, the targets for the obese sportsman seen with the Honourable Mrs Henry Davenport (below) were pheasants. A dead bird can be seen lying behind the end of the barrels of his twelve-bore shotgun. Two loaders stand behind him with his second and third guns ready to be passed to him so there need be no break in the barrage of lead that he might send in to the flushes of pheasants when they start coming over thick and fast. The beaters at the shoot of the mustard-manufacturing Colman family near Norwich (left) wear light-coloured coats so that they will stand out from a woodland background and thus avoid being shot as they advance towards the guns, driving the game before them. Here the drive is over and they carry dead birds to the game cart.

**Tally-Ho!** *The elegant horsewoman (right) is at a meet of the Cottesmore Hunt – Oscar Wilde's 'unspeakable in pursuit of the uneatable' – is after the fox. The apron-like divided skirt with breeches underneath was worn to facilitate riding side-saddle. This was the expected mode for all women until some sensible souls started riding astride after the First World War. The net over her face would have helped to keep her top hat from flying off as well as adding greatly to her appeal to male members of the hunt.*

**The Henley Regatta,** *the high point of the rowing man's year, was also an important fixture during the 'Season'. Phyllis Court (left) had lawns stretching down to the Thames at Henley, where the river is thick with punts and canoes (right) during the regatta. A water-borne conjuror provides what is probably welcome light relief for the ladies during an interval between races.*

[PHOTOS: HORACE NICHOLLS]

Lady Violet Brandon, the daughter of a marquis, found the number of rooms in her father's house in Norfolk beyond her powers and patience to calculate. It had two grand halls, a large and small dining room, a library, several parlours and drawing rooms, 'innumerable' bedrooms with a 'bachelors' row' for single guests, family and servants' bedrooms, a nursery, a schoolroom, a lamp and a china and a laundry room, and a stable block. Distances were so great that the lamp man had a huge wheeled truck on which he hauled food from the kitchens to the dining room. Not that this was the Brandons' only home; they also had an Irish estate, a house in London and a villa on the Mediterranean. They were in Norfolk only for the autumn, for the shooting, between the London season and wintering abroad.

With the house came the house party. The Edwardian weekend, 'Saturday to Monday', it struck the diplomat and writer Sir Harold Nicolson, was 'the most agreeable form of social intercourse the world has ever known.' The guest was called at 8.30 am by his valet, 'silent but hostile', carrying a brass can of shaving water in his left hand and a tray in the right laden with tea, toast and Marie biscuits. The last were plain and thin, ornamented only with small indentations, the simplest food to pass the lips. 'Blinking plethoric eyes above his pink silk eiderdown', the guest would nibble the biscuits and sip the tea before adjusting his teeth, his hair and his Afghan dressing-gown, and padding off to the bathroom.

Only the most louche Edwardian, Nicolson observed, would take Sunday breakfast in his room. The others met in the dining room. Here were tables with hams, eggs, tongues, galantines, cold grouse and pheasant and partridge, and hot or cold ptarmigan – 'no Edwardian meal was complete without ptarmigan', the mountain-dwelling grouse from the northern uplands – and fruits and porridge and jugs of lemonade. The pots of tea had little ribbons, yellow for China, and red, 'indicating, without *arrière pensée*, our Indian Empire.' No newspapers were allowed at this stage; guests were expected to talk, with the 'pleasant sense of confederacy and sin' that came from avoiding the family prayers with which their Victorian parents had welcomed each day.

True, they then attended church for matins, where the sermon might be tediously long, but that was followed by luncheon, and an afternoon drive in an open car, and tea, and bridge, and dinner – 'ptarmigan and champagne' – and more bridge, and finally at midnight, devilled chicken. On Monday morning, after their valets had packed away their medicinal salts and their shooting sticks, they regained London by train, leafing through the pages of *The Times* and *Morning Post* to find references to themselves and their fellow guests. 'They returned to Curzon Street feeling very pleased,' Nicolson observed. 'And next Saturday it would all begin again.'

The rich toiled hard at being idle. After Easter they dined and danced at the balls given in London to facilitate the marriage market at the heart of each year's 'Season'. Then they watched their horses run in the Derby and at Ascot. In August, after

**The age of elegance** is caught even by a child (above), the son of the Duke and Duchess of Hamilton, self-confidently astride his pony in Highland dress. Grace and charm were part of an ideal which Constance, Marchioness of Ripon (near right), had no difficulty in maintaining into her forties. She was a great patron of the opera and was famous for her parties where she daringly mixed leading singers with nobility and royalty. Someone described the atmosphere at the parties as 'Bohemia in tiaras'. When the native coffers ran dry, they could be restocked by importing an American heiress, like the Duchess of Marlborough (far right), who poses with her children in her coronation robes. Her slight stiffness is due either to the jewelled choker round her neck, or to her consciousness that she was not to this British manner born. She was the former Consuelo Vanderbilt, who brought with her money from American steamships and railroads.

[Photos: Lafayette]

taking part in Cowes Week on the Isle of Wight, sailing in the regatta themselves or watching from the Royal Yacht Squadron, they had to traverse the country to shoot grouse or stalk deer in the far North. The moors were followed by the coverts, for pheasant and fox, before a winter in France.

A lady invited to a weekend at a great house needed to take several trunks with her; she was expected to change her outfit half a dozen times a day. A gentleman needed tweed suits for the country, plus fours for shooting and golf, a frock coat for business, a dinner jacket for an evening in, a tail coat for an evening out. He had to wear the right combination for every event, or tongues would wag about lack of breeding; an experienced valet was an essential part of the parvenu's defences. Brown boots, for example, could be worn as far as Ascot, but no nearer to London. Society people were not supposed to be in town in August and September. A man who found himself in this predicament made it clear that he was only passing through on his way to the country by wearing country clothes, a light thin lounge suit with a straw hat. Life was all very free and easy in principle, the astute Yorkshire novelist and playwright J. B. Priestley observed, but 'in practice it was more highly disciplined and more wearing than the life of a recruit in the Life Guards.'

Liver salts – Eno's, Epsom, Andrew's – or Carter's Pills were essential, for Edwardians were Gargantuas. A guest at one dinner party for twenty-four counted 362 plates and dishes and six dozen wine glasses in use. The menu of a dinner Sir Charles Petrie recollected his father giving, began with caviar and anchovies to work up a thirst, moved on to *Tortue Claire* and salmon and filet of sole, gathered pace with chicken and asparagus, rolled through lamb and filet of beef, paused briefly with water ice flavoured with Kummel, resumed with wild duck and Russian salad, and entered a frenzy of puddings – *pouding Imperial, pouding glacé à la Chantilly* – before reaching a final dessert.

Sport was the best antidote to this prodigious intake, dieting being a necessity of the poor and not a fad of the rich, and it was a passion for the British as a whole. Whatever interest there was in politics, the writer G. K. Chesterton remarked in 1904, 'we have a much greater love of cricket and C. B. Fry represents us much better than Mr Chamberlain.' The latter was merely a cabinet minister and leading imperialist; Charles Fry was a member of the English cricket, soccer and athletic teams, a man who had scored six successive centuries at cricket and who later refused the throne of Albania, offered to him by the feuding people of that Balkan country on the grounds that only an English sportsman could have the sense of fair play they themselves so sadly lacked; an all-rounder, in short, of such talent that, when he lamented that he had never become involved in the Derby, a friend retorted: 'What as, Charles? Trainer, jockey or horse?'

The notion that the British had invented sport was a conceit, but they had created more games than any people, before or since, and they devoted more time to them. A test match at cricket, with play interrupted at frequent intervals for soft drinks, luncheon and afternoon tea, lasted for five days, a luxury incomprehensible to foreigners, who also had the greatest difficulty in grasping its rules and the arcane vocabulary of its field placings, 'silly mid off', 'cover point', and its deliveries, the 'yorker', 'the chinaman' and the 'googly'. Regattas and race meetings also consumed several days; Henley, Cowes and Ascot had their own Weeks.

**The Sporting Life** *had a place for women, as demonstrated by one hurtling down the Cresta Run in St Moritz in 1908 (left). A heavy skirt is tied round her to protect her from the ice. A brace of Honourables (above left) attend a ballooning meet at Hurlingham near Fulham in London. Frank Meadow Sutcliffe photographed this game of tennis (above) at Whitby on the Yorkshire coast, with the windmill of the Union Mill Society, a cooperative founded in 1900 to provide cheap flour, in the background. Invented in the 1870s, the game soon became hugely popular with both sexes, though it is a men's doubles in action here.*
[PHOTO, ABOVE: FRANK MEADOW SUTCLIFFE]

The first rules for football had been drawn up at Cambridge in 1848, whilst the benighted foreigners in Europe were undergoing their year of revolutions. Prizefighting with bare knuckles, the great sport of 18th-century England, was made respectable by gloves, the public school ethos and the rules laid down by Oscar Wilde's tormentor, the Marquis of Queensberry. Lawn tennis was created by a Major Clopton Wingfield during a Christmas house party in Wales in 1873. Most country houses had a billiard room, which also proved a convenient home for antlers, tusks, lions' heads, the pads and brushes of foxes, bearskins and other proof of hunting prowess. The older sport of rackets, played against the walls of London buildings, was modernised into squash.

American crews had a firm grasp on the America's Cup, in spite of patriots like Sir Thomas Lipton, a Glasgow errand boy who was a millionaire at thirty from a grocery chain, and who poured much of that fortune into a series of challenges against the New York Yacht Club. Patriotism, however, was not enough; he tried five times between 1899 and 1930, and lost each time. Killing things remained the greatest sport, however, and the earlier the child started the better. It did not much matter what was shot as long as the quantity was high. 'We have slaughtered many rabbits,' Winston Churchill wrote to his mother

as a young teenager from a manor house near Newmarket. 'About eleven brace altogether. Tomorrow we slay the rats.' It was all character-building: 'Pipes are frozen', he added. 'Oil freezes in the kitchen… We exist on onions and Rabbits.'

'Living like a Duke' had entered the language, and small wonder, for one of them, Westminster, inherited an estate estimated at £14 million at the turn of the century, spread over four continents and including the heart of Mayfair and Belgravia, London's most expensive residential areas. The Earl of Derby was hardly a lesser creature, with an income of £300,000 a year from coalmines, city rents and his 70,000 acres. He was known as 'the King of Lancashire', seventeenth holder of a title conferred more than four centuries before, grandson of a prime minister, with political clout felt from London to the Liverpool slums.

It is easy enough to multiply the Edwardian pound into dollars – the exchange rate was stable at $4.15 to the pound – but less easy to convert it to modern values. It sells the Edwardian millionaire short to increase his wealth the hundredfold that is justified in terms of average wages. He had a style of living beyond that of the modern billionaire, for he had few equals on earth, and the earth knew it and loved him for it, or pretended to.

**Upstairs, Downstairs:** *more than two million domestic servants toiled in Edwardian houses. The pay was miserable – maids on £12 a year like this one (left) getting the silver breakfast service ready before dawn, and gardeners (centre) on little more – but they were fed and sheltered and a happy home was thought a good billet. The Traill family in Northern Ireland (right) thought it natural to include their parlour maid, house-keeper, butler, carpenter and coachman in this family portrait.*

Lord Derby's income was 25,000 times higher than that of a 'tweeny' housemaid on £12 a year; the question of overstaffing Knowsley Hall, his great house outside Liverpool, did not arise.

Splendour was not only ducal. Industrialists, shipbuilders, locomotive makers, the owners of chemical plants and steel and woollen mills, were making fortunes. The 'Cottontots' of the Manchester textile trade, snugly installed in their great Cheshire villas, thought of themselves as a class apart; the money amassed by big brewers, duly translated into titles and seats in the House of Lords, led the 'beerage' to become a distinct part of the peerage. These men could well afford the elegant and expensive Silver Ghost, designed for them in 1906 by the new partnership of Rolls-Royce. The car reflected its maker; Charles Royce, Cambridge-educated, was the son of a peer, the first man to

make a non-stop flight across the Channel and back. In Oxford, William Morris, a former bicycle repairer, founded a company that had started to make cars that sold to the different but thriving middle-class market.

Edwardians with more than £400 a year, the average income of a country doctor, could live well. A good London house could be rented for £100, and equipped with two live-in servants, and a housekeeper to relieve the mistress of the tedium of arranging housework, for a further £80 a year. A bank manager might have an income that was one five-hundredth of the Earl of Derby, but his £600 still stretched to a housemaid, a cook, a 'knife-boy' to clean boots and chop wood, a governess, a part-time gardener and one of the new Model Ts that Henry Ford was producing for £135 from his new plant at Trafford Park in Manchester.

In the provincial towns, businessmen breakfasted heartily – porridge, bacon and eggs, kidney and steak, often washed down with beer – put in a morning's work at the office, met their friends for a pre-lunch drink in the town club or its best hotel, took a heavy lunch at home, had a nap, worked a little in the afternoon, took tea with cakes and scones, and at 7pm were ready for a sherry before dinner. A man's paunch was not a source of shame; it was known as his 'corporation', a sign of status.

The better-paid employees – managers, senior clerks,

foremen – were abandoning the city centres for new housing in leafy suburbs. These were places of halfpenny journalism and penny bus rides, 'gramophones, bamboo furniture, pleasant Sunday afternoons', recitals of the Glory Songs of empire, golf, tennis, high school education, picture postcards, 'miraculous hair restorers', prize competitions – 'and all the other sorts of 20th-century claptrap', a critic said, that gave the Edwardian suburbs their prosperous and self-contented air. 'Like the Arabs,' the *Birmingham Mail* reported in 1903, 'they are folding their tents and stealing silently away in the direction of Knowle or Solihull… a little revolution is taking place.' The city poor and their habitat – 'endless streets of undistinguished houses,' wrote H. G. Wells, author of *The War of the Worlds*, 'undistinguished industries, shabby families, second-rate shops, inexplicable people who in one fashionable phrase do not "exist" ' – were no longer visible. Each day, in a train high on an embankment or deep in an underground tube, middle-class man 'hurried through the region where the [poor man] lives. He gazes darkly from his pleasant hill villa upon the huge and smoky area of tumbled tenements which stretches out at his feet.' In this 'uncouth laboratory', he dimly sensed that the dark forces of socialist revolution were fermenting.

Like one of the flying machines that were now taking to the air – Charles Royce was killed in an aircraft crash shortly after his Channel triumph – the apparently unblemished lifestyle of the middle and upper classes could not defy gravity for ever. Landowners were already in trouble. Even the largest of them could not compete with wheat from the virgin prairies of North America. Transatlantic freight prices fell thanks to steamships – by 1910, their number reached that of sailing ships and their tonnage was greater – and the price of homegrown wheat halved. Refrigeration, with cheap Danish bacon, Argentine beef and Australasian mutton, had the same effect on livestock prices.

Noblemen who felt the pinch carried on the tradition of marrying heiresses. A new ploy was to tap the American market. Consuelo Vanderbilt brought a dowry estimated at £2 million to replenish the coffers of the Duke of Marlborough; another member of the family, Lord Randolph Churchill, married Jennie Jerome, the daughter of a New York businessman, a bargain that brought the British their son Winston. The Duke of Manchester married the daughter of a Cincinnati railroad magnate. Lesser men had no such lifelines. The market towns of the South were half-ruined. They still held yearly 'hiring fairs' where labourers wanting a new job stood in the market square – shepherds with their crooks, milkmaids with pails, carters with whips – waiting for a farmer

**Days at the races:** *a group of industrialists (right) enjoy a light snack, with the limousines that have conveyed them effortlessly to the racecourse behind them; (left) the poor wash themselves at Epsom, having walked from London to see the Derby.* [PHOTOS: HORACE NICHOLLS]

to choose them. Fewer were wanted; the farm labour force of two million dwindled as men abandoned the countryside for city factories or the colonies.

'A village which once fed, clothed, policed and regulated itself cannot now dig its own wells or build its own barns,' a Somerset clergyman lamented. 'It is pathetically helpless in everything… England is bleeding at the arteries, and it is her reddest blood which is flowing away.' The blood was not English alone. In Wales, still with many Welsh-speakers, the poor who could no longer meet the *dyled tato* – the 'potato debt' paid in labour to landowners who allowed them to plant potatoes in their fields – left for the sheep stations of Patagonia. From Scotland, with its 'unspeakably filthy privy middens… incurably damp labourers' cottages on farms, whole townships unfit for human occupancy in the crofting counties and the islands', the ambitious young escaped to Canada.

In industry, Germany and the United States had removed steel from the long list of items – coal, gold, timber, tea, textiles, ships – in which Britain was 'first among the Powers'. It was thought intolerable that German steel should be going into battleships that could threaten British naval supremacy. The First Sea Lord, Admiral Jacky Fisher, responded with a new type of all-big-gun battleship. The first, HMS *Dreadnought*, almost 18,000 tons with ten 12-inch guns, was built in less than a year. As it began its sea trials in 1906, the German navy in turn ordered its own Dreadnought. The programme was so expensive that the government had difficulty in funding it – 'the Royal Navy always travels first-class', Fisher said – but the public was not content with the three other Dreadnoughts on order. 'We want eight,' the cry went up, 'and we won't wait.' Erskine Childers's spy novel *The Riddle of the Sands*, about a German invasion across the North Sea, caught a national imagination fevered by threat of 'the Hun'. Fisher twice proposed a pre-emptive strike to catch the German fleet at anchor and destroy it. It did not happen – 'My God, Fisher, you must be mad!' the rattled Edward VII told the admiral – but it was clear that the Germans had skills and pockets deep enough to challenge Britannia's rule of the waves.

There was concern, too, at the Germans' progress in business. 'He is a glutton for work,' the *Daily Mail* warned of 'our German cousins', bolting his simple breakfast of coffee and rolls and clocking into his factory whilst his British relation was still ruminating over his bacon and eggs. 'He out-hustles even the Americans… It is the German's love of work, love of business, that makes him, and his thoroughness of scientific training, a menace to easier-going rivals.'

Labour relations in Britain were notoriously bad. Up to 40 million working days a year were being lost to strikes.

Observers recognised that the 'everlasting feudalism of master and man' was damaging. They pointed out that American bosses worked with their men, not over them, and that in America 'the man is colleague of his master.' Little notice was taken. The school leaving age was twelve, and children laboured from that age. Safety standards were primitive; molten metal and chemicals spilled on flesh, chips of steel flew into unprotected eyes and the air reeked with dust and fumes. It was so noisy in the Lancashire textile mills that the weavers had to learn to lip read. Few plants had canteens or indoor lavatories; the men took in their own food and heated it on boilers or, in the rolling mills, on a length of glowing metal; and a coat of whitewash passed for hygiene. There were enlightened industrialists, who built airy model towns for their workers: the soapmaker Lord Leverhulme at Port Sunlight, the Quaker chocolate tycoon George Cadbury, with his Bourneville village near Birmingham. More were happy to enjoy a godlike status, masters of their labourers' lives, with their foremen in attendance as demi-gods, hiring and firing, fining for sloppy work or promoting, and rejoicing in song:

*The working class can kiss my arse*
*I've got the foreman's job at last.*

Union power was anathema, and they attacked it vigorously, celebrating the arrival of the Edwardian era with a famous

**In the mills.** *Girls (left) were particularly valued for their nimble fingers in the huge Lancashire cotton industry, in whose damp mills much of the world's cotton was spun and woven. Pay was no more than a few shillings a week.*

triumph in the Taff Vale case. A local railway company in Wales was awarded £23,000 from the railwaymen's union in compensation for losses caused by a strike. It had been thought that the unions, as voluntary bodies, were immune from prosecution. The ruling in the House of Lords opened any union to financial ruin if it called a strike; it was seen as a 'heads I win, tails you lose' decision in favour of the bosses, for if the union failed to achieve its objectives in a strike, it lost, and if it was successful but was sued, it lost too. The victory was Pyrrhic, however; working-class anger gave the unions and the new Labour Party impetus. The decision could only be reversed through parliament, and the unions agreed to pay a penny a member a year to support pro-labour candidates for the House of Commons. This, too, was ruled illegal but the unions were putting on enough muscle to have the ban lifted with the proviso that they balloted their members and allowed them to opt out of the political levy if they wished.

The miners saw themselves as the front line in the class war, distinctly unEdwardian figures, battered, instantly recognised by their blue scars where coal dust had filled a wound. They won campaigns – they were the first workers to get an eight-hour day and a minimum wage, after a series of strikes from 1908 – but they paid a constant price to the pits. Several hundred were injured each day, 493 killed in the disaster at Senghenydd in

**The 'workshop of the world'** *was Britain's claim, but its dominance as the world's leading exporter of manufactured goods was under increasing threat from Germany and the United States. Little of the equipment used in this forging shop (right) can have changed in more than half a century. The British were already slow to adopt new methods and machines in old industries.*
[PHOTO: ALVIN LANGDON COBURN]

South Wales in 1913. In Yorkshire, some seams were seven feet high and near the surface. The faulted seams deep under South Wales and Durham were sometimes only eighteen inches thick, so that the men worked lying on their sides, in a filth of water and dust, hacking at the coal with pick and shovel, with a lad – perhaps twelve – to haul the coal from the face to the tub in a box. Working by the guttering light of a candle pushed into a clod of clay, in a gas-free pit, the miner cut and heaved wooden pit–props for his tunnel as he advanced, alert for the tell-tales of a roof collapse that would entomb him, a creaking timber, a puff of dust. Productivity was falling as the easier seams were worked out, and more labour was drafted in to compensate. The coal industry was employing 1.2 million by 1913, the year when an absolute record of 278 million tons was mined.

For all its squalor and danger, mining paid a living wage. Face workers averaged just over £2 a week. A ploughman trudged twelve miles a day through the heavy soil for half that, though his tied cottage might be free. Two million domestic servants toiled in Edwardian households, fed, uniformed and sheltered in basements or attics, but expected to work 'all hours' six days a week for £12 or £15 a year. The great industries based on coal and steam were flourishing, if vulnerable to turndowns in world trade. It was hard for casual labourers hired by the day – port workers paraded through

**Putting their backs into it.**
*Labourers lay the first electricity cable under the River Esk at Whitby in 1910 (above). The men seem to be bending before the imposing and erect figure of the foreman. It was already observed that the 'everlasting feudalism of master and men' was damaging, unlike America where men had* greater equality with their bosses. Strikes took a huge toll of working days a year.
[PHOTO: FRANK MEADOW SUTCLIFFE]

**Shipbuilders,** *here fitting the starboard propeller shaft of the ill-fated Titanic (right), were relatively well paid but the work was dangerous. As the ship grew, riveters worked 100 feet up in biting winds on fragile scaffolding.*

Trafalgar Square with fish heads to show their diet before they succeeded in winning the 'dockers' tanner' of sixpence an hour – but those in regular work made the northern cities more prosperous than the South. This wealth was reflected in the solid vastness of their town halls, the speed with which they copied Bradford in opening the world's first public swimming baths, and the size of their football stadiums. The 'works outing' by charabanc to the seaside, and the annual Wakes Week holidays to the pleasure palaces of Blackpool, were northern phenomena.

Lancashire had dominated the world cotton industry for a

century, exporting so much – loincloths and saris for India, turbans and bernouses for the Middle East – that it was said that 'they weave the home trade before breakfast, and weave for the world the rest of the day.' The well-paid spinner went to work in hat, collar and tie, with an umbrella; at weekends, he bicycled, went ballroom dancing, fancied pigeons or coursed greyhounds. The shipyards centred on the Tyne and the Clyde; scores of them, mainly family-owned, were producing six in ten of the world's ships. Riveters were paid by the hundred rivets they knocked down; in a good week they could make £3, as much as an engine driver on the booming and still expanding railways. They earned it. They worked in pairs, one left-handed, one right, with a 'holder-up' who held the rivet in place for them after a 'heater-up' had tossed it to him from a coke fire. A fifty-four-hour week was the norm, spent standing on a couple of planks seventy feet up or more as the ship grew, tying themselves to the scaffolding with ropes when gales whipped in from the sea. Though the process was largely based

on 'Armstrong's Patent', as the men called muscle-power, the big yards worked with smooth efficiency. The *Mauretania*, the biggest ship then built on Tyneside, nine decks of luxurious cabins and immense public rooms, served by new electric lifts, was launched in 1906 within eighteen months of the contract being signed. These were aristocrats of labour, already sensitive to that most British of industrial problems, the demarcation dispute between members of the twenty unions working in the yards. A plumber could join a two-inch pipe; if he touched anything larger, the boilermakers would walk out.

Then, hidden away in the Edwardian slums, were the truly poor. London had become the greatest metropolis in the world; it had doubled its population to 7.2 million in forty years, and it had not enough beds to go round. Children slept in banana crates, on mattresses of cotton rags and sackcloth. Some lodging houses let each bed to three tenants, who slept in eight-hour shifts. The novelist Jack London wrote of such a

**'Sink or swim'** *had a special
meaning for a sea-going race, as these
children of the well-to-do discovered
when being taught how to stay afloat
in the Thames at Wallingford.*

**The leisure industry** *was well under way and townspeople now had the means of getting out into the countryside, whether in a motor charabanc in 1913 (top), or on a Sunday-morning bicycle ride in 1911* *(above). Mass-production techniques, and the fact that Britain was still the richest country in the world, meant a bike was within reach of much of the population.*

place that 'the walls and ceilings were literally covered with blood marks and splotches. Each mark represented a violent death – of an insect, for the place swarmed with vermin.'

As the Plimsoll line marked the limits of a ship's lading, beyond which it might founder, the Yorkshire chocolate maker and philanthropist Seebohm Rowntree wrote of the 'poverty line' below which physical survival was threatened. Families with an income of round about a pound a week were under the line. His findings were based on visits to fish-fryers, tailors' pressers, feather-cleaners' assistants, railway-carriage washers and others of the London poor who had a weekly twenty shillings or so to make ends meet. They shocked bourgeois Britain. A shilling, sometimes two, of this pittance was paid out in burial insurance; these poignant pennies added up to an annual business of £11 million a year for the insurance companies. It was economic nonsense, for a shilling spent on extra food for half-starved children would in itself have prevented many a premature funeral, and the rich mocked it. They knew, however, little of what lay behind it – the infantile death rate in wealthy Hampstead was eighteen per thousand, but it reached 140 in the slums of Hoxton.

To have a child buried 'on the parish', a pauper's funeral, was

to add utter humiliation to family grief. It was something to be avoided at all costs, and the cost was heavy; a penny or tuppence a week for each child, tuppence for the mother, thruppence for the father. If the payments stopped for any reason, so did the insurance cover irrespective of previous payments. It was a disaster if a baby breathed before it died at birth, for it had then been a living soul and must be buried in a cemetery, though there had been no time to start payments; mothers often claimed that their children were stillborn to avoid this. The money bought little enough. The villa-dweller's vision of the poor squandering money on funerals as elaborate and sentimental as their own was an unkind myth. Slum undertakers charged a minimum of thirty shillings for a burial, unless they were able to slip a coffin into the common grave at another funeral and avoid the cemetery fees. A child who died at six months of infantile cholera in London's 'deadly month' of August 1911 had been insured for tuppence a week. The insurance pay-out was £2; it covered placing her in a common grave with three others, but the family had to find sixpence for flowers and a shilling for the father's black tie.

The respectable poor had good reason to fear disgrace. It was much closer to them than to others; a few weeks' illness or lay-

**Dockers' children** *in the East End of London (left) are waiting for food hand-outs from charities when their fathers are out on strike for the 'dockers' tanner', a minimum wage of sixpence an hour. The dockers paraded through Trafalgar Square with fish heads to show what they were reduced to eating. Though they won their 'tanner', the life of casual workers like dockers remained a hand-to-mouth affair, and children had to make their own amusements, swinging in circles round a lamp post (right). Recreation grounds, with slides and swings paid for by the rates, were a thing of the future.*

[PHOTO, RIGHT: PAUL MARTIN]

off from work was enough to tip them into it. The parish provided only 'the House', the place of final degradation, the workhouse. There were many pawnbrokers in the slums who tided over families in hard times, and enabled them to avoid this fate. But some families had nothing to pawn; no watch, no clothes or bedding of any value, no furniture, for there were indeed families who had not so much as a chair, and ate standing up. These people had no resort but 'the Lender', whose terms were a penny a week on every shilling loaned. The annual interest rate was thus 433 per cent.

The practice was outrageous enough to be illegal, but the lack of alternative made it widespread, particularly among women who had been widowed or deserted. One such, in Kennington in London, had three shillings a week after paying her rent. She slept in the same bed as her three children. Each day, they had half a loaf of bread with dripping or margarine for breakfast and tea. Their Sunday lunch, sausage and greens, was repeated cold the following day. On Tuesdays, they had flour pancakes and sugar; on Wednesdays, a quarter pound of bacon was stretched round the four of them, on Thursdays they devoured a halfpenny worth of fish and the same of potatoes. On Fridays they scrimped on bread and margarine to be able to

feast the next day on three salted herrings.

A boy could run away to sea. Many girls fled the slums by selling themselves on the streets. The pretty found a ready market for their bodies. Edwardian gentlemen married late, often in their mid-thirties, and pre-marital sex was taboo; eighty per cent of all Edwardian brides were virgins, and the proportion among the middle classes was larger still. A girl in the West End of London could make £1 a man, more than some servants cleared in two months. At the rougher end of the trade, sailors at half a crown a trick still gave a feeling of relative wealth and independence. 'I was a servant gal away down in Birmingham,' a prostitute told the Rev. G. Merrick, a priest working among the fallen. 'I got tired of workin' and slavin' to make a living and getting a bad one at that, what of five pun a year and yer grub, I'd sooner starve, I would.' She took herself to London; 'I soon found my level there.'

It was, as the serial killer Jack the Ripper had shown, a dangerous trade. Virtually all the girls had syphilis, ulcers or gonorrhoea, for which the only treatments, crude and painful, were mercury and caustics. Girls as young as twelve were abducted and sold into foreign brothels for between £18 and £32 a head. 'The facts are horrible,' the Archbishop of

Canterbury declared in 1910, 'but they are plain.' English and French *placeurs* found a ready supply of girls in tea shops and cafés, where a waitress could work twelve hours a day, without being allowed to sit down or accept tips, for a wage of a few shillings a week after she had paid her rent. The brothels of Buenos Aires were one destination, where English girls were said to fetch a high price; others went to Asia, to distributing houses in Pondicherry and Singapore's infamous Malay Street. The children of the very poor, half a million and more of them, would have been healthier if they had been orphaned, abandoned or reduced to 'the House'. Orphanages and workhouses reckoned to spend a minimum of six shillings a week to feed, clothe and lodge each child. Many mothers in the slums had to budget on less than half that sum; Seebohm Rowntree found that a quarter of the families in York lived at below-workhouse levels. These 'saddened, weakened, overburdened wives' struggled to keep their children clean and decent. They washed their hair in soda, for it was cheaper than soap, and bathed them in the same bowl, for fuel was expensive. They joined boot clubs, and calico, stocking, crockery and Christmas dinner clubs, run by local tradesmen, paying a few pennies a week into each to be able to clothe their children and give them one good meal each year and the plates to serve it on. 'You get a bigger bit of meat on your plate than you ever seen before,' a boy said to explain what he thought of Christmas and the birth of Christ. 'When He dies,' he added of Easter, 'you get a bun.'

The middle class could control pregnancies with sheaths and douches. No such luxuries existed for working-class women, for whom continual childbirth was a fact of life. They might fashion their own pessaries, from lard, margarine and cocoa butter, but abstention from sex was the only guaranteed way of limiting the number of mouths to feed. It was approved by the Church, which condoned intercourse only when 'the procreation of children is intended', but the size of working-class families showed that it was seldom practised. Resorting to a back-street abortionist was possible, but expensive and illegal. Women often tried to induce miscarriages with compounds of aloes and iron or ergot of rye – purgatives with traditional names, Penny Royal, Slippery Elm – or by combining a bottle of gin with a hot bath and running up and down steps or deliberately falling down stairs. It was, by its nature, a most dangerous business. Ergot poisoning could result in gangrene or convulsions. After an accidental outbreak of lead poisoning in Sheffield resulted in miscarriages, the deliberate use of the lead plaster diachylum spread among women in the North.

On their visits, the Fabians – gradualist social reformers – were shocked to realise that 'these women who look to be in the dull middle of middle age are young.' Mothers of twenty-six looked to be forty. The children were polite, and well-behaved; 'thank God fer me dinner' they said after a meal of suet pudding and treacle, eaten standing up. They were not stupid, or ugly, but 'puny-sized and damaged in health'. They suffered rickets from their diet and weak lungs from the damp; since they slept in the same beds, measles, whooping cough and influenza went swiftly through a family. They had no

**Children of the slums** *in 1910 gaze at a window display that, though cheap enough, is utterly beyond their means. Their bare feet reveal that they are living at home with their families. It was often healthier for a child to be orphaned or abandoned since charities clothed, shod and fed their young charges properly, spending a minimum of six shillings a week on each. Many 'saddened, weakened, overburdened wives' had half or less than that; a quarter of the families in York lived below the level of the workhouse.*

books, no toys and no space; at twelve, they became wage-earners, taking their grave, thin faces and inflamed eyes to work. The boiling resentment that the rich imagined in their nightmares was absent; the poor were too exhausted to rebel.

Revolution there was; it came not from the depths, but from the stirrings of conscience above. Recruiting during the Boer War had made the ill-health of the poor shockingly obvious. Four in ten were rejected by the army as unfit. The farm boys held up well enough, but only a tenth of the 12,000 men who volunteered in Manchester were accepted. Articles on the degeneration of the race alarmed politicians. The catalysts were a barrister, Herbert Asquith, a radical Welsh solicitor, David Lloyd George, the son of a younger son of a duke, Winston Churchill; men who, as the howls of anger that echoed around the House of Lords and the businessmen's clubs had it, should have known better. The Liberals – Churchill was a Tory turncoat – won a landslide victory in the 1906 elections. The first Labour members were swept in with them. A period of great social reforms began; the poor acquired at least a fig leaf against their nakedness.

A schools medical service was set up to monitor the health of the young. An Open Spaces Act allowed for more parks where city dwellers could take exercise. The Liberal programme called for the protection of union funds against damages for strike action, for free school meals for needy children, and the payment of old age pensions. Wages were

fixed in 'sweating' industries, and Churchill introduced labour exchanges to help get the jobless back to work. The moves were modest enough; the old age pension was set at five shillings a week from the age of seventy, which was beyond average life expectancy. Nevertheless, with increased military spending and the new reforms, Lloyd George had to raise £16 million in new taxes in his 1909 budget. Income tax at one shilling and tuppence in the pound – about six per cent, with a threshold income of £160 a year so that most of the country paid no direct taxes at all – was not enough. Lloyd George wanted to increase death duties, to impose a new 'supertax' on incomes of more than £3,000 a year, and to levy a tax on land values.

The House of Lords would have none of it. 'Should five hundred men, chosen accidentally from among the unemployed,' Lloyd George scoffed, 'override… the deliberate judgment of millions of people who are engaged in the industry which makes the wealth of the country?' He attacked the landowners: 'Who made them owners of the soil, and the rest of us trespassers in the land of our birth?' The Lords flung the budget out; the Commons declared that unconstitutional. An election was held and the Liberals were returned, if with a much reduced majority.

At the height of the crisis, on the evening of 6 May 1910, the King died. The rich mourned him with special regret; the Continent, where he was affectionately known as 'l'oncle de l'Europe', would miss him too. He approved of the *Entente*

**The great Liberal reforms** *from 1906 helped to improve conditions. Winston Churchill left the Conservatives and joined the Liberals in that year and the first Labour MPs were elected to Parliament. Keir Hardie (right), seen here addressing the faithful, was one of the founders of the party. A schools medical service was established to check the health of children in infants' schools (left) like this one in London's Chelsea. New parks were opened to give slum dwellers the chance of breathing fresh air. To the fury of the rich, income tax was increased to six per cent to help pay for the reforms.*

*Cordiale* with France, having enjoyed several intimate *ententes* with Parisiennes during his café society days as Prince of Wales, whilst keeping up family ties with his wife's nephew, the Russian Tsar Nicholas II, and his own nephew Kaiser Wilhelm, though disapproving of the latter's 'dangerous antics'.

Asquith had introduced a bill under which the Lords would lose any powers to amend or reject the budget or other money bill. Any bill passed by the Commons in three successive sessions − normally after three years − would become law even if their lordships rejected it. The Lords prepared to do battle. Under Edward, they believed they might have won; his son, now George V, was less amenable. He gave an undertaking to Asquith that, provided the people approved of the proposals at a fresh election, he would create enough new Liberal peers to outnumber the 'ditchers', the diehard Tory peers. A second election was held, with the same result as the first, and the bill was brought back again. 'Hedgers', peers fearful of being swamped, succumbed; the Parliament Act became law. The affair was bloodless − faced with domestic crisis, the British instinctively preferred to bend rather than be broken − but it was nonetheless a revolution.

More followed. The cult of the amateur was entrenched, in politics as well as sport. It was part snobbery − amateur cricketers used a separate gate at Lord's to underline their social superiority over professionals − and part morality. The well-bred acquired duties with their wealth; they sat on magistrates' benches, charity boards and in parliament without payment.

Many MPs no longer had independent means, however, and the new intake included the sons of railwaymen and steelworkers. From 1911, they became professionals, paid £400 a year; hardly a fortune, equivalent to a doctor or country lawyer, but handsome enough for a man like Ramsay MacDonald, the new leader of the Labour Party, and the son of a Scottish labourer. The change had been on the Liberal agenda since 1880; it was overdue. So was the crude safety net for workers erected by the National Insurance Act the same year. It provided the insured with free treatment and medicine from local doctors − charity hospitals already provided free hospital care for those who could not afford to pay − and a weekly allowance for those off work. Unemployment benefit was also provided for 2.5 million workers in construction, shipbuilding and engineering, where cyclical lay-offs were common.

High society was losing its Edwardian impregnability. It had to transfer more money to the less privileged, through taxes; it could no longer silence them politically, or ensure their social deference. 'What is the life of the rich man today?' mocked Lady Dorothy Nevill. 'A sort of firework! Paris, Monte Carlo, big game shooting in Africa, fishing in Norway, dashes to Egypt, trips to Japan.' In April 1912, the White Star liner *Titanic* sailed for New York on her maiden voyage; she had been designed for such people, a giant sparkler with her ballroom, jazz band, cocktail bars and staterooms. Her captain was so certain of her impregnability − she had sixteen

## Bitter industrial disputes

spread as the trade unions battled their employers. In Leeds (above) shopkeepers swept the streets after municipal workers came out on strike. During a coal porters' strike in July 1914, an amateur coalman is seen (left) at St Pancras in London. One of the worst years for strikes was 1912, when these children in London's East End (top left) made a rush on the baker's cart. In that same year full-scale rioting broke out during strikes at Tonypandy in South Wales, where non-striking stokers slept in the powerhouse (below left) to keep the pumps going to prevent the mine being flooded whilst police and strikers fought outside.

watertight compartments and was advertised as unsinkable – that he pressed on at 22 knots through the icy waters south of the Grand Banks. Four hours after striking an iceberg, the majestic firework and the lives of 1,513 passengers and crew, including a clutch of multi-millionaires, were extinguished. It seemed to some to be divine retribution on the rich and powerful – 'our forefathers were content with a Heaven after death,' Lady Dorothy had added, 'we demand a Heaven here.'

The comfortable and clubby world of all-male politics was also under threat. Women were increasingly well-educated; girls' public schools had opened, and women's colleges at universities, from which they emerged with the same inbred

confidence as their brothers; women were becoming doctors and architects, they ran charities and local constituency parties. They did not, however, have the vote. Emmeline Pankhurst, wife of a radical barrister, and her daughters Christabel and Sylvia, had formed the Women's Social and Political Union in 1903 to acquire it. Waving banners demanding 'Votes for Women', the suffragettes tried to break up a meeting in London's Albert Hall attended by the prime minister and much of the cabinet. 'In the midst of the uproar and conflicting shouts the women were seized and flung out of the hall,' an observer recalled. 'This was the beginning of a campaign the like of which was never known in England or for that matter in any other country.' The exaggeration was excusable; the suffragettes were mistresses of publicity. They chained themselves to the railings outside Buckingham Palace, slashed the famous 'Rokeby Venus' painting by Velazquez recently acquired by the National Gallery, and set pillar-boxes on fire. 'What we have done,' Sylvia Pankhurst snapped at a heckler in Hyde Park, 'is only child's play compared to what men have done in the past.'

When they were arrested, they went on hunger strike. The prison authorities force-fed them; this led to attempted suicides, and fresh outbreaks of window-smashing. The government wanted no deaths on its conscience; it passed the 'cat and mouse act' under which self-starved suffragettes were released from gaol when their lives were in danger, only to be re-arrested later. The example of Charles XI of Sweden was much quoted by men irritated by women straying into territory they thought was theirs; 'Madame,' the monarch had told his wife when she mentioned politics, 'I married you to give me children, not to give me advice.' One backwoodsman argued that the suffragettes were sexually as well as intellectually embittered, for the drain of young men to the colonies had left Britain with a large surplus of women; he said that they represented this excess female population, 'that million which had better long ago have gone out to mate with its complement of men beyond the sea.' These were determined women, however, not easily frightened by Neanderthals, and they acquired a martyr. Emily Davison was a brilliant Oxford graduate, much-imprisoned, with a formidable stone-throwing arm and much sometimes ill-directed courage; she once attacked an innocent Baptist minister whom she mistook for Lloyd George. During the 1913 Derby, she ran from the crowd, wearing her WSPU banner, and tried to catch the reins of the King's horse. She fell and was trampled so severely that she died a few days after the race.

Middle-class women, working-class men; diehards had no end of bugbears to torment them. By 1914, the trade unions had four million members. A 'triple alliance' of railwaymen, other transport workers and miners was powerful enough to contemplate a national strike to bring the nation to a halt. In the early summer, striking London construction workers gave flesh to social nightmares. They greeted the Princess Royal, when she arrived to lay the foundation stone of Marylebone Town Hall, by singing the Red Flag and calling for three cheers for Socialist Revolution, and three boos apiece for Blacklegs and Royalty. There was a development though, across the Channel, that would place all this on hold; darker and more sinister, it was something that the British instinctively shied from, war on the European mainland.

**A flair for publicity** *helped suffragette leaders in their campaign to get the vote for women. They tried to chain themselves to the railings of Buckingham Palace (left) to make sure that the world knew when they were arrested.*

**Emmeline Pankhurst,** *who launched the militant suffragette campaign in 1906, is carried off from Buckingham Palace (right) after one of her many protests there, in 1914.*

**Music halls and theatres** *were full. Curtsying coyly (above) is Lottie Collins, whose song 'Ta Ra Ra Boom de Ay!' epitomised Edwardian high spirits. Harry Lauder, with his Scots songs like 'Roamin' in the Gloamin'', had immense popularity abroad as well as in Glasgow and London. He toured the United States, Canada and the other dominions almost annually after 1907. Marie Lloyd, eldest of the eleven children of a waiter, with an ear for the wittily coarse and songs like 'Oh, Mr Porter' and 'The Boy I Love Sits Up in the Gallery', played to packed houses all over the country as well as in America, South Africa and Australia until a few days before her death in 1922. Straight theatre was becoming more respectable. At a matinée in London's Haymarket Theatre (right), a special entertainment was mounted for the boys of Charterhouse, a public school, and their parents and relations.*

CHAPTER FOUR

# IN FLANDERS FIELDS

'THE WAR TO END WAR', THE BRITISH CALLED IT; a cataclysm so unimaginable to a secure and stable people that only a claim of such - unfounded - magnitude could explain it. God went into it an Englishman, or so they had thought, and during it He disappeared. 'Personally, I held it my one true form of courage,' an infantryman noted, 'that I never once called on God for help.'

Its landscapes were a denial of the divine, a signal that the British were no longer touched by grace. 'This country stinks of corruption,' a Guards officer, Oliver Lyttelton, wrote from Flanders. 'As far as the eye can reach is that brown and torn sea of desolation and every yard is a grave, some marked with rifles, others with crosses, some with white skulls, some with beckoning hands. But everything is dead: the trees, the fields, the corn, the church… it is all dead and God has utterly forsaken it.'

It came out of an alien summer sky on the last Sunday in June 1914: two shots into a motorcade, a teenage gunman, a dead princess and a dying archduke, the flowers on her picture hat catching in the braid of his uniform as she fell. The murder seemed infinitely remote from the lives of the millions of young men in Britain and her possessions. The site, Sarajevo in Bosnia, was obscure to them. The victim, Franz Ferdinand, was heir to the throne of Austria-Hungary, an empire rickety and feeble in comparison to their own. The terrorist, the Serb Gavrilo Princip, was set on throwing Austria out of Bosnia so it could join Serbia; the British were indifferent to his cause.

Austria sent a provocative ultimatum to the Serbs; the Russians, traditional protectors of such orthodox Slavs, growled angrily whilst Berlin warned St Petersburg not to go too far. For the British, this was familiar ground. They had watched Europe rack itself with war and revolution since Waterloo a century before. Only once, in the Crimea in the 1850s, had they left their islands and become involved. Europe was the only continent on earth in which they had no territorial ambitions.

If they had a serious worry that summer, it was Ireland. Arms were being smuggled in by both the southern Irish and the Ulster volunteers in the north. Lloyd George thought that the risk of civil war between them was 'the gravest threat to this country since the days of the Stuarts'. Then he watched with horror as Europe 'stumbled and staggered' towards war. On 28 July, Austria declared war on Serbia. This prompted Russian mobilisation; in turn Germany declared war on Russia on 1 August, prompting French mobilisation.

The British had no desire to join in. They were not formally obliged to do so by the terms of the double entente with France and Russia. They could have remained in their glorious

**The body count,** *in the end, was what mattered most. The aim was to reproduce by the million what was done to this German soldier, who lies outside his dugout in Beaumont-Hamel in November 1916. They had such pretty names, the hamlets and farms of Flanders, and one, Passchendaele, where British casualties numbered 400,000, seemed to ring with the grief of the very Crucifixion.*

*Alone of the combatants, the British had no territorial ambitions in Europe. They had, indeed, not long before ceded the North Sea island of Heligoland to Germany – in return for Zanzibar. The Continental struggle upon which they embarked with such disinterested enthusiasm degenerated in three months into a war of attrition, in which the side with the deepest pockets in men and morale would win. It was a matter in which tactical flair and strategic brilliance counted for little. Dash, firepower and modern technology had won the British their remembered victories at sea and in the empire. The one great naval battle of the war, at Jutland, was inconclusive; the Germans were at least equal in weight of shell and scientific innovation, and dash was merely dangerous in trenches where the best advice was to 'keep yer bleedin' head down'.*

isolation. It was what the Germans expected of them. Twelve out of eighteen cabinet ministers declared on 1 August that they were opposed to giving the French any assurance of support in the event of war. Winston Churchill, the First Lord of the Admiralty, was alone in demanding that the navy be mobilised; his request was denied. Crowds jammed the trains to the seaside resorts for the August Bank Holiday weekend. They played beach cricket and watched Punch-and-Judy shows. Yachts raced in light airs at Cowes, where so recently the royal relations – George of England, Nicholas of Russia and Wilhelm of Germany – had strolled arm in arm.

Eight million men were under arms across the Channel. How could the British, with an all-volunteer army of just 200,000 men, plus some 'seven and fives', ex-regulars serving five years in the Special Reserve, compete with these conscript masses? Why should they, since they were in any event protected from invasion by Fisher's Grand Fleet? It might be an axiom of British policy to prevent Europe from falling under the sway of one nation, once the French, now the Germans. 'If Germany dominated the Continent,' Sir Edward Grey, the foreign secretary, declared with sublime understatement, 'it would be disagreeable to us as well as to others...' But policy was not enough in itself. Grey needed a moral basis for war. Belgium, 'plucky little Belgium', provided it. It was not a country of which the British were particularly fond. They disapproved of its brutish colonial regime in the Congo, and thought its people mean. Since 1839, however, Britain had been committed to defend Belgium.

The German war strategy, the Schlieffen plan, involved surging through Belgium into northeastern France, swallowing Paris, and then swinging into the rear of the French right wing. Count Schlieffen had calculated that the war would be won in six weeks. His timetable depended upon the neutral Belgians allowing German troops safe passage through their country. It was essential that the French be quickly knocked out, as in 1870, so that the Germans could then give their attention to the Russian masses in the east. But the Belgians refused to play ball. The Germans threatened to invade.

On Bank Holiday Monday, 3 August, Grey warned a packed House of Commons that he must respond to the German menace to France and Belgium; Britain must not 'run away from these obligations of honour and interest...' There were still objections – Ramsay MacDonald said Britain must remain neutral – but the die was cast. Early the following morning, German cavalrymen with twelve-foot steel-tipped lances rode into Belgium, below the black eagle of the German empire. Grey finally sent the ultimatum, demanding a 'satisfactory reply' by midnight. After lunch, some women golfers on the Suffolk coast drove their ball into a group of senior officers watching the North Sea for signs of an invasion fleet. 'My dear young ladies, the Germans are expected to land this afternoon,' a general told the startled players. 'Do you know what rape is? I advise you to head for home...' Officers playing cricket were informed of mobilisation by spectators waving white handkerchiefs at them. In the evening, a mob of Berliners stoned the British Embassy. 'Rassen-Verrat!' they screamed; it was 'race treason' that Britain's Anglo-Saxons were at war with their German cousins.

## OLD CONTEMPTIBLES

The decision involved all the territories of the empire and its 425 million people. Half a million men in Britain enlisted in the army in August alone. Ulster and Irish volunteers forgot their differences for the moment, and joined up; thousands of

**The summer of 1914** *was hot and glorious. Young girls (left) – 'sea urchins' the photographer wrote affectionately – race along a Channel beach without thought for the Continent across it and what it would do to the boys they might marry. Their parents and grandparents, back to the Napoleonic wars a century before, accepted it as an axiom of policy that the British should wherever possible avoid entanglement in the mainland of Europe. When war came, young soldiers (right) like these – Privates Raper, Crocket and Beckham – faced it with cheery self-confidence. How could the German Empire, an upstart of forty-three years' standing, compare with their own, centuries old?*

[PHOTO, LEFT: JAMES B. WELLINGTON]

[PHOTO, RIGHT: MRS ALBERT BROOM]

southern Irishmen served in the British army. Troopships were readied in the dominions and India. Thirty thousand Canadians, many in the kilts of their Scottish ancestry, had sailed by the autumn. 'Our duty is quite clear,' the Australian prime minister, Andrew Fisher, remarked. 'To gird up our loins and remember that we are British.'

It seemed to most, however, that the war would be over before the volunteers had learned to shoot. The Kaiser promised his departing troops: 'You will be home before the leaves have fallen from the trees.' The Germans were deploying 1.5 million men in Belgium and France, the largest force in history. The British Expeditionary Force which sailed from Portsmouth and Southampton to meet them on 9 August numbered just eighty thousand. The Kaiser called them 'contemptible', or so the black propaganda department at the Foreign Office put it about; they dubbed themselves the 'Old Contemptibles' and prepared to halt his advance among the slagheaps and winding gear at Mons.

They fought well on 23 August, their rifle fire so rapid and

causing so many casualties that the Germans mistook it for machineguns. They savaged a German regiment – 'shot down, smashed up – only a handful left' – but they were wholly outgunned and outnumbered, two corps against the German lst Army of 320,000 men. The BEF commander, Sir John French, was in danger of being surrounded and ordered a retreat next day.

It continued for a fortnight, a desperate affair, the men 'so dead asleep that we officers had to shake them to wake them.' The public knew little of the setbacks. Truth, throttled by DORA, the Defence of the Realm Act, had been the first casualty of war. The French were falling back, too, everywhere north and west of Verdun as the Schlieffen plan unrolled. The two British corps separated. Smith-Dorrien, commander of the second corps, checked the pursuing Germans at Le Cateau, his men taking heavy casualties in shallow 'scrapes', indentations clawed into the earth. The commander of the first corps, Douglas Haig, shared the gloom of French, who wanted to pull the BEF out of the line altogether. Kitchener, whom Asquith had made war minister in deference to the mystic feeling the public had for the hero of the Sudan, travelled to Paris on 1 September to order French to stand.

The Germans now suffered the problems of success. As they advanced, their flank was exposed to the French and the BEF. They wheeled to take Paris, but were squeezed east of the capital instead of rounding on it from the west. It was the German commander, von Moltke, who now lost his nerve as Marshal Joffre rallied the French on the Marne and counter-attacked. Through the autumn, both sides fought for a decision around Ypres. The Germans mauled the BEF's regulars and the French conscripts, but they failed to break through. The front line stretched from Switzerland to the sand dunes on the Belgian coast. Deep trenches replaced the scrapes. Movement was over; the terrible stalemate of the Western Front was born.

Militarily, it became a war of attrition. Kitchener alone, clairvoyance behind his fierce moustaches and blazing but ambivalent pale eyes, had predicted from the start that it would last for three years – perhaps longer, but 'three years will do to begin with. A nation like Germany, after having forced the issue, will only give in after it is beaten into the ground. That will take a very long time. No one living knows how long.' He had its instant measure, recognising that the German lines 'cannot be carried by assault, and they cannot be completely invested.' They had to be worn down by weight of men and metal; 'we must be prepared to put armies of millions into the field.'

Politically, it was a struggle to the death; German atrocities – and inventions of German atrocities, such as the deliberate mistranslation of 'tallow factories' into 'corpse-conversion factories' in which the Germans were alleged to be rendering the bodies of humans rather than animals into fats and oils – ensured that there would be no diplomatic solution. Snipers, or rumours of snipers, drove the Germans into a frenzy of retribution just as the *francs-tireurs* had stung them into brutality during their campaign in France in 1870. In Belgium, in August, they herded the townsfolk of Tamines into the church square and opened fire on them, bayoneting the wounded and killing 384. At Dinant, they lined up the men and women in groups, forced them to kneel, and shot 612. Louvain, with its

**A family affair.** *Queen Victoria had been the dynastic 'grandmother of Europe', and the war set her descendants at each other's throats. One of her grandsons, the wing-collared Kaiser Wilhelm II of Germany, is seen here (above) enjoying the hospitality of another, George V of England. Queen Mary stands between them. The sailor-suited royal children include the future*

*Edward VIII and his younger brother George VI. Field Marshal Hubert Horatio Kitchener (left), in his martial splendour, who routed the Sudanese dervishes at Omdurman in 1898 and finished the second Boer War, recruited the great armies of the First World War before being lost at sea off Orkney in 1916.*

[Photo, left: Bassano]

[Photo, right: Lafayette]

magnificent town hall and university, burnt for six days. 'We will teach them to respect Germany,' a German officer told the first secretary from the US Legation. 'For generations people will come here to see what we have done!'

The world indeed saw, and was sickened. In London in September, the British, French and Russians signed a pact pledging not to conclude peace separately. In Brussels, the

Germans arrested a British woman, Edith Cavell. The daughter of a Norfolk clergyman, she was the director of the first Belgian school of nursing. She had tried to help Allied soldiers caught up in the retreat from Mons to escape from behind German lines. For this, she was later tried by a military court, and shot. A humane and handsome woman, who loved dogs and the sick, she was a custom-made martyr.

The King struck the German princes off the roll of the Order of the Garter; the dynasty was to change its name from Saxe-Coburg-Gotha to Windsor, as Admiral Prince Louis Battenberg was to translate his to the English-sounding Mountbatten. Spy mania spread. Concrete tennis courts, status symbols of the rich, were said to be gun emplacements cunningly inserted by the Germans in advance of invasion. Oompah bands had been a feature of pre-war street life; their German trumpet and tuba players were interned on the Isle of Man. Wagner was no longer played at concerts. German-owned shops were looted until the supply ran out, whereupon any shop with a foreign name was in danger.

The troops at the front would have none of it; until the end, men going on leave were shocked by the bloodlust of civilians at home. 'There was no hatred of Germany,' a cavalry commander said. 'We were quite ready to fight anybody...' The mutual misery of the trenches produced mutual respect. At Christmas, the front fell so silent that the birds returned; a captain counted fifty sparrows chattering around his dugout. Near Armentières, the Germans shouted to the Gordon Highlanders opposite them: 'You no shoot, we no shoot.' Men from both sides wandered into no man's land. The corpses of those killed earlier in the month were buried by a Scots padre with a German divinity student in attendance. A German swapped his Pickelhaube helmet for a tin of British bully beef. On Boxing Day, he asked for it back because a kit inspection had been sprung on him. Once it was over, he kept his promise and returned it.

Near Ploegsteert, an improvised game of football was held. A slender young rifleman in the Queen's Westminster Rifles was delighted to find that the Germans were not as strong-looking as the English fellows. 'I feel much more confident about a bayonet charge now,' he noted.

## PALS

Kitchener's glaring face and jabbing finger on recruiting posters said simply: 'Your Country Needs YOU.' By the end of 1914, more than a million men had responded. In a week in August, a brigade of four infantry battalions – almost four thousand young men – was raised in Liverpool from the offices of the great business houses, shipping clerks, insurance agents, cotton brokers. The Earl of Derby built huts for them in the grounds of his stately home, Knowsley Park, for there was nowhere else to house them. Officially, they became 17, 18, 19 and 20

**So many volunteers** (right) *flocked to the colours – a million in the first three months – that they had to wear civilian clothes and use dummy weapons for training. They spent much time on bayonet drill: 'In... out... onto the next.' Yet bayonets accounted for a mere one per cent of war casualties.*
[PHOTO: HORACE NICHOLLS]

**Infantry subalterns,** *leading men against machineguns with no more than a revolver or walking stick, suffered terribly. As a rule of thumb, the public schools which supplied many of the young officers had as many casualties among Old Boys as they had current pupils. This photograph (left) shows the headmaster of Radley College, Warden Selwyn, and his prefects in 1913. This was their fate by the end of the war: back row from left: Nuge, retired wounded; Richardson, died of wounds; Gibbons, awarded Military Cross, killed; Cotton, wounded; Bennet, survivor. Middle row: Keller, survivor; Reid, winner of the Victoria Cross, the highest award for gallantry, three times wounded; the Warden; Whitfield, wounded; Westmore, killed. Seated left: Groves, twice wounded.*

Battalions, King's (Liverpool) Regiment, but they called themselves simply the 'Liverpool Pals'.

All the British passion for joining and belonging poured into affectionate battalions of Pals, united by regions, interests and ancestry – Newcastle Scots, Church Lads, Artists, North East Railway, 1st Football. Many men from the mines, steelworks and shipyards of the North were slight and skinny. They failed to meet the minimum height requirement, but so keen were they to serve that special Bantam battalions of undersized men were formed.

There had never been volunteering like this before. The notion of a citizen army was alien to the British. They regarded the soldiery as brutal and licentious – the 'mere scum of the earth' as Wellington put it – and the army as a form of outdoor relief for paupers and the deprived. Occasionally, they redeemed themselves with a distant victory, or by climbing out of the ranks; even so, as the mother of the most famous ex-ranker, Sir William Robertson, had put it: 'I would rather bury you than see you in a red coat.'

It was entirely beyond the regular army, much of it already dead in France, to train and command this flood. The huge shortfall in officers was made up with men from the public schools. R. C. Sherriff, who was to write the war's most popular play, *Journey's End*, applied for a commission as an eighteen-year-old in August 1914. The adjutant asked him a single question: 'School?' Sherriff had just left Kingston Grammar School. The adjutant searched through a printed list. He looked pained. No matter that Kingston had been founded in 1567 and was one of the country's great rowing schools. 'I'm sorry,' he said. 'But our instructions are that all applicants for commissions must be selected from the recognised public schools and yours is not one of them.'

Casualties made the army less fussy – grammar schools were acceptable soon enough, Sherriff becoming a captain in the East Surreys, and before long many were promoted directly from the ranks – but the public school ethos dominated the officer class, as the younger public schoolboys, the subalterns, dominated by proportion its casualty lists. The Old Etonian roll of 1,157 dead was the same as the number of boys at the school at any one time; as a rule of thumb, each school lost five years' worth of pupils.

It was assumed, on the whole correctly, that the qualities of self-reliance and leadership they had acquired at school would serve them well. As they had looked after junior boys as prefects, now they drilled their men, took them to church parades, organised sports for them and minded their health and welfare. Patronising it might be, but they knew what was expected of them. They died well, and the depth of mutual affection between them and their men – 'what a wonderful bunch of fellows they were, and how damned lucky one was to

**Daddy's boy.** *Lord 'Charlie' Mercer Nairne was killed in France in October 1914. 'Madam, Your Majesty was so kind to us about the photograph of Charlie's grave that I am tempted to send you a picture (left) of his little two-year-old son,' his father, Lord Lansdowne, a former Foreign Secretary and Viceroy of India, wrote to Queen Mary early in 1915. 'George, who is His Majesty's godson, is a dear little boy, and it is something that he should be left to us.' The poignancy in the picture is saved from propaganda by Lansdowne's lack of jingoism; he turned his home, Bowood Park, where it was taken, into a hospital and argued unfashionably during the war for peace without retribution. The boy in due course became eighth Marquess of Lansdowne.*

**Flanders was distant** *beyond the imagination of most at home; yet it was physically so close that a man could be seen off to the front (right) at London's Victoria Station, as if he were taking a day trip to Brighton.*

have such men to command,' an officer remarked; 'never a better lad or soldier ever stepped on a field and what I say every word true,' a private wrote as typically to his dead lieutenant's mother – inspired the survivors to narrow Britain's social divides after the war.

They and their men were, however, amateurs. They trained through the winter of 1914–15 largely in civilian clothes and with walking sticks instead of rifles. They spent much time on bayonet practice. To survive long enough to get on hand-to-hand terms with the enemy required other and more complex skills – the use of dead ground, covering fire and leapfrogging by section, reconnaissance, achieving a flank, maintaining communication to gain protection from friendly artillery. They did little of this. The Liverpools had one full-scale manoeuvre before they sailed for France. Five thousand of them charged an equal number of Manchesters across Salisbury Plain.

There was a terrible innocence to these 'Kitchener battalions'. They believed in their cause; the poet Rupert Brooke urged that 'God be thanked who has matched us with His hour.' They sailed to France in great excitement on cross-Channel ferries, with reassuring names like *Empress Queen*. There, they were slaughtered. Their pals buried them, huddling around the hole, tin hats awkward in their hands.

## WIRE AND WHIZZ BANGS

As Kitchener realised, trench warfare was a brilliantly effective method of defence; once men were dug in, it required a colossal effort to shift them. A trench was dug to a depth of some six

feet and lined with sandbags; it was traversed, dug in zig-zags, to prevent the enemy from firing straight down its length. A parapet was raised with sandbags at the front, with a similar raised parados giving protection at the rear. A firestep ran along the front of the trench, high enough for the men to be able to shoot out. A second trench line ran some 200 yards back from the front line, with a third a quarter of a mile behind that. A breakthrough thus involved the enemy in fighting his way through three lines of trenches. Communications trenches ran between the lines.

At intervals the front line was sapped forward to an excavated observation post, where lonely men listened for signs of enemy activity. The latrines were tins or pits in diggings off the main trenches; the scent of the trenches was chloride of lime. Shovels and pumps were often unable to cope with the mud and water that lay stagnant in the trenches, and they had to be shifted by bucket. The damp caused trench foot with suppurating sores; the only preventative was to keep the feet washed and dry and to rub in whale oil. Some men wore waders and firemen's thigh boots.

The men slept and sheltered from shells in dugouts bored deep into the clay or chalk, reinforced with timber joists and sandbags, to provide a cocoon sometimes thirty feet below the dangerous surface. All life was hidden from the enemy; when, each sixteen days, a battalion rotated into reserve or rest, the change was made at night. An observer, using a periscope to peer safely through the parapet, would see nothing of the army close in front of him but its earthworks, as though the enemy was some gigantic collection of moles. No man's land was the gap between the front lines. The troops, herded in their claustrophobic earthworks, called it simply 'the open'. In places, it was less than 200 yards across and in others half a mile.

Barbed wire entanglements were planted in no man's land, not the genteel stuff used to keep cattle in a field but thick, with long spikes that slashed and castrated, fixed rigidly on stakes screwed deep into the ground, in belts four feet high and twenty feet wide.

Though some sections of the line never saw any large-scale action, and others were quiet for months on end, the trenches were always dangerous. Sniping was a field sport. 'I did what the best snipers do and went into hiding places outside the trench,' a British subaltern wrote enthusiastically to his mother, after a 'regular little gem of a rifle' with telescopic sights had been loaned to him. Snipers slid their way to within yards of enemy positions, waiting for a head to appear, able to see their victims clearly – 'an old German, white haired with spectacles and a red band round a blue cap.'

Artillery fire was a constant peril; the men tried to soften the awfulness of incoming shells by giving them nicknames, almost affectionately – 'whizz bangs', 'coal boxes' for large and visible trench mortar shells, 'Johnny Johnstons', 'sausages'. Louis Maude, an officer in the King's Own Yorkshire Light Infantry, recorded casually how a 'sausage' fell outside his dugout and removed a man who had been standing there. Part of his water bottle was found a hundred yards away, 'but otherwise he has not been seen since.' Later, as he was going down a disused trench, Maude 'smelt the man I mentioned who left his water bottle behind last week… In the evening I had a look round on top and there he was right enough, which shows that German sausages have some pepper in them.'

Trench raids were mounted, vicious affairs of hand grenades and stabbings, often to take prisoners to identify a new enemy unit. Patrols crawled beyond the parapets at night, to check on enemy positions; chewing gum was issued to stop the men from coughing. Laying wire was another hazardous occupation, done at night, the men carrying the coils forward and winding them through the loops in metal picquets that had to be screwed quietly into the ground. Then there was the underground mine or sap, where, toiling in dark and foetid air, engineers dug forward under no man's land to cut out a cavern under the opposing line, to stuff it with explosive, and then to blow the enemy above to eternity. Men could follow the progress of an enemy sap by putting their ear to a bucket of water buried in the earth.

Gas was first used by the Germans in April 1915. The British watched a greenish-yellow cloud drifting towards their trenches. It choked them as they were enveloped in it, burning their throats and causing uncontrollable weeping. The sun turned 'a ghastly green'. After several hours, word came down the line that the best protection was to urinate into a handkerchief and tie it over the mouth and nostrils. The following day, the infantry officer F. P. Roe was sent back to the nearest town to buy gauze for his battalion. The town square was full of gassed victims, many of whom had died during the night, lying with 'a quite appalling blueness/purpleness of the skin'. Gas masks were soon issued.

**Before the battle.** *The foreknowledge of certain terror is deep in the face of this young soldier (right) of the Durham Light Infantry before an attack goes in towards Veldhoek. Only officers were thought mentally refined enough to suffer from 'shellshock', or breakdown. Front-line officers and physicians found for themselves that this was a nonsense. 'What a lesson it is to read the thoughts of men,' a Balliol-educated subaltern wrote after censoring his men's mail, 'often as refined and sensitive as we have been made by birth and education, yet living under conditions much harder and more disgusting than my own.'*

*'Men wear out in battle like their clothes,' wrote a young medical officer, later to become Lord Moran, Winston Churchill's personal physician. 'Courage is the willpower whereof no man has an unlimited stock; and when in war it is used up, he is finished. A man's courage is his capital and he is always spending. The call on the bank may be only the daily drain of the front line or it may be a sudden draft which threatens to close the account.'*

[PHOTO: JOHN WARWICK BROOKE]

## FEAR OF THE OPEN

It was 'the open', however, and its mud, and machinegun and artillery fire, that was most lethal. The British machinegun, the Vickers, was efficient enough to last in service for another fifty years. It fired 600 rounds a minute, ten a second. In a second and a half, it fired more rounds than an infantryman with a rifle could manage in a minute, and it did so with far greater accuracy. The Machine Gun Corps school near Grantham taught men how to keep it fed with belts of ammunition and cooling fluid, and how to adjust the angle of the barrel so that the bullet stream was set at the correct height to strike the advancing infantry. They were trained to sit cross-legged, and to tap the stock to traverse the barrel from left to right and

back. During an enemy artillery barrage, the machinegunners survived in deep dugouts, like submariners below the violent surface of the sea, ready to rise swiftly when the bombardment lifted and the enemy infantry appeared.

Artillery came in three broad bands. The lighter guns, eighteen-pounders and 4.5-inch howitzers, threw a shell of shrapnel, high explosive or gas to a range of six thousand yards. Medium guns, sixty-pounders and 6-inch howitzers, extended the range to 10,000 yards. The heavies, ranging up to fifteen inches in calibre, had little more range, but their high trajectory gave their shells greater penetration of the soil as they arced down. Trench mortars lobbed bombs across no man's land, a task also performed by hand grenades launched by catapults.

In the assault, the lighter guns cut the enemy wire, whilst the heavies sought out the dugouts to destroy the enemy in his burrows. That, at least, was the theory. In practice, the initial barrages merely redistributed parts of the wire, and rarely killed enough of the enemy to ensure the success of the foot soldiers, whose advance was hindered by the cratered moonscapes caused by the shelling. A unit going over the top launched itself into a maelstrom of noise and smoke in which their position was rapidly obscured from their own gunners, who were unable to offer them protective fire. But the guns were splendid in defence. They had merely to be ranged on no man's land, filling it with shrapnel and explosive shock at the moment of attack.

There was soon evidence enough of the price to be paid in

**Mud, mud, inglorious mud:** *so thick that pumps and shovels could not deal with it, and troops often had to bail out a trench by bucket like stricken seamen. It drowned; it also entombed, like quicksand. The trench (above) seems unfit for human* *habitation; yet it was preferable to the dangerous surface. The troops became subterraneans, the artillery observer (right) setting up his lamp to signal back to his battery crouches amid earthworks over which he will peer only with a periscope.*

**A working party** set off to shore up a trench (above) in trench waders and waterproof sheets. Even with thigh boots, the damp caused the condition known as trench foot, with suppurating sores. The conditions made it difficult to evacuate the wounded. Here (main picture) stretcher bearers toil with a casualty during the battle of Thiepval Ridge in 1916.

[PHOTO, ABOVE: JOHN WARWICK BROOKE]

[MAIN PHOTO: ERNEST BROOKS]

attack. At Neuve Chapelle in March 1915, Captain E. C. Deane, an army doctor attached to the 2nd Leicesters, recorded that his regiment 'had the honour of being the first to attack.' The company commanders called out the minutes before going over the top. Deane had his stretcher bearers ready to go into the open to pick up casualties. Many men did not get that far; they were cut down on the parapet itself and fell back. 'I ran along the trenches,' Deane wrote, 'jumping over pools of blood, severed limbs with no owner, shattered corpses and groaning wounded.' A Gurkha tried to hand him his left arm, torn off above the elbow; a wounded company commander 'seemed shrunk to about half his usual size and was very blue… five wounds, mostly in the lung and probably all one shell.' The assault achieved nothing; for the doctor, it was 'a nightmare of bandaging and iodine and blood – always blood – working in the dugout with bent back…'

At Loos, in the summer, the British were again easy meat from the moment they emerged into the open. 'Never had the machinegunners had such straightforward work to do, nor done it so effectively,' a German regimental diary read. 'They traversed to and fro along the enemy's ranks unceasingly. The men stood on the firesteps, some even on the parapets, and fired triumphantly into the mass of men advancing across the open grassland…' No moment was safer to the defender than the start of an enemy attack; the artillery barrage had lifted, the British infantry had no time to aim and fire as they stumbled

forward. They filled 'the entire line of fire' for the Germans, who had a clear view of them 'falling in hundreds'.

The fruitless attacks were the handiwork of Sir John French. Short and florid, he had a natural disdain for social inferiors, his own men, Irish Volunteers, and the Sudanese fuzzy-wuzzies and Boer farmers against whom he had acquired his 'practical grasp of minor tactics'. He had little interest in the techniques of mass warfare; he 'never displayed any bent for abstract knowledge nor even aspired to pass into the Staff College' to acquire some. George V found him 'not particularly clever and he has an awful temper.' He was a Hussar with a cavalryman's mercurial temperament, alternately elated and depressed. He was all dash or defeat, dangerous qualities in an infantry war in which calmness was a general's greatest virtue. General Smith-Dorrien, by contrast a happy man with a happy division, now protested at the futile waste of life and was removed and made governor of Gibraltar. Though it was a German general who said it, the idea that the British were 'lions led by donkeys' was in the making.

## HEROINES AND 'ORRIBLE WOMEN

French blamed his failures on the shortage of shells. The government blamed overpaid and drunken munitions workers; 'we are fighting Germany, Austria and Drink,' Lloyd George said, 'and as far as I can see, the greatest of these deadly foes is Drink.' The lack of progress in the war was evident enough by mid-May 1915, even with censorship, for Asquith to reform his government in coalition with the Conservatives. Pubs were ordered to close in the afternoons, an 'emergency' measure that would last for sixty years; those in Carlisle, a major munitions town, were taken over by the State. More positively, Lloyd George was made Minister of Munitions. Politicians interfered little in the war; by and large, the generals ran their own show. The Welsh Wizard was an exception. He neither liked nor trusted the brasshats. Haig thought that the machinegun was 'much overrated' and that two per battalion were enough; Kitchener was shrewder, but thought that anything above four was a luxury. Lloyd George took Kitchener's maximum, squared it, multiplied it by two and then doubled it again for good measure. That gave sixty-four machineguns a battalion.

The suffragettes welcomed the new minister with a march down Whitehall. 'We demand the right to work,' their banners said; Lloyd George gave it to them, together with a ministry grant to help them into industry. Agreement was reached with the unions to allow male labour to be replaced by women for the duration. They operated lathes, riveted ships, turned aircraft propellers and overhauled truck engines. The whistling errand boy on a bike was replaced by delivery girls. They worked in tanneries and sugar refineries and soon made up four in five of the workers in rubber plants. More than a hundred thousand were to join the Women's Land Army, toiling to bring in the harvest. Women schooled army horses and mules; the Countess of Airlie, a lady-in-waiting to Queen Mary, was killed in a fall.

Others enlisted in the services. The Women's Army Auxiliary Corps emerged from the Women's Legion, which freed men for the front by working as clerks, telephonists, cooks, waitresses and drivers. By the end of the war, there were 40,000 WAACs. Stationed in the great rear bases in France, they were forbidden to go into bars or even cinemas, to smoke in public, or to drink alcohol; no man was allowed into their hostels without written permission.

There were few pregnancies, but they enjoyed themselves. 'A lovely old place,' one wrote from Calais. 'Six of us went out and got an Aussie. Bea and I had a car ride with our two...' They dressed in khaki frocks, and an officer found them 'very picturesque and delightfully English'. He thought them excellent for morale, for they gave the troops on leave 'good female company when Tommies get down here'. In the air force, women worked on airframes and engines; they could take flying instruction, though they were not allowed to qualify as pilots. The navy seemed less keen on the 'Wrens' of the WRNS. 'Of all the 'orrible things this war 'as done, these 'orrible women are the worst,' one tar exploded.

They served, too, as nurses, largely in unpaid Volunteer Aid Detachments, VADs, or, in pith helmets, webbing belts and tunics, as FANYs in the First Aid Nursing Yeomanry. Though nurses were torpedoed, and bombed in Zeppelin raids on bases, the more adventurous were frustrated that they could not serve at the front. Flora Sandes, daughter of a Suffolk clergyman, is the only British woman known to have formally enlisted as a soldier and to have fought in combat. At thirty-eight, she went to Serbia with a Red Cross team. Separated from her unit during a retreat, she joined a Serb regiment and became a sergeant-major. Another heroine was the Scots suffragette Dr Elsie Maud Inglis, who – told by the British to 'Go home and sit still' – organised suffragette medical teams for allies. She refused to leave the Serbs she was tending amid the Bolshevik chaos on the Russian front. 'If you want us home,' she wired, 'get them out too.' When she was at last free to go, she wired Edinburgh: 'Everything satisfactory and all well, except myself.' Although dying, she insisted on walking down the gangplank at Newcastle. A hundred thousand attended her funeral in Edinburgh.

In a manner, the women who were closest to the killing fields were those who filled the shells. They were called 'munitionettes', or 'canaries' – the amatol used in shells gave them yellow faces and hands. Ten women were employed in the Woolwich Arsenal at the start of the war; by the end, there were 24,000 of them. They earned good money, as much as £2 10s a week. That, and the equality of male pay that women

**Ladies of the lamp.** *The British did not allow women to nurse in the front line. Eighteen-year-old Mairi Chisholm (right) drove a motorbike from Scotland to London to help the war effort, but became bored with life as a despatch rider. With a trained nurse, Elsie Knocker, she sailed for the front where she set up a first-aid post in the shell-battered village of Pervyse in the Belgian sector. Both women were gassed; the 'madonnas of Pervyse' survived to win Belgian Military Medals. Sister Jane Trotter (left) served as a nurse with the Serbian army in a hospital she defended herself with small arms. She was decorated with the Serbian Golden Eagle.*

doctors extracted from the astonished War Office, was a portent of times to come. Women were not only infiltrating male preserves – in the police force, as bus conductresses and guards on the London underground – but were earning enough money to become independent, to eat out and go to pubs on their own. They looked the part; whalebone, corsets and frills gave way, and in came shorter skirts and bobbed hair. They were aware of what they wanted from the post-war world as a reward for their efforts. 'Votes for Heroines as Well as Heroes,' the new suffragette slogan ran.

Men still earned more than women in the munitions plants, but that was little comfort to the infantry in the trenches. An infantry private earned a shilling a day, enough to buy a pint bottle of Bass and a bar of chocolate. The best paid, sappers in the Royal Engineers, made 1s 8d a day, which bought them the Bass and a tin of sardines. It rankled. Australians – 'fucking five bobbers' to the Tommies – made five shillings a day, the same as a woman stenographer in the WAACs. Most scorn, though, was reserved for civilians. 'A munition worker works five hours per day, five days a week and draws £5 per week,' a regimental magazine posed a satirical exam question. 'Compare the scale of pay of those who make the shells with those who deliver them.'

The soldier, as the War Office pointed out, had his board and lodgings paid (a subaltern had to pay his own mess bills out of his 7s 6d a day). That added to the bitterness. The lodgings in the line were dugouts, damp, dark pits shored up with timbers and wattle, often flooded, dimly lit by lamps, with wire mesh cots or canvas camp beds. They were infested by lice and rats. Some units brought in terriers and ferrets to chase the rats, or shot them with revolvers by torchlight; but more always appeared, feeding on the dead and the other detritus of war. On warmer days, it was common to see men strip themselves naked, their fingers working as if they were sewing as they moved along the seams in their uniforms crushing the lice.

Board was basic. A goo called 'Pozzy' was made from jam poured into a mixture of water and biscuit given the consistency of porridge by boiling it in a mess tin. There was bacon, and bully beef, and meat and vegetable stew. In the mornings, under the eye of an officer, rum was issued. Tea was ubiquitous, strong, laced with sugar and condensed milk. As to the terms of employment, leave was rarely more than ten days a year, with travelling time deducted at both ends. It was often an unsettling experience, for the civilians had little idea of the 'cess of war'.

**Womanpower.** *'We demand the right to work', the suffragettes insisted at the start of the war. They became essential to the war effort. In Coventry, a girl is placed (top left) in the muzzle of a 15-inch gun to clean the rifling. Girls in shell-filling factories*

(above) were known as 'canaries' because the chemicals turned their faces and hands yellow. Women operated lathes, riveted ships, turned aircraft propellers and overhauled truck engines. They toiled on the land. They served in uniform in the women's auxiliary services; these women are with the army in France (left), tending the graves of the British dead at a cemetery in Abbeville.

[PHOTOS, TOP LEFT AND ABOVE: HORACE NICHOLLS] [PHOTO, BOTTOM LEFT: DAVID MCLELLAN]

## GALLIPOLI
### *'Death grins at my elbow…'*

The casualties and apparent futility of the Western Front led to a split over British strategy. The 'Westerners' held that the war would be won only by wearing down the German forces in France. They accepted that the price would be high, but they saw no alternative; kill enough Germans, and the enemy would crack. The 'Easterners' felt this meatgrinding to be alien to the island tradition. They wanted to use British seapower to achieve a much cheaper victory elsewhere. They believed that the Royal Navy could, at a stroke, force a passage through the Dardanelles straits in the eastern Mediterranean. The great ships would then steam on for Constantinople, and so bring down the rotting Ottoman empire which had misguidedly thrown in its lot with the Germans. Turkey would be knocked out of the war, and Bulgaria and Italy coaxed into it. Germany and Austria would be encircled by hostile armies; a warm sea passage would be opened to Russia, and the defence of Egypt and the Suez canal assured.

The Navy was not so sure; it remained a force of global splendour, its mere existence giving it immense influence, but it had not had a major engagement for more than a century, and it was cautious. The First Sea Lord, 'Jacky' Fisher, had visited the Dardanelles in 1900 and knew how well they were defended. The straits, the ancient Hellespont, divided Turkey's remaining foothold in Europe from Asia. They ran for forty-one miles from the Aegean to the town of Gallipoli where they opened up into the Sea of Marmara. Its waters led to Constantinople, the Bosphorus and the Black Sea. The Dardanelles ranged from two to four miles in width, but also with narrows of less than a mile. A line of forts, some ancient, some modern, ran their length; there were fixed and mobile guns, and minefields. A Franco-British fleet of ten battleships, with attendant cruisers and minesweepers, attempted to blast through the straits on 18 March 1915. At 1.54 pm, the French battleship *Bouvet*'s magazine exploded; she capsized and sank in three minutes. The British battleships *Inflexible* and *Irresistible* were mined later in the afternoon; HMS *Ocean* circled helplessly, her steering gear damaged. At 5 pm, the fleet withdrew; it had lost three capital ships and 700 men.

The Turks awaited a fresh assault the next day. It never came. Fisher resigned. 'Damn the Dardanelles!' he said. 'They will be our grave!' Churchill was for continuing the naval action; he was overruled. Though Churchill was bitterly attacked over the campaign, the strategy was not foolish. The Turks themselves thought it 'most probable' that the fleet would have overwhelmed them had the attempt been made 'with greater vigour and repeated several times'. Instead, a huge seaborne invasion was planned, to land an army on the Gallipoli peninsula, the western shore of the strait, and thus to open the way to Constantinople.

The hills of the peninsula have an arid beauty. From the central spine, the Aegean is seen to the west, and, to the east, the narrow blue ribbon of the straits and the gunmetal mountains of Anatolia. In spring and early summer, it is an aromatic place of scented shrubs and wild flowers, hyacinths and heathers, clear blue skies and blazing sunsets. The men would remember 'the smell of thyme mixed with cordite'. In high summer, it is desiccated, deadened by heat and haze, the ravines and gullies that scour it choked with a fine dust. In autumn and winter, rain drives in with storms and temperatures fall below freezing.

An imperial army was assembled, including the Australian and New Zealand Army Corps, 30,000 of the finest troops from the Antipodes. The force commander was General Ian Hamilton, who had a shrivelled left hand from the battle of Majuba Hill in Africa, and a shortened left leg from a wound on India's North West Frontier. He expected to capture the lower half of the peninsula in three days, and then clear the minefields so that the Fleet could storm through the narrows. He anticipated light fighting. The Turk was, the troops were assured in a notice issued before the landings, 'of very little use and has a very small power of initiative…' But the invasion had been telegraphed in advance; the greatest amphibious assault force in history was being assembled and every dock worker in Egypt knew it. Experienced German officers were in place to advise their allies and when US Ambassador Morgenthau visited the Gallipoli forts, 'German not Turkish was the language one heard and the Germans thought Johnny Turk: "Brave, trustworthy, content with little…"'

The invaders were happy. 'Oh God!' Rupert Brooke had written of the prospect of action. 'I've never been so happy in my life, I think…' On the way to Gallipoli he disembarked on Skyros with his naval division on Saturday 17 April. He roamed the island and its olive groves, where Theseus was murdered and Achilles had been hidden by his mother, but by Friday he was dead of an insect bite and buried 'in a foreign field'.

The Australians and New Zealanders were landed before dawn on 25 April, Anzac Day, a day of collective grief on which an Australian lieutenant, Phillip Schuler, thought that his country 'attained nationhood by the heroism of her noble sons.' They were caught by machinegun and rifle fire as they grounded in the shallows. Many were dropped a mile from the landing zone, finding themselves not on a gently sloping beach from which they could move inland, but pinned in an inlet under steep cliffs. Anzac Cove was a trap, blocked by sharp cliffs forward and the dangerous shoreline behind. Boats full of the dead drifted along the beach for several days. The Australians got one Turkish sniper and watched the corpse, caught on the cliff-face by a foot, slowly shed its arms and then its head as it decomposed in the rain and sun.

Irish troops were landed on V Beach south of the Anzacs. Two thousand men were packed aboard an old collier, the *River Clyde*, and had to jump into the water from her decks. The Munsters, with sprigs of shamrock in their caps, were 'literally slaughtered like rats in a trap' by rifle and machinegun fire. The

**On Anzac Beach** *at Gallipoli, a soldier snugs down out of sight of snipers. The Australian and New Zealand Army Corps, the Anzacs, suffered terrible casualties in the* landings on the beach. The campaign by 'Easterners' to shorten the war in the West by defeating Turkey and rolling up the Austrians failed.
[PHOTO: ERNEST BROOKS]

Dublins struggled ashore. Their chaplain held his wounded right arm in his left whilst he gave Absolution, until he was killed trying to reach a wounded man in the light surf. As fresh lighters were towed in, the arriving men jumped onto submerged corpses. The survivors huddled on the slopes of sand dunes for protection from Turkish machinegunners. They were killed, a Turkish officer said, 'like a shoal of fish'. At W beach, the Lancashire Fusiliers had 190 killed and 279 wounded in the few minutes before they could dig in. Hamilton felt himself penned in by mortality. 'Death grins at my elbow,' he wrote. 'I cannot get him out of my thoughts. He is fed up with the old and the sick – only the flower of the flock will serve him now…'

The fleet gave the men ashore some comfort, shelling Turkish positions, until the *Triumph* was torpedoed by a German submarine. The fleet withdrew. 'All the ships disappeared as if God had taken a broom and swept the sea,' a German officer wrote. Gallipoli became as trenchbound as France. In places, the lines were only a few yards apart; some trenches were shared, with a pile of sandbags as a divider. It was so easy to throw hand grenades that fences of wire netting were put up to intercept them. The brutal and flyblown summer – 'there are about twenty flies per square inch and one corpse per yard' – bred dysentery. Snipers shot men as they raced for the latrines. A small group of British and Gurkhas reached the top of the central ridge and looked across the monotone scrub to the blue of the narrows five miles away. It was a first and only glimpse of the objective; they were soon forced back. The Turks equally failed to hurl the invaders into the sea. In one attack, the Anzacs cut down three thousand of them in front of their trenches.

In August, reinforcements were landed at Suvla Bay in the north. These were 'Kitchener men' with no combat experience, under General Stopford, whose last command had been of the Beefeaters at the Tower of London. Success depended on moving swiftly inland and seizing a ridge five miles from the beach. The landing was achieved without loss; the Turks were taken by surprise. Stopford congratulated his men and settled down for an afternoon nap; he was still asleep when Hamilton called on him later, as the Turks furiously moved troops to meet the new threat. Stopford's force took 8,000 casualties and never reached the central ridge; he returned to the Tower of London. Putrefaction drifted in the heat; offshore, the supply boats cut up floating horses and mules with their propellers.

In truth, Hamilton was too much a gentleman, too happy to delegate and listen to others, too reluctant to drive his men, indeed too gentle, for he refused point-blank to use poison gas against the Turks, who had no masks. On 15 October, he received a message from Kitchener advising him to decipher the

next message himself. He found himself replaced, and his successor then recommended that the campaign be closed. The evacuation, at night, was a brilliant success. Destroyers trained searchlights onto Turkish observation posts to blind the watchers. Candles were lit which, as they burned down, ignited fuses which caused explosions as though an active foe remained in its trenches and dugouts. The sailors used muffled oars. Not a man was lost. 'Es war ein Meisterstueck,' said an admiring German officer, a masterstroke. The campaign itself was another matter. The Australians had 26,094 casualties, 7,594 of them killed, the New Zealanders 7,571 casualties and 2,431 dead. In all, 36,000 soldiers and sailors of the British Empire died.

## SIDE SHOWS

A few days before his death in France, a subaltern wrote that generals were 'nothing but brass and red tabs, all riding about and criticising.' By now, reputations were being ruined. Asquith needed fresh faces to justify the casualty lists. French took his fellow cavalryman, the smooth and ambitious Douglas Haig, to be his ally. The two had served together in the Boer War, and French had presented his subordinate with a gold flask in tribute to 'our long and tried friendship'. Haig, however, had written in his diary that his friend 'is quite unfit for this great command', and missed no opportunity to say as much to the King and Asquith. 'If anyone acted like that at

school,' George V muttered, 'he'd be called a sneak.' It was effective, however; French was given a viscountcy to sugar the pill, and put out to grass at home, while Haig inherited the Western front. Kitchener remained too popular to be sacked as war minister. Instead, Asquith sidelined him by appointing Sir William Robertson as Chief of the Imperial General Staff and sole government adviser on strategy.

The two men now principally responsible for the conduct of the war were very different. Haig was effortless superiority made sleek flesh, good-looking and gracious. He took his own pack train with him to the Sudan in 1897; it included a camel freighted with claret. The Boer War was kind to him; he was a major-general at forty-three and used his position as ADC to Edward VII to meet senior politicians as well as his wife, the daughter of a lady-in-waiting to the Queen. Robertson was self-made, the son of a Lincolnshire villager who joined the 16th Lancers at seventeen. He educated himself, paying a fellow trooper a few coppers to read to him whilst he cleaned his kit. After ten years, he was commissioned in India; cash awards were given for proficiency in native languages, and he made up for his lack of funds by mastering first Urdu, then Hindi, Persian, Pushtu, Punjabi and Gurkhali. Badly wounded on the North West Frontier, he had become commandant of the Staff College – 'a ranker officer in that position was indeed a novelty' – before returning to high command.

It was the few things they had in common that made the duo formidable. Both were convinced Westerners; they had scorned Gallipoli. They were painstaking over detail – ''Ope for the best and prepare for the worst' was Robertson's maxim, delivered forcefully with dropped aitches. Their strategy was simple: attack and attrition. They believed in themselves, and had no time for politicians. Haig thought the very word to be 'synonymous with crooked dealing and wrong values.' Kitchener was drowned in June 1916 when the cruiser *Hampshire* was mined off the Orkneys, and his death meant that the only military counter to them had gone. The new War Minister, Lloyd George, found himself a civilian amateur among the professional heavyweights.

The politicians had problems enough of their own. The war was costing £5 million a day; inflation was rising and income tax reached twenty-five per cent. There was much talk of speculators; in truth, the country was living beyond its means and the government had turned to the printing press.

Ireland had seemed quiescent and Home Rule had been suspended for the duration. Nationalists had fought with the Dublins at Gallipoli; Erskine Childers, who had landed a cargo of arms for them at Howth harbour in 1914, was a decorated lieutenant commander in the Royal Navy. A splinter group of the Irish Volunteers, however, was determined on a rising. Sir Roger Casement, the ex-British consul and humanitarian, visited Germany to try to raise an Irish Legion from the prisoner of war camps. He failed, but planned an insurrection for Easter 1916. He counted on 10,000 Volunteers and German arms. When German help proved niggardly, he was landed from a German submarine to call off the rising, but was found wandering on the shore and arrested.

Though the Volunteers' chief of staff ordered the rising to be cancelled, a remnant seized the Central Post Office in Dublin on Easter Monday and proclaimed the Irish Republic. They failed to take Dublin Castle, though its garrison was only twenty men. British reinforcements shelled the post office; on the Friday, the surviving Volunteers surrendered. They were hissed as they were marched away; many Dubliners had relatives in the British forces, and thought the rising ill-timed at best, treason at worst.

What changed attitudes was the treatment of the captured men. The seven who had signed the proclamation of the republic were shot; one, badly wounded, was carried out to the execution yard in a chair. The volunteer commandants were

also shot, with the exception of Eamon De Valera.

The greater war took precedence. The Germans had declared a blockade of Britain and were using submarines to enforce it. It was diplomatically dangerous for it involved neutrals. A hundred and twenty-eight Americans had been drowned (and over 1,000 others) when the great liner *Lusitania* was torpedoed in May 1915. On the surface of the North Sea, the Grand Fleet finally met the Germans off Jutland at the end of May 1916. It was a clash of titans – 250 warships, including forty-two battleships, with twenty-five admirals aboard them – but it was inconclusive. The British claimed victory, on the basis that, although the navy could not win the war, it could lose it in an afternoon, and the Grand Fleet had survived whereas the German fleet retreated to port and was not seen again. From the air, Zeppelin airships bombed cities. They did little damage, but Britain was blacked out at night and work stopped when a raider was sighted.

Beyond France, there were other and more exotic campaigns that soaked up troops. A group of British intelligence officers was persuading Hussain, the Sharif of Mecca, to raise an Arab

**Big shots.** *The British duo of Sir Douglas Haig and Prime Minister David Lloyd George (above left), respectively commander-in-chief and prime minister, with the French commander General Joffre and munitions minister Albert Thomas completing their circle. Haig was polished and unimaginative; he thought the machinegun 'overrated' and maintained a simple and bloody belief that the next 'big push' would stave in the Germans. Joffre also believed in attrition; unlike Haig, he resigned after his failure to make adequate preparation for the defence of Verdun. Lloyd George was horrified at mounting casualties. The torpedoing of the liner* Lusitania *in 1915 – a survivor (right) is escorted ashore at Cork in Ireland – helped to bring the Americans into the war.*

**'Conchies'.** *The pacifist movement was small in number but large in intellect. The mathematician and philosopher Bertrand Russell (far left) takes the sun in 1915 next to two fellow conscientious objectors, the brilliant economist Maynard Keynes and the waspish writer and Victorian debunker Lytton Strachey. In spite of his stance Keynes remained at his post in the Treasury until the end of the war. The troops themselves, though fighting on, became bitterly disillusioned with staff officers, here (right) riding in comfort whilst they march forward for another offensive on the Somme in 1916.*

[PHOTO, LEFT: LADY OTTOLINE MORRELL]

revolt against the Turks. They included a young captain, who, as the Arab forces moved north-west up the desert, earned the sobriquet of Lawrence of Arabia. In Mesopotamia, modern Iraq, a force was landed at Basra to protect the Persian oilfields. The Turks fled and General Charles Townshend, a dashing and impulsive man 'with a passion for theatrical society', set off in pursuit up the Tigris with a fleet of paddle steamers and ancient barges. It was, to begin with, a light-hearted affair, 'Townshend's Regatta'; villages put out white flags as the flotilla passed, and barges full of Turkish troops were captured when their officers cut them adrift from their steamers to beat a hastier retreat. Townshend was within twenty miles of Baghdad when he was halted by stiffer Turkish resistance. He fell back on the river town of Kut, and there he was besieged. After four months of sniping and dysentery, and a final doomed effort to break the siege by gunboat, Townshend surrendered. Half his men did not survive Turkish captivity.

The British still planned to take Baghdad, and simultaneously to fight the Turks in Palestine. Other troops faced the Bulgarians in Macedonia, miserable and cold; in China, they forced the Germans out of Shantung with Japanese help, and slowly dislodged them from East and West Africa, and Togo and Cameroon. By the end of the war, these 'sideshows' had mopped up more than 1.5 million troops. The government worried that it would run out of men.

Conscription was introduced in 1916. It was a historic shift for a country that had survived so long on seapower and a few regulars, designed to flush out the 650,000 shirkers who were thought to be skulking at home. The mood was bellicose; 'Over the Top', a military two-step, was danced in music halls, and white feathers were handed to young men in civilian clothes, some of whom were soldiers on leave. Most of the shirkers turned out to be men in vital war industry jobs, however, or conscientious objectors. A new word, 'conchie', was coined for them; they drove ambulances or were put to work in stone quarries and cultivating the barren soil of

Dartmoor. The Australians rejected conscription in two referendums; in Canada it caused riots in French-speaking Quebec when it was introduced.

In fact, three million responded to Kitchener's advertisement for volunteers – Lady Asquith called him 'the Great Poster' – and by the summer of 1916 the number of British divisions in France had increased from four to 57. It was as well. In the desperate cauldron round the fortress of Verdun, the French lost 315,000 casualties and much of their fighting spirit. Bled too white for a fresh offensive, they pressed for a sacrifice from their allies. Haig and Robertson laid plans for a great attack in France, and they had the men. A disaster was in the making.

### THE SOMME
*'My men! My men! My God, my men!'*

The offensive was planned for an eighteen-mile stretch of front on the Somme. Thirteen divisions would attack simultaneously on 1 July. The greatest artillery barrage of the war would obliterate the German trenches and wire in the week before they went into the open. That was the theory. If it went wrong, the intimate composition of the Pals meant that the loss of a battalion would, at home, devastate a pit village, a shipyard or a small complex of city streets.

They swam naked in the rivers and ponds, and fished, and played football and cricket and had blindfold boxing. The rolling landscape was little touched by war, the cornfields amber and the stands of oak and beech a deep green. A subaltern was billeted in an old farmhouse, its garden filled with roses and lupins and bees; there was plenty of cream and eggs and good beer. It was like England. 'What more could you ask for...' he wrote to his little sister. Nobody was reporting sick any more; 'no one', he wrote, his own epitaph, 'wanted to miss it.'

The barrage was fired by an army of 50,000 gunners, continuing day and night. The inexperienced Pals, impressed by the dust and thunder, thought it impossible to survive such

an onslaught. But, deep in bunkers carved out of the chalk forty or fifty feet below the surface, the concussive changes in air pressure dousing their acetylene lamps, the atmosphere acrid with explosive and gas fumes, sleepless, the Germans lived.

At 6.30 on the morning of 1 July 1916, every British gun on the front fired continuously for an hour. The earth rose in the air and fell slowly back into the craters. The forward German trenches were destroyed, but no Germans were in them. From their dugouts, they watched the British lines through periscopes and saw the gathering of an army of steel helmets. The men were being given a final tot of powerful Navy rum. As the barrage lifted at 7.30, the Germans were ready.

The British did not charge; they jogged as best they could over the torn ground under heavy loads. An officer described himself as got up 'like a small Christmas tree', with water bottle, haversack, maps, wire cutters, entrenching tool, clasp knife, binoculars, compass, mess tin, great coat, periscope and telescope. His only offensive equipment was a revolver and four hand grenades. Soldiers carried their rifle and equipment, hand grenades, extra bandoliers of ammunition, two days' rations, a waterproof cape, four sandbags, a shovel to fill them, gas masks, goggles, water bottle and mess tin.

They had most need of their field dressings. They had between 500 yards and a mile of open ground to cover. Some were hit climbing out of their trenches. 'I could see, way to my left and right, long lines of men,' a sergeant in a Tyneside Irish Pals battalion recalled. 'Then I heard the "patter patter" of machineguns in the distance. By the time I had gone another ten yards there seemed to be only a few men left around me; by the time I had gone twenty yards, I seemed to be on my own. Then I was hit…'

Units went forward, and disappeared in the noise and smoke and craters, as if they had gone to the moon, beyond their commanding officer's ken. 'Two hours after zero, no news whatever was received from the front,' Colonel Dickens, a grandson of the novelist, reported. The wires of field telephones were cut by shrapnel; pigeons and semaphore flags were no substitute. Ten miles behind the front, in his advanced headquarters in the Château de Beuaquesne, Haig had only the vaguest notion of events.

The Germans opposite the 16th Northumberland Fusiliers stood on their own parapet in delight at the target offered to them. They 'waved to our men to come on,' the regimental war diary reported. 'The enemy's fire was so intense that the

advance was checked and the waves, or what was left of them, were forced to lie down…' A further wave was cut down as it clambered out of the trenches. The commander, Lieutenant-Colonel W. H. Ritson, had to be pinioned to prevent him from joining them. 'My men! My men! My God, my men!' he howled in desolation as he saw them 'fall as if tied to the same steadily drawn string.'

Each company of the 23rd Battalion, a unit of Tyneside Scottish Pals, advanced behind a piper who 'continued to play until killed or wounded.' The men were told 'on no account whatsoever to assist the wounded'; there were so many that the battalion would have become motionless if it had paused to help them. It went into the open with 750 men. After nightfall, the Fusiliers 'found in several places straight lines of ten or twelve dead or badly wounded as if the Platoons had just been dressed

for Parade.' A roll call was held the following morning. A hundred men answered their names, with a further twenty appearing during the day. Nineteen out of twenty-one officers were dead, missing or wounded; sometimes armed with nothing more than a swagger stick, a malacca cane or ashplant, their casualties were seven times higher than those of the other ranks. The battalion had suffered eighty per cent casualties, most of them in the first few minutes. It was not the worst hit; that sad honour belonged to the 1st Newfoundland Regiment, which took ninety-five per cent casualties. Every officer was killed or wounded; only thirty-five men emerged unscathed.

Sixty thousand men were hit on 1 July; twenty thousand were killed. The losses were the worst recorded by any army in a single day – half a day, in fact, for the survivors were back in their trenches by early afternoon apart from a small gain in the

**Calvary with cavalry.** *Horses and men of the Duke of Lancaster's Own Yeomanry (left) move through the devastated landscape of the Somme in March 1917. Many such regiments were dismounted and sent into the trenches later that year or in 1918.* [PHOTO: ERNEST BROOKS]

**The Red Cross** *did nothing to protect horses, caught in the shafts of ambulances (right) or harnessed to gun limbers, utterly unable to take cover, helpless victims of shelling.*

southern sector. The three thousand Germans of the 180th Regiment lost 280 men defending their positions; the twelve thousand British attacking them lost more than five thousand. Nevertheless, Sir Henry Rawlinson, commanding the 4th Army on the Somme, continued the offensive for 136 days. Tactics changed. On 14 July, the attack was put in before dawn with no preliminary bombardment, and the German first and second lines were overrun before the machinegunners in the intact third line cut down the British cavalry trying to exploit the breach. Nowhere was the advance more than five miles.

In the last assault in November, rain and shellfire produced mud so deep that a Northumberland Fusilier sank to his neck in front of his parapet. He was fed with bread and meat stuck on a bayonet pushed over the parapet, and drank from a tin on a stick. The mud was too liquid to shovel. On the second day, he was hit in the shoulder by shrapnel. Eventually he was dragged out, minus his boots, puttees and trousers. The offensive was called off on 13 November 1916. The British had taken 419,000 casualties.

## THE PITY OF WAR

The greatest fear was to be wounded. 'Death has no terror for me in itself, for (like Cleopatra) "I have immortal longings in me,' a Gloucesters subaltern, Ernest Polack, wrote from the Somme on 30 June, a few hours before his death. 'The prospect of pain naturally appals me somewhat, and I am taking morphia with me into battle…'

The ratio of shell and bomb wounds to bullet wounds was usually 70:30; there were more bullet wounds on the Somme because of the exposure to machinegun fire. The vaunted

8776

bayonet, in whose use the Pals had been well-trained, accounted for less than one per cent of casualties. Both shrapnel and high velocity bullets, which tumbled as they struck bone, caused terrible tissue damage. Infection followed. Anaerobic bacteria, in particular *clostridium welchii*, were present in the earth on which the men fell. They need deep and dirty wounds to prosper, thriving in damaged tissue in airless conditions. As the flesh was attacked, it gave off a bubbling gas, which gave the condition its common name, gas gangrene. It causes septic shock, an overwhelming infection. Trench warfare provided it with a feast. A surgeon had to be bold to deal with it, either amputating or removing all damaged flesh and leaving the enlarged wound open to the air and to other infection. Many survivors of the Somme owed their lives to the necessarily ruthless surgery performed on them. Seventy years later, in the Falklands, the British found that Argentine surgeons had not learned the lesson.

Shrapnel or bullet wounds to the abdomen could perforate the viscus, thus allowing the acid in the gut to escape into the abdominal cavity. When the chest cavity was pierced, the wound acted as a valve, in which air was sucked into the lungs through the chest and could not escape. The surgeon had to insert a tube into the lungs so that the air could get out, placing the other end of the tube into water so that air could not re-enter. As to head wounds, without X-rays to diagnose blood clots, surgeons were in uncharted territory and the fatality rate was high.

Each battalion had thirty-two stretcher bearers, who could carry sixteen wounded between them. They could not cope with casualties on the scale of the Somme. Many of the seriously wounded crawled into a shell hole, wrapped their ponchos round them, and died alone. Those who were recovered went first to a regimental aid post, where the battalion medical officer bandaged and sedated those whom he could not treat. From there, they were taken to a casualty clearing station. Those who were fit to travel were sent on to base hospitals. The surgeons operated on those who might survive; the rest were placed in a special tent where nurses gave them morphine and washed and comforted them before they died.

**City of dead youth:** *a cemetery is seen under construction on the Western Front. A temporary wooden cross is laid on each corpse, to be replaced after the war by a carved headstone. Behind can be seen stacked stretchers, waiting for the next batch. The bodies here are those of men of the Australian Corps killed in the battle of Guillemont, named for a ruined farmhouse, in October 1918. A month later, at the Armistice, the meatgrinder at last stopped its work after the Germans lost the will to feed men into it. The Allies may have endured better than the Germans, but it was a close-run thing. By the summer of 1918, when the photograph below was taken, the British army was accepting conscripts previously thought too young or too weak.*

A corporal of the Suffolks was hit in the head by shrapnel after going to ground behind two dead cows, 'green and stinking', in no man's land. He was blinded in one eye but got back to the line. Stretcher bearers carried him for three miles under shellfire to an ambulance depot. He was taken first to a church full of wounded, and then to a school where he lay on a mattress as paralysis set in. At 2 am he was taken to an ambulance train for a 14-hour journey to Boulogne. He had had neither food nor drink since he had been hit, and he was in great pain. In Boulogne he was given morphia and a clean bed; the following day his eye was taken out.

When the troops felt they could take no more, they called it being 'done up'. It was inevitable after a long period in the line. 'The men broke down slowly, most of them,' William Strang, a subaltern in the 4th Worcesters, wrote of the Somme campaign. 'Some of my men stood firm... Sergeant W stuck to the end but only just. He was nearly beaten two days from the end and burst into tears as he told me so... We remember the

1st Newfoundlanders. It makes me feel eerie at night. I am not brave and I think about things too much. Much shellfire would drive me mad. I am disappointed with myself and am terribly afraid of giving way…'

As a rule of thumb, a division might mutiny when its death roll overtook the number of men still active in its ranks. The French passed that stage after another fruitless offensive on the Aisne in April 1917; fifty-four out of a hundred divisions refused orders and one regiment marched to the front bleating like sheep; order returned only when Marshal Pétain made it clear that the *poilus* would not have to take part in further great offensives. The month before, the Petrograd garrison had mutinied, precipitating the Russian Revolution. The Italians collapsed at Caporetto; ultimately, well beyond their due point, the Germans on the Western Front also declined to fight on.

The British no longer sang 'Tipperary' with cheery resignation as they marched. The new song had a bitterness behind it:

*It's the same the whole world over,*
*Ain't it all a blooming shame,*
*It's the rich wot gets the pleasure,*
*It's the poor wot gets the blame.*

As a whole, though, they did not desert the battlefield. Individuals did; particularly Australians. Twelve times as many went absent without leave as the British, four times as many for long enough for it to count as desertion. A feral gang of Australian deserters evaded the provosts marshal in the abandoned dugouts and trenches of the Somme battlefields in 1917, scavenging for food from old supply dumps. The Australians were fine troops (though the Canadians were thought the best on the Western Front); they were independent-minded, so difficult to lead by the nose that Haig kept them isolated from British units, lest their example spread. They also had no death penalty.

The British shot 312 men after courts martial, the great

prolong these sufferings for ends which I believe to be evil and unjust,' Owen's fellow-poet Siegfried Sassoon famously declared.

They did not fight for politicians; though, had they known it, Lloyd George was their ally after he became Prime Minister in December 1916, rowing with Robertson and Haig over the endless casualty lists. They did not fight for their generals, either. 'To crown our troubles the Acting Brigadier-General came round the trenches,' one wrote, 'and found a smelly latrine, an officer who didn't salute him and sentries who didn't

majority for desertion. Their families were informed merely that they had 'died of wounds'. Private Albert Ingham of the 3rd Manchester Pals was executed after he was found stowing away on a Swedish ship at Dieppe. His father was one of the few to discover the truth; angry at the deception, he insisted that his son's headstone be inscribed: 'Shot at Dawn One of the first to enlist A worthy son to his father.' The enthusiastic amateurs became cynical and hardened professionals, loyal only to themselves. They did not pretend that those at home understood, their loved ones as much out of touch as the jingo patriots and shrews who handed out white feathers. On leave, they brought with them experiences which, like the poet Wilfred Owen's sight of a gassed man, left them intruders from an alien world:

> If in some smothering dreams, you too could pace
> Behind the wagon that we flung him in,
> And watch the white eyes writhing in his face…
> If you could hear, at every jolt, the blood
> Come gargling from the froth-corrupted lungs,
> Bitter as the cud
> Of vile, incurable sores on innocent tongues, –
> My friend, you would not tell with such high zest
> To children ardent for some desperate glory,
> The old Lie: Dulce et decorum est
> Pro patria mori.

Owen yearned for a public that had some vision of the pity of war. He knew it had none; that it still thought it sweet and proper that men should die for their country. He and his like felt they were dying for old men. 'I have seen and endured the sufferings of the troops, and I can no longer be a party to

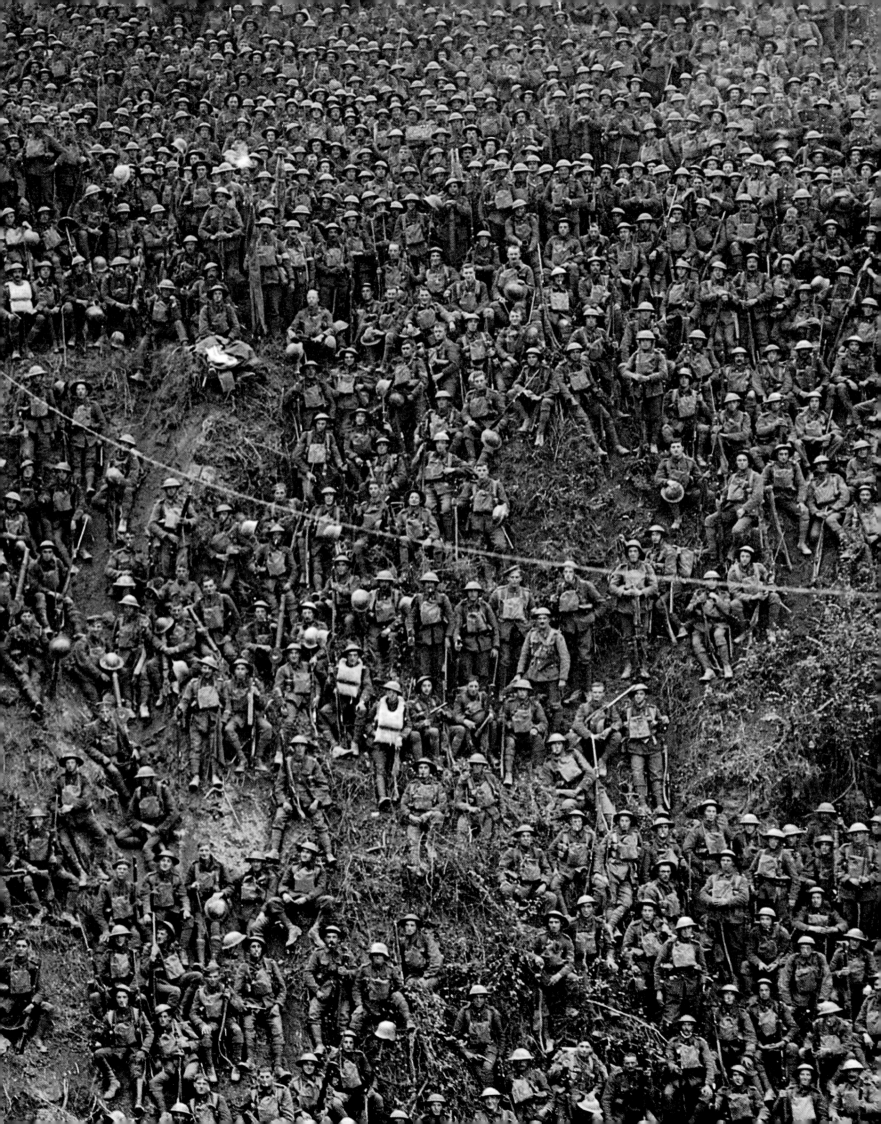

stand up as he passed. As though anyone ever paid compliments in the trenches...' Sassoon put it as succinctly in a verse about The General:

*'He's a cheery old card,' grunted Harry to Jack*
*As they slogged up to Arras with rifle and pack...*
*But he did for them both with his plan of attack.*

If the generals saw no option other than battering at the enemy lines, they had the defence that no French or German commanders saw it differently; and, in the end, the British army had been trained – or trained itself – from scratch into

the steadiest and most effective force on the Western Front. It did come down to attrition, as the Westerners had predicted; the British lost fewer men than the French and Germans, and their side won. It was the remoteness of the brasshats, their ignorance of conditions, that was inexcusable. Haig's Chief of Staff visited the fighting zone for the first time at the end of the ruinous Passchendaele offensive in 1917. 'Good God,' he said in tears as he saw the mud. 'Did we really send men to fight in that?' In the past, the British had, by and large, trusted their superiors. They had been visible; an admiral, after all, shared the same ship as his men and might expect to go down with it if it sank; colonial skirmishes were best led from the front; and politicians, at least in peacetime, appeared on the hustings and were vulnerable to the ballot box. The Western Front changed the perception of authority.

The men knew why they were there, however, and it gave them a grim satisfaction to know the truth. 'Some people at home seem to think that we are only trying to gain ground and that because we haven't broken through we have failed,' one wrote. 'It is a wrong idea. We are simply killing Bosch...'

### THE ELEVENTH HOUR OF THE ELEVENTH DAY OF THE ELEVENTH MONTH

The German U-boat campaign came close to success; in April 1917, more than a million tons of shipping was sunk, and one in four ships that left British ports failed to return. Only Lloyd George's insistence on a convoy system, imposed over the

**Breakthrough** *(previous pages). The end, when it came, was swift and unexpected. In the summer of 1918, the Germans had threatened once more to break through to Paris. It proved the last flailing of an exhausted army. The British now poured forward and here, Brigadier-General Campbell, VC, addresses men of the Staffordshire Brigade from a bridge over the St Quentin canal. The men had won the battle for the canal by 2 October 1918.*

**Lawrence of Arabia** *(below) led the Arabs in revolt against the Turks with all the old imperial panache. He is the dismounted figure in this photograph taken in the summer of 1918 at Akaba with the levies of Emir Faisal which he commanded. By October, this strange and tormented man had taken Damascus; already legendary, he turned his back on 'the shallow grave of public duty' and joined the RAF as a humble aircraftman under an assumed name.*

heads of the Admiralty, staunched the losses. The new Prime Minister was less successful with his generals. Haig demanded a summer offensive, the third battle of Ypres (or Passchendaele), the 'battle of the mud' to the Welshman. When Lloyd George visited the front to try to have it called off, all fit-looking Germans were removed from the prisoner-of-war stockades to convince him that the enemy – malnourished from the British blockade of German ports and the hungry 'turnip winter' – was at his last gasp. Three hundred thousand casualties bought a few square miles of shattered woods and wrecked buildings.

At the end of the year, Leon Trotsky negotiated Bolshevik Russia out of the war; German troops were freed for the Western Front, and German hunger assuaged by the wheatfields of the Ukraine. If the Americans were now in, their presence took time to be felt and they had to be supplied with British and French aircraft and artillery. The tank, a development in which the British placed much hope, would come close to winning a war; but the next one, and for the Germans. It was too unreliable to be decisive in this one.

Meanwhile, the old weapons of Empire – dash, subterfuge, cavalry, irregulars, brawn and brain – were carving through the Middle East. The campaign in Palestine had started badly; the British were held at Gaza, when, as Lloyd George put it, 'nobody could have saved the Turks from complete collapse but our General Staff.' A big, shambling, raw-boned general, Sir Edmund Allenby, 'the Bull', was given command. He

encouraged the unorthodox. His first victory in the Sinai followed a stratagem by one of his young intelligence officers, Richard Meinertzhagen, who rode into the desert alone and sought out a Turkish patrol. When it fired at him, he acted as though he had been hit; he dropped his binoculars and an already bloodstained haversack, and galloped off holding his shoulder. The haversack held orders for an attack at Gaza, with a feint at Beersheba. The Turks were fooled; Allenby duly attacked at Beersheba and had soon broken through to Jaffa.

The most exotic of Allenby's officers was T. E. Lawrence, ex-archaeologist and intelligence agent, a nervous and slender figure, sexually ambivalent, who had raised the desert tribes in revolt. 'In walked an Arab boy dressed in spotless white, white headdress with golden circlet; for the moment I thought the boy was somebody's pleasure boy but it soon dawned on me that he must be Lawrence whom I knew to be in camp,' Meinertzhagen wrote of their first meeting. 'I just stared in silence at the very beautiful apparition.' Allenby recognised the charisma beneath the flamboyance, and the value of the Arab irregulars with whom Lawrence had a mystical affinity. At twenty-nine, Lawrence was a colonel. The Bull advanced by outflanking the Turks and keeping them off-balance; the raids by Lawrence's horsemen and cameleers on forts and railway lines preserved momentum. 'I have covered 925 miles in forty days,' Lawrence wrote. 'I really believe I have worried the Turk no end…'

Near Christmas 1917, Allenby closed on Jerusalem. It was agreed that there would be no fighting in the city itself, holy to

Muslims as well as Christians and Jews. The Welsh Division had stiff combat in the fields and stone walls on the Mount of Olives. The mayor of Jerusalem – a formal figure in morning coat and pepper-and-salt trousers, with a tarboosh and a white flag – brought out the keys of the city for its new conquerors on 9 December. Allenby, a descendant of Cromwell, entered it three days later, in sweaty khaki and dusty boots, unarmed; the last Christian armies to enter Jerusalem had been the Crusaders seven centuries before.

At home, meat, sugar and butter were rationed in February 1918. On 21 March, under cover of dense fog that blinded the machinegunners, Ludendorff broke through the line south of Ypres. The British 5th Army was almost overwhelmed, staggering back towards the Channel ports, in danger of losing contact with the French on its flank. Haig suggested putting himself under Marshal Foch, who became supreme commander of Allied forces in France. The British tripled the number of cross-Channel sailings to fling in all available troops; the line steadied.

In April, the Germans attacked again, driving a breach thirty miles wide in the line. The British were forced to abandon Passchendaele, bought at such cost. Haig feared he would lose the Channel ports. 'With our backs to the wall,' he ordered, 'and believing in the justice of our cause each one of us must fight to the end.' It impressed the public; the men whistled at its melodrama. They had contained the Germans by 29 April. Ludendorff tried again, on the Aisne on 27 May. He fell on five British divisions, exhausted by the fighting in Flanders. The Germans advanced ten miles in a day, a rate unseen since the first month of the war. By 3 June, they were fifty-six miles from Paris and shelling the city with their Big Bertha guns. Foch held them, and counterattacked when Ludendorff launched his last offensive around Rheims on 15 July.

On 8 August – 'the black day for the German army', Ludendorff said – British, Canadian and Australian troops ripped into the Germans with 456 tanks. The Germans fell back six miles; it was a turning point, the moment when, exhausted by constant attacking, they knew for the first time

**Exhausted prisoners** *captured by the Canadians (left) during the attack on Cambrai on 27 September 1918. The end was close, though the British did not yet sense it. By rule of thumb, a unit can be expected to lose its morale and approach mutiny after it has lost as many men as it still has active soldiers. The Germans were well past that point when, with revolution breaking out at home, their officers judged that no more could be asked of them and sought the Armistice.*

[Photo: William Rider-Rider]

**A poem** *was written by Siegfried Sassoon for men like these (right), amputees at Roehampton Military Hospital:*

*Does it matter?... Losing your
    legs?...
For people will always be kind,
And you need not show that you
    mind
When others come in after hunting
To gobble their muffins and eggs.*

that they had nothing more to give. In September, the British broke through the Hindenburg Line; on a single day, they fired 943,000 shells. There was no sense of elation; half the British infantry were under nineteen years old, and the loss of a foot or hand no longer guaranteed discharge, for some amputees served in supply units behind the front. 'None of us will ever live to see the end of this war,' was the gloomy prediction of Lord Northcliffe, ultra-patriotic owner of the *Daily Mail*.

In forgotten Salonika, the Bulgarians collapsed and asked for an armistice. The way to the Danube and Austria was open to the allies. Allenby had pushed on from Jerusalem to Amman, building the still standing Allenby Bridge on the way, and to Damascus, Beirut, Homs and Tripoli. In September, at Megiddo, the Armageddon of the ancient world, the remaining Turkish armies were destroyed. The Turks, the Ottoman Empire ruined, sued for peace. Austria-Hungary was going the same way, the Czechs and Hungarians declaring their independence, regiments melting away. On 3 November, the Austro-Hungarian High Command sought an armistice; the army it represented had already passed into oblivion.

Ludendorff sought an armistice, too; the Kaiser dismissed him. Warship crews in Kiel mutinied. On 9 November, a republic was proclaimed in Berlin. At Spa, the German headquarters, it was explained to Wilhelm II that his troops would no longer follow his orders; he was driven to the Dutch frontier. He died in 1941 without seeing Germany again. At

5 am on 11 November, in a railway carriage in the forest of Compiègne, the Germans signed an armistice. It was due to come into effect at 11 am. Shortly before that, Canadian troops entered Mons; the forces of the British Empire, at a cost of 956,000 lives, were back where they had begun.

Wild rejoicing swept Britain. Women 'seemed to go out of their heads'; in Oxford, a group lifted their skirts above their heads. Cambridge undergraduates celebrated by ransacking the rooms of the pacifist Bertrand Russell in Trinity Street. There was public copulation, and the drunkenness went on in places for a week; the police were reluctant to intervene. Fires were started, windows smashed, people lay in stupor on the pavements.

At the front, there was incredulity. The men were still faced by Germans along the line. They themselves had recovered after the German breakthroughs of the summer; they thought the Germans quite capable of doing the same. Only a week before the end, Wilfred Owen had been killed in heavy fighting on the Oise-Sambre canal. Many units did not hear of the Armistice until 9 am. The orders were guarded, with no note of congratulation. 'Hostilities cease 1100 November 11,' the notice from staff headquarters ran. 'Defensive precautions will be maintained. There will be no intercourse of any description with the enemy.' A stretcher bearer said that, after the announcement was made, 'not a word was spoken, everyone went their several ways...'

**Wild revels** *greeted the Armistice at home; women 'seemed to go out of their heads'. These partygoers are at the Ritz Hotel in London. At the front, there was no rejoicing; just silence and disbelief. 'Everybody wore an air of complete, if somewhat bewildered satisfaction, as one who rises from a thoroughly good dinner,' Sir Alan Lascelles, later secretary to four sovereigns, wrote in his journal near Mons on 13 November 1918. 'That within five months of that nightmare last spring the Beast should be broken body and soul; that his armies should be in rout, his emasculated fleet in English harbours, the Kaiser in exile, the Crown Prince the jape of Europe, Ludendorff a broken imbecile; that all the wild jingo-hopes we used to toy with in the early days before jingoism died and stank, and hope itself almost withered, should in one thunderclap become stark reality… can you wonder that we were dazed and slow of comprehension?'*

## CHAPTER FIVE

# 'NO MORE WAR... FOR THE MOMENT'

**The landscapes** *of Old England may have survived the war intact but the pre-war ethos was in full retreat. Here (left), under an ilex tree at Ham Spray in Wiltshire with the artist Dora Carrington, the writer Lytton Strachey prepares fresh assaults on the morals and pretensions of the Victorian past. His book* Eminent Victorians *appeared in 1918 and was indeed a ruthless and daring attack on the nation's pantheon.*

*He dug up legends – the nurse Florence Nightingale, Cardinal Manning, Thomas Arnold, headmaster of Rugby School, General Gordon, killed by dervishes in Khartoum in 1885 – and stripped them, with a mordant eye for whim and smugness, of their reputations. Strachey, son of a British India civil engineer and soldier, was himself a product of the very circles at which he aimed his elegant libels. The ménage at Ham Spray was just as much an attack on Victorian mores, with Strachey in love with Carrington's husband, Ralph Partridge, and Carrington in hopeless love with Strachey.*

THE LOSSES FROM THE GREAT WAR WERE NOT overwhelming and, in a biological sense, they were more sustainable than the pre-war drain of 300,000 people a year by emigration. But, discriminating in their cruelty, they had fallen largely upon a single group. Three in ten of the boys and young men aged between thirteen and twenty-four in 1914 were killed. The feeling of a 'lost generation' was palpable; the best and the bravest had gone. It was felt, too, that the armistice could be no more than its name suggested; a pause, in the event, of twenty-one years, so that those who were conceived in the nights of its wild celebration would be the first to be called up when the normal business of butchery was resumed. 'No more war!' an artilleryman had written on 11 November, and added: 'At least for the moment.' Britain was to survive the inter-war years well enough in comparison to others, but they had nonetheless a feverish and nervous quality, as though the country was merely in remission from the violent psychoses that swept mainland Europe. Robert Graves, poet and survivor of the trenches, gave the period a bittersweet name: 'The Long Weekend'.

Two popular pledges dominated the 1918 election, in which, for the first time, women householders of thirty and above had the vote. Lloyd George promised to 'build homes fit for heroes', and to 'make the Germans pay'. They worked well as slogans; perhaps too well, for his Conservative-Liberal coalition outnumbered an opposition rump of Labour and rebel Liberals by almost six to one. The nationalist Sinn Feiners in Ireland, who might have given some bite to Westminster debate, refused to take their seats. The promises themselves proved impossible to keep. Few homes were built, for heroes or anyone else. Skilled builders were scarce; the apprenticeship system had lapsed during the war and materials were expensive. Families lived in converted railway carriages and barges and huts. There was plenty of money around – wartime profits were released and spent, factories and real estate fetched record prices in anticipation of a return to the good times – but it bypassed those who felt they deserved it. Troops angry at their slow discharge from the army rioted and burned down Luton Town Hall. Returning union men were angry at the women who had taken industrial jobs, while there were race riots in seaports against West Indians recruited into the merchant navy; their lodging houses were sacked by mobs of whites and three were killed in Cardiff.

Policemen went on strike, demanding their own union; taking advantage of their absence, hooligans looted shops in Liverpool until troops opened fire, killing one and arresting several hundred. Railway engine-drivers, angered at prospective pay cuts, came out on strike. Lloyd George called it an 'anarchist conspiracy' and sent a cruiser to the Mersey and troops to main stations. Volunteer strike-breakers were used; chiefly, said *The Times*, 'the public school type of man. Many were ex-officers, and nobody could have wished for a more cheerful, courteous and considerate body of public servants.' A skeleton service was maintained, but the government agreed to a minimum wage of fifty-one shillings a week.

The mood was surly; the government kept a nervous eye on the reaction to events in Russia, where British forces were fighting on the White side in the civil war, attempting with no great enthusiasm to 'strangle Bolshevism at birth', as Churchill put it. Royal Navy torpedo boats attacked the Red fleet in dashing raids, sinking two battleships and a cruiser; RAF pilots flying a de Havilland bomber tried to kill Trotsky in a bombing raid on a hall where he was due to speak, but he failed to keep his appointment. British troops, however, came close to mutiny and at home dockers refused to load the *Jolly George* steamer with munitions for Polish opponents of the Communists. 'I'm not going to ask the dockers to put a gun in the ship to carry out this wicked venture,' Ernest Bevin, a former van boy and transport union leader, declared. 'The workers have a right to say how their labour should be used.'

It smacked of revolution. Thirty-five million days were lost to strikes in 1919. Calls for a mass strike in Glasgow were met by baton charges. There was talk of 'Red Clydeside' and 12,000 troops were sent to the city with tanks in support. 'Had there been an experienced revolutionary leadership of these great and heroic masses,' claimed Willie Gallagher, the leading Scots leftist, 'we could easily have persuaded the soldiers to come out and Glasgow would have been in our hands.' The government half believed him; a draft bill was prepared giving powers to arrest union leaders and to prevent unions from having strike funds. Plans were made for commandeering 40,000 trucks and 100,000 cars to keep the country fed and mobile in the event of an all-out strike by the Triple Alliance of miners, railwaymen and transport workers.

In the upper classes, Robert Graves noted, 'anyone who merely visited Russia... was socially ruined'; a Balliol undergraduate and ex-officer who spent his vacation there was asked to leave Oxford on his return. Two other undergraduates were rusticated for 'Russian Communism'; the fear of people who had murdered their tsar, and who, according to the Conservative press, had 'nationalised women for sexual purposes', ran deep. In truth, the fear of a Red rising was a mere alarum. The British remained a deeply stable people; Bevin, a former lay preacher and a robust pragmatist, was no fire-eating extremist. But the post-war euphoria quickly eroded; Britain was seen as a land more fitted to the speculator and the striker than the hero.

As to 'making the Germans pay', an attempt was indeed made. The terms imposed on them at Versailles were harsh. Germany was disarmed, the crews on the warships held by the Royal Navy at Scapa Flow scuttling them; her colonies were transferred to France and the British Empire; her frontiers were shrunk and the Saar coalfields taken from her. On top of that she was to pay massive reparations. Hatreds were being stored

**Is the strike justified?** *asks the poster on the wall, as railway strikers come to blows with volunteers who offered their services to keep the trains running in September 1919. It was feared that Communism would spread from Russia where British troops were fighting in the civil war on the side of the Whites against Trotsky's Red army in a forlorn attempt, as Winston Churchill put it, to 'strangle Bolshevism at birth'. Germany, too, was violently unstable, prey to Anglo-French insistence on reparations and the transfer of territory. 'She is stripped naked and then told to turn out her pockets,' the Daily News commented. Europe was already setting towards extremes. Fears of 'Red Clydeside' and revolution at home were misplaced, however. Britain remained an instinctively stable society.*

*The advertisement for the magazine John Bull has a fraudulent charm. Horatio Bottomley MP was the owner and publisher and in truth one of the great charlatans of the age, who cheated his readers with lotteries that had no winners and 'bonds' that were never repaid. A precursor of another swindler-publisher, Robert Maxwell, he was convicted of fraud in 1922.*

up; the *Daily Herald* ran a prescient cartoon of a child crying outside the conference chamber, wearing a sash marked 'Class of 1940'. In the event, the Germans defaulted on their payments, as the British, reduced by wartime spending from creditor to debtor nation, would themselves later default on their American loans in 1947; the mark was reduced to 15 million to the pound, the French occupied the Ruhr and an ex-corporal named Adolf Hitler first came to the attention of British newspaper readers. 'Hitler, the tub-thumping patriot, may be heard from again some day,' the *Daily News* man in Munich reported. 'It is not generally known that this man, who is Austrian by birth and a signpainter by profession, was badly gassed on the British front. Previously he had been badly wounded, but after he recovered from the gas-attack he stated he had seen a vision and received a message. He had been summoned as the Saviour of Germany!'

The normal stance to the Continent was resumed; the public turned their back on it. They subscribed to appeals to buy British transport horses left in France and Belgium 'out of Continental slavery', and to a Soldiers' Dog Fund so that the troops could bring their pets home with them. Everyone knew that animals had a rough time of it across the Channel. But towards the people there, they were indifferent. When the Germans complained that they were starving, which indeed some were, *The Times* correspondent dismissed it as 'proof of a mean and lying and greedy spirit'. The British had unfinished business closer to home.

'That cloud in the West,' Gladstone had called Ireland, 'That coming storm! The minister of God's retribution upon cruel injustice!' It had done for him, his Home Rule bills thrown out; it had split his Liberal party and caused the first and only

mutiny of the British officer corps at the Curragh in 1914, when officers indicated that they would refuse to fight Ulster Protestant rebels. During the war, in 1916, it had produced the Easter Rising, that lethal blend of the idealism and savagery that so marked Irish nationalism; gunmen commandeering a tram had insisted on paying their fares in full, and had then shot down defenceless and elderly part-time soldiers. The Rising itself had been so unpopular that Dubliners had given the British troops chocolate and fruit as they marched in to put it down. It was the executions that followed it that turned opinion, in Ireland and the many places where the Irish had emigrated. There were sixteen shot. It was 'like watching a stream of blood coming from under a closed door...' an Irishwoman wrote – and on days when there were several, the evening papers in Chicago brought out special editions with a different name headlined in each.

It was abnormal that people should find the execution of armed rebels in wartime to be repellent. But normal moral rules did not apply between Britain and Ireland. Too much history intervened. The British had been in Ireland for 750 years, and as a result of their presence, or interference, it had three distinct breeds. The native Irish Catholics, stripped of much of their land, brutally reduced in numbers by the starvation, disease and emigration that had followed the Potato Famine seventy years before, felt themselves servants in their own home. To them, the Catholic Emancipation Act of 1829 had been mere window-dressing; after Gladstone's failures Home Rule had been proffered, again, and then withdrawn at the start of the war in 1914, at the whim of Westminster MPs and peers. At Versailles, the Irish saw small nations attain statehood, Czechoslovakia, Estonia, Latvia, with the support of the British who, with malign discrimination, refused it to them. The main reason why the British dragged their feet was the Ulster Protestants in the northeast around Belfast, many of them the descendants of Lowland Scots shipped in and 'planted' on land confiscated from Catholics in Jacobean times, leery and contemptuous of the 'Papists' and 'Fenian rebels' to the south. Each year they celebrated the Battle of the Boyne, at which, in 1690, William of Orange had confirmed Protestant domination. They were linen manufacturers, shipbuilders and engineers, and called themselves Orangemen. Then on estates great and small, in grand Georgian houses in varying states of repair, were the Anglo-Irish of the Protestant ascendancy, some the descendants of Norman warlords, most more recent arrivals, two or three centuries old. They were a dashing, military and literary people. Their generals included Wellington, Kitchener and French, their writers Sheridan, Goldsmith, Oscar Wilde, the creator of Dracula, Bram Stoker, and W. B. Yeats. Where Ulster Protestants were prepared to fight to maintain the Union with Britain, the Anglo-Irish were more ambivalent. Jonathan Swift, author of *Gulliver's Travels* and Protestant Dean of St Patrick's Cathedral in Dublin, had urged his fellows to burn everything English except English coal; as Ulstermen ran arms into the north in the months before the war, an Anglo-Irishman, Erskine Childers, had sailed his yacht into Howth with a cargo of arms for the nationalists.

Sinn Fein – 'Ourselves alone', the nationalist party – had won seventy-three of the 105 Irish seats in the 1918 election. Boycotting Westminster, they set up the Dail Eireann, the Irish assembly, in Dublin and declared an independent Irish Republic. The British were hoping to restrict the Irish to the long-delayed Home Rule, under which London would have retained control of taxation, defence and foreign affairs; the worst-case scenario was Dominion status, in which Ireland, like Australia or Canada, would become effectively independent within the British Empire. The Dail went far beyond either.

**Shadow of a gunman.** *It was the title of the play Sean O'Casey was writing in 1922; it was the reality on the streets of Dublin (right) that year. Here armed IRA men patrol during the civil war that* *followed the fighting against the British. The emerald isle had split in two; and, within each half, the green eyes of jealousy were glaring. Ireland, wrote James Joyce, 'is the old sow that eats her farrow'.*

**'The Big Fella'.** *Michael Collins leaves Ten Downing Street (left) in December 1921 after negotiating a treaty which gave southern Ireland independence within the British Commonwealth. 'Early this morning I signed my death warrant,' he said. The treaty required members of the Dail, the Irish parliament, to swear: 'I will be faithful to HM King George V... in virtue of the common citizenship of Ireland with Great Britain and her adherence to... the British Commonwealth.' He knew that republican diehards would kill fellow Irishmen rather than keep this verbal link to the British crown.*

*He became head of the military forces of the Irish Free State in the fratricidal war with the IRA. In August 1922, Collins was ambushed by republicans in his Rolls-Royce tourer in the wilds of County Cork, and murdered. Here (right) his body lies in state.*

Early in 1919, it set up ministries and called on the people to boycott the Royal Irish Constabulary as 'agents of a foreign power'.

In January 1919, two RIC men were shot dead as they escorted a load of gelignite to a quarry in County Tipperary. The Irish Republican Army began a guerrilla war against the police and army. Its strategy and fundraising were organised by Michael Collins, the thirty-year-old son of a Cork farmer, who had been briefly interned after the Easter Rising. 'The sooner fighting is forced and a general state of disorder created throughout the country,' he declared, 'the better it will be for the country.' The favoured targets were RIC men. The British declared Sinn Fein illegal. By early 1920, with raids on isolated police stations and barracks escalating, it was clear that the RIC could no longer cope.

The government advertised for British volunteers willing to 'face a rough and dangerous task' attached to the RIC for 'ten shillings a day and all found'. There were not enough green RIC uniforms to go round so they wore a mixture of khaki and dark green with black belts. The get-up reminded people in Limerick of the colouring of a local pack of foxhounds, the 'Black and Tans'. The loathing between them and the Irish was mutual; most had been in the trenches, and they remembered the Easter Rising as a stab in the back. They were joined by a special auxiliary division – the 'Auxis' – of 1,500 men whose task was to deal with IRA flying columns, groups of twenty to

thirty well-armed guerrillas. The Auxis were impoverished ex-officers who had spent their wound-gratuities and Victory bounties on high living or failed business schemes, and preferred this to humdrum civilian jobs or re-enlisting in the ranks of the Army of Occupation in Cologne, especially since they were paid double the rate of the Black and Tans.

Cruising the country in their big armoured trucks called Crossley tenders, the 'Tans' – the word was used for both Auxis and British RIC men – were ruthless. The Lord Mayor of Cork, Thomas MacCurtain, was shot by masked men in civilian clothes. They cut out the tongue of one IRA Volunteer they captured, cutting off the nose of another, the heart out of a third and bashing in the skull of a fourth. They set the centre of Cork afire and cut the hoses of the firemen, whilst they lashed onlookers with whips they had looted from saddlers' shops. After the great fire, they sauntered through Dublin with half-burnt winecorks in their caps. Their conduct became an international scandal. 'You do not cast out Beelzebub by Beelzebub,' the archbishop of Canterbury warned the government, and the nationalist leader Eamon De Valera raised $5 million on a tour of the United States on the back of their conduct.

They seemed effective enough for Lloyd George to claim that he 'had murder by the throat' in November 1920, but he was premature. 'You cannot,' T. E. Lawrence said, with the experience of the Arab revolt behind him, 'make war upon rebellion.' On 21 November, Michael Collins located the

lodgings of British intelligence officers in Dublin. Fourteen were shot dead in their beds or as they dressed. In the afternoon, a group of Tans opened fire on the crowd at a Dublin football match. One player and eleven spectators were killed. In the evening, in further retaliation, two senior IRA men and a Sinn Fein sympathiser were murdered in the guard-room of Dublin Castle; Michael Collins, the most wanted man in Ireland, laid a wreath at the funeral. On 28 November, an eighteen-strong Auxi patrol was ambushed and killed to the last man at Kilmichael by a Cork flying column.

Among the atrocities and counter-atrocities – old Anglo-Irish ladies shot, country houses burnt by the IRA and cottages and creameries torched by the Tans, cattle maimed, IRA men hacked with bayonets and shot in barracks – there were moving gestures. Major Compton Smith, about to be killed in retaliation for the executions of IRA men, wrote to his wife: 'I am to be shot in an hour's time. Dearest, your husband will die with your name on his lips, your face before his eyes, and he will die like an Englishman and a soldier. I leave my cigarette case to the regiment, my medals to my father, and my watch to the officer who is to execute me, because I believe him to be a gentleman, and to mark the fact that I bear him no malice for carrying out what he sincerely believes to be his duty.' Both sides knew how to die: Terence MacSwinney, the new Lord Mayor of Cork, was given a two-year sentence for possession of documents 'likely to cause disaffection to His Majesty', a

catchall charge that could have been applied to any nationalist. 'I have decided I shall be free or dead within a month,' he declared when sentenced. It took rather longer, seventy-five days, to starve himself to death in Brixton prison in London. When his coffin, in the nationalist colours, green, white and orange, left Euston station for Ireland, an onlooker said of the crowds: 'Are we to take it that all these people are Sinn Feiners?... I never guessed we had so many of them and right in our midst!' There was an intimacy between the two people – Collins had been a bank clerk in London, the commander of the Cork flying column, Tom Barry, had served in the British army – and it was as much a civil war as a war of independence, for the Irish would move seamlessly from killing and being killed by the British to doing the same with each other.

The British, though still hoping to cede no more than Home Rule, proposed partition. Two parliaments would be set up, one in Belfast for the six predominantly Protestant counties of Ulster in the north-east, and the other in Dublin for the remaining three Ulster counties and their Catholic compatriots in the twenty-three southern counties. In the north, elections returned the Unionists and the King opened Stormont, the Belfast Parliament, in June 1921. Westminster retained control of taxation, defence and foreign policy. In the south, 124 Sinn Feiners with very different views of sovereignty were returned unopposed to the Dail. A truce in the fighting was declared in July, to the relief of Michael Collins, who had lost 120 men

**Black and Tans.** *The two men with trench coats and pistols (left) were volunteers for 'a rough and dangerous task'. They assumed responsibility for security in Ireland from the Royal Irish Constabulary (in the British 'bobby's' helmet) and the regular steel-helmeted army. Their uniforms reminded people of a pack of Limerick foxhounds, hence the 'Black and Tan' tag attached to these well-loathed symbols of British supremacy.*

*Far from the troubles, in peaceful England, the guests of Viscount Wimborne (right) arrive for the weekend at his country house.*

[PHOTO, RIGHT: CECIL BEATON]

when they took and burnt the Customs House on the Liffey quays only to find themselves surrounded. 'You had us dead beat,' he told the British. 'We could not have lasted another three weeks.' The British offered the equivalent of Dominion status. Collins and Arthur Griffiths, a former goldminer on the Rand and a founder of Sinn Fein, went to London to negotiate. An agreement for an Irish Free State – not a republic, independent in all policy but still owing at least technical allegiance to the King – was reached on 6 December 1921. 'When you have sweated, toiled, had mad dreams, hopeless nightmares, you find yourself in London streets, cold and dank in the night air,' Collins wrote. 'What have I got for Ireland? Will anyone be satisfied with this bargain?... Early this morning I signed my death warrant.'

De Valera warned that the treaty was 'in violent conflict with the wishes of the majority of the nation.' That was untrue; it was passed by a majority, if a narrow one, in the Dail and pro-treaty candidates won three-quarters of the seats in the subsequent election. Collins called the treaty 'the freedom to win freedom'. He was right; De Valera was later to proclaim a republic without much British ado. Collins was right, too, about his death warrant. Ireland was split down the middle in the south, as well as being severed from the north, as De Valera and his republican diehards precipitated a purely Irish war against Collins's pro-treaty forces after the British withdrew. In April 1922, republicans seized Dublin's Four Courts, and were shelled by Free State troops. Collins was warned not to return to County Cork. 'Sure, they won't shoot me in my own country,' he said. On 22 August, his open Rolls-Royce tourer, escorted by an ex-Tan Crossley tender and an armoured car, ran into an ambush in the wilds of West Cork set by a party of republicans. Collins was killed.

Seventy-seven executions of republicans followed; the

Anglo-Irish Erskine Childers was among them. During the war, he had served in British naval intelligence, taken part in a famous Royal Navy raid on Cuxhaven and won the Distinguished Service Cross. He was minister of propaganda in the Dail government, but he was a passionate republican and opposed to the treaty. The Free State now sentenced him to death, ironically for possession of a pistol given to him by Collins. He was shot at dawn in the Beggar's Bush barracks in Dublin on 24 November. 'My beloved country, God send you courage, victory and rest, and to all our people harmony and love,' he wrote. 'It is six a.m.... it all seems perfectly simple and inevitable, like lying down after a long day's work.' He shook hands with each member of the firing squad.

Republicans set out to avenge him by shooting any Dail member who had voted for the emergency powers under which he had been executed. In retaliation, the government had four leading republicans who had been captured at the Four Courts removed from their cells in the middle of the night and shot without trial. The whole cabinet agreed, though one had been best man to one of the victims. Green was a bloody colour. Thirty-four republicans were shot by firing squad in January 1923 alone, and 13,000 were in prison, before De Valera in May ordered republicans to 'dump arms'. For the time being, Ireland was quiet.

The British lost their oldest colony because, in the end, they had no stomach to keep it; the implications for the rest of their empire were enormous. In India, too, the British were no longer so prepared to shoot. Nationalist demonstrations escalated beyond Gandhi's control in the Punjab in April 1919 and a mob seized the centre of Amritsar. Europeans were murdered and banks set on fire so the Punjab governor, Sir Michael O'Dwyer, himself Anglo-Irish, imposed martial law. The military commander, General Reginald Dyer – a man, a brother officer remarked, 'happiest when crawling over a Burmese stockade with a revolver in his mouth' – was faced by a crowd of 10,000 with sticks and Sikh swords. He ordered his Indian troops to open fire. They killed 379 in ten minutes with volleys of rifle fire and wounded more than 1,000. Unrepentant, Dyer regretted that he had not been able to use machineguns; he had suspects flogged and ordered Indians to slither like snakes on their bellies down a street where a woman missionary had been assaulted.

Dyer explained to the court of inquiry: 'I thought I'd be doing a jolly lot of good.' He was effectively dismissed from the army. There was a great sense of outrage among Conservatives and officers, but Winston Churchill, the War Secretary, would

have none of it – 'frightfulness is the inflicting of great slaughter or massacre… such ideas are absolutely foreign to the British way of doing things' – and neither would Edwin Montagu, Secretary of State for India. He castigated Dyer for 'racial humiliation' and turned on his supporters in the parliamentary debate. 'An Indian is a person who is tolerable so long as he obeys your orders,' he told them, 'but if he thinks for himself, if once he takes advantage of the education… you have provided for him, if once he imbibes the ideas of individual liberty which are dear to the British people, why then you classify him as an educated Indian and an agitator.'

But – and this was the rub – if an Indian, or an Irishman, imbibed those ideals of liberty, and then demanded independence upon that basis, how could he be denied?

The post-war boom burned as bright and brief as a firework. The stock market soared and wages and inflation let rip; the post-war pound lost half its value. The national debt had risen twelvefold to £8 billion since 1914; income tax had reached thirty per cent partly to service it. Death duties on estates were raised to a maximum of forty per cent and land flooded onto the market. The Duke of Sutherland sold more than 250,000 acres of Scotland and the Duke of Rutland parted with half his Belvoir estate, getting £1.5 million for 28,000 acres. A knell was tolled by *The Times* for the county families. 'England is changing hands,' it said in 1920. 'Will a profiteer buy it?… For the most part, the sacrifices are made in silence… The sons are perhaps lying in far away graves, the daughters are secretly mourning someone dearer than a brother.' To the death in action of the son was added the slaughter of assets on the death of the father. By 1921, a quarter of England had changed hands. It was, the historian John Stevenson pointed out, the largest and most rapid transfer of land 'at least since the dissolution of the monasteries and possibly since the Norman Conquest'.

With the easy money came easy virtue. The coalition government was a cosy affair, inbred and full of pals – 'Lloyd George knew my father,' as the ditty had it, 'Father knew Lloyd George' – and the parties were not scrupulous about their sources of income. They sold honours and found eager buyers. The whistle was blown by a Colonel Parkinson, a member of a rich construction family, who sued for damages after handing over £3,000 to a fixer for a knighthood that did

**Heart of the north.** *The industrial towns of the north were distinct in character, in work and in sport. These photographs were taken at Bolton, a textile and chemicals town near Manchester, by Humphrey Spender. He found Bolton so typical of the north that he called it simply 'Worktown'. The men are playing 'crown bowls' (left), so*

*called because the centre of the green was raised a few inches higher than the edges – effete Southerners played 'flat green bowls'. The green belongs to a pub, the imperiously named Gibraltar Rock. Women also played bowls, but not on pub greens; in the pub itself, cards, dominoes and darts were played in the tap room, a men-only bar. 'It's quite possible,'*

*a northerner commented of the washerwoman (right), 'that she's done this washing, but it's somebody else's — either to get half-a-crown [12.5 pence] for a basket of washing, or she's borrowed the clothes and washed them free, because she'll put them in the pawn and use the money until next Friday…'*

[PHOTOS: HUMPHREY SPENDER]

not materialise. Men with deep enough pockets had long been able to acquire honours; what was new was the precise tariff now put on them. The Duke of Northumberland said that knighthoods were being sold for £10,000, suggesting that Parkinson had underpaid, and baronetcies for £40,000.

Corruption was personified in the portly figure of the MP Horatio Bottomley, raised a poor orphan, promoter, gambler and publisher of the bellicose magazine *John Bull*, and swindler of genius. He had charm and an eye for the catchy phrase – he called the Germans 'Ger-Huns' and the teetotal Lady Astor a 'hypocrite of the first water' – and an utter lack of scruple. He promoted monster competitions in his magazine, keeping most of the prize money raised by readers for himself. He kept all but £10,000 of the £90,000 they subscribed for his 'Premium Bonds', but lost half of it when his horse failed to win the Manchester Cup and spent the rest on women and champagne.

The issue of a post-war Victory Loan gave him a chance to restore his fortunes. The government set a minimum investment of £5; Bottomley attacked this as elitist. He promised that any reader who sent *John Bull* £1 would have a fifth share of a Victory bond, and the chance of winning a big prize from the pooled interest on the bonds. He took in £650,000, an immense sum. The 300,000 investors waited for prizes with increasing suspicion. His method of clearing the air was to have a crony libel him as a fraudster, and then apologise to him in a court surrounded by demonstrators whom he paid five shillings a day to shout: 'Three cheers for Mr Bottomley'. His bluff was called when one of his stool pigeons was asked who had written the apology he was reading out in court, and blurted out: 'Mr Bottomley'. As thousands demanded repayment of their bonds, Bottomley challenged the Director of Public Prosecutions to examine his books, after shredding most of them. He was charged with fraud, pleading 'decidedly not guilty'. The jury did not believe him. After a final weekend spent watching a boxing match and drinking champagne, he was sentenced to seven years and lost his parliamentary seat. When he was released, he became a music hall turn.

**For richer, for poorer.** *The Depression was selective in its victims. The very rich — like this lady (left), fresh from a canter in Hyde Park and taking a stirrup cup in Mayfair — were often little affected if they lived on secure investments such as government stocks. Mergers and takeovers softened the blow for industrialists whose own companies ran into difficulties. Scores of pubs were still called The Jolly Farmer; but the living article had become hard to find. Many were ruined as wartime subsidies on crops were revoked, and agricultural labourers' wages halved.*

*The plight of ex-servicemen, once promised a 'land fit for heroes', had a particular poignancy. These (right) are busking for coppers in London. 'Unable to Work', the notice on the trumpet-player reads. 'Acute Asthmatic Attacks. Bronchitis and Emphysema. I have proofs in pocket.' They did not, however, coalesce into political gangs as their former German foes were now doing. Hard times produced resignation, but little street violence or extremism.*

[PHOTO, RIGHT: EDITH TUDOR HART]

Like Bottomley, the boom came to an abrupt end. Unemployment rose from 1.3 million in the spring of 1921 to more than two million by Christmas. Markets lost in the war were not regained. The Japanese paid their workers eightpence a day to weave cotton on electric looms, where Lancashire girls earned £2 a week in an industry still powered by coal. The aircraft industry had become the largest in the world, employing 350,000; workers had celebrated Armistice Day by dragging a biplane from a Hendon factory down the Edgware Road and abandoning it in Hyde Park. The triumph was premature; half the industry was now bankrupt and the rest on short time. Lloyd George's heroes stood on corners in London's West End with collecting boxes; ex-officers became door-to-door salesmen and, as world trade fell away, a quarter of Britain's merchant seamen and a third of iron and steel workers lost their jobs as more efficient American plants took what market was left. 'The British industry turns out steel as a by-product,' an observer wrote, 'its main product being self-pity.'

Unemployment insurance had been extended to cover most manual workers. Originally set at 15s a week for men and 12s for women, it was hardly manna but it overwhelmed the Boards of Guardians in the worst-hit areas who were responsible for poor relief. In Poplar, in the London slums, the Guardians refused to place a maximum amount on the payouts to large families, so that dockers in the borough with many children were better off than if they were at work. The cost was borne by local rates; the Labour members on the Poplar council refused to levy a rate large enough to pay for it. This was illegal. Thirty of them, pleading 'Guilty but proud of it', were imprisoned. They made popular martyrs, however, and they struck a chord with their demand that the poor rate should fall on London as a whole rather than on the East End. The government gave way; they were released, and a pooled metropolitan poor fund was set up. Strikers fared less well. Policemen who came out after their demand for a union was refused were dismissed from the force without pensions. Miners struck when coal owners imposed wage cuts. They appealed to the transport unions for solidarity but this was turned down on 'Black Friday', 15 April 1921; they struggled on until the end of June before throwing in the towel.

Guaranteed prices for corn were abandoned. Cheap imports flooded in and agriculture was devastated. A quarter of corn that had fetched 80s in 1920 was worth 47s by 1922. In the post-war bubble, farmworkers had made £2 10s a week. The government scrapped the minimum wage – farmers could not meet it – and pay was halved. In Norfolk, farmers tried to cut that back to £1 a week. Ten thousand men went on strike for six weeks, singing *The Red Flag* – and *Onward Christian Soldiers*, for insurance – until the farmers gave in under government pressure. Strapping West Country boys in Devon became 'pale-faced, anaemic-looking, with eyes lacking lustre, undersized, underfed and sad-faced.'

Lloyd George's handling of the Irish crisis had delighted the King, but not the Conservatives in the coalition. In the 1922 election a Conservative administration was formed under Andrew Bonar Law. He made so little impact that, when he died the following year and was buried in Westminster Abbey, Asquith remarked that the Unknown Prime Minister was being buried next to the Unknown Soldier. He was succeeded, not as expected by the glamorous Curzon, but by the equally obscure Stanley Baldwin; Max Beerbohm caricatured him as a Harrow schoolboy looking at his older self and exclaiming: 'Prime Minister? *You?* Good Lord!!'

Though he was a survivor, calm, pipe-smoking, reliable and extremely rich – he gave £120,000, a fifth of his fortune from the family steel business, to put a small dent in the National Debt – Baldwin's first administration did not last long. At the beginning of 1924, Labour took office with Liberal support. In deference to the country's first working-class administration, the King agreed to relax the rule that cabinet ministers should wear black knee-breeches and white silk stockings at royal levees. At their first meeting with him, the new ministers wondered at the historic change that had brought 'MacDonald the starveling clerk, Thomas the engine-driver, Henderson the foundry labourer and Clynes the mill-hand to this pinnacle.' The middle classes shuddered at the prospect of Reds in power, but had no reason to. The railwayman became J. H. Thomas, the utterly respectable Colonial Secretary, who loved evening dress and cigars so much that the cartoonists called him 'The Right Honourable Dress-Shirt'. The radical Sidney Webb accepted a peerage as Lord Passfield. As to Ramsay MacDonald, the new Prime Minister invoked the Emergency Powers Act to deal with a transport strike with as much aplomb as any Conservative, despite the fact that his party had described it as a 'sinister instrument of Capitalist tyranny'.

Labour did not bring in a much-feared levy on capital; it was a minority government and, as Asquith observed, 'its claws were cut'. The only vaguely left-wing action it took was to make Britain the first country to recognise the Soviet Union. The Liberals had no wish to 'shake hands with murder' or to sit with those who did, so they withdrew support from Labour and an election followed in the autumn. Eight days before the polls opened, the Foreign Office made public a letter that appeared to be from Zinoviev, the President of the Communist International, to the Communist Party of Great Britain. The letter urged the party to stir up the workers, propagandise the army, and foment trouble in the knowledge that the British treaty with the Soviet Union would revolutionise the proletariat. It was a forgery; the British Communist Party had as few members as the British Geoplanarian Society, which believed the world was flat. The delighted Conservatives seized on it and said that a vote for the Liberals was a vote for Labour, and a vote for Labour a vote for Communists. In the event, it

**'Bright Young Things'.** *Society between the wars was racy and daring, or thought itself so; it discovered cocaine and cocktails, wore its skirts short and its checks loud, and perfected the art of the elaborate hoax. Fun was a natural antidote to memories of the trenches, and it was had in full. These guests (right) are at a ball held by Sir Oliver and Lady Hart Dyke at Lullington Castle in Kent to raise funds for a historic church close by. The castle and church were floodlit, and a cabaret, bridge games, a darts parlour and an Egyptian fortune teller were laid on for their entertainment; the attention span of the flapper and her beau was not great.*

did Labour little harm but it helped finish the Liberals. They were left with forty-two seats, in Wales and the wilds of Scotland, reducing them from a great party to a Celtic fringe. The much-feared Communists had a single member, the Indian Sharpurji Saklatava, in Battersea. The Conservatives had 415 seats. Baldwin was Prime Minister and Winston Churchill – having returned to the fold after his outing with the Liberals – became Chancellor of the Exchequer.

The fashionable young, the 'Bright Young Things', had little interest in politics. Noël Coward's 'poor little rich girl' was too exhausted by late nights, mixed drinks and jazz percussion to think of anything. As well as the Charleston they danced the Twinkle, the Jog Trot, the Vampire, the wonderfully named Elfreda, the Canal Walk and the Shimmey. They drank Manhattans, Sidecars and White Ladies in American cocktail bars. The papers ran sizzling accounts of their 'Nights in the Jazz Jungle', where 'women dressed as men, men dressed as women; youth in bathing drawers and kimonos. Bald, obese, perspiring men. Everybody terribly serious; not a single laugh, or the palest ghost of a smile.'

Free invitations were given to 'bottle parties' to get round the licensing laws. The police raided commercial nightclubs that were open after hours, but they had no power to intervene with private parties. Professional hosts thus flung open their apartments and houses, issued printed invitations, hired dance-bands and waiters, and charged whatever the well-heeled market would bear for whisky, champagne and bacon-and-egg breakfasts. It was discovered, too, that the Lord Chamberlain, the censor responsible for upholding decency in public performances, had no control over private entertainment. Semi-nude cabarets were held. The tubular shape of the early Twenties

**The wedding of the year.** *Edwina Ashley has her train arranged by the verger (above) as she arrives to marry Lord Louis Mountbatten in 1922. The bride was a noted beauty; the groom was a great-grandson of Queen Victoria, and a naval lieutenant with all the elan of the Senior Service. The honeymoon pictures come from Mountbatten's private albums. In Santander, the newlyweds swing together (main picture) before moving on to America. It was a saying that 'the Royal Navy always travels First Class'; the Mountbattens had their own private railway car (right above) to carry them in style.*

*They had a superstar aura themselves, and showbusiness friends. They dined with Jerome Kern in New York, met the baseball hero Babe Ruth and rode the Roller Coaster at Coney Island. In Hollywood, they stayed at the home of Mary Pickford and Douglas Fairbanks. Charlie Chaplin's wedding present was a film called* Nice and Friendly. *He directed and starred in it; in this scene (right below), Chaplin, the Mountbattens and a naval friend and his wife appear. After six months' leave on half-pay, the young lieutenant returned to a glittering naval career.*

**English roses.** *A model (left) catches the mood of youth – knowingly sexy, mock-decadent and slinky – in an outfit by the couturier and court dressmaker Norman Hartnell, who made his name dressing*

*Queen Elizabeth, later the Queen Mother. Cecil Beaton's picture of Georgia Sitwell (centre) was taken in 1930 when* Vogue *described her as 'one of the prettiest young marrieds' in England. She*

*was the wife of Sacheverell Sitwell, who was the brother of Osbert and Edith. The three were 'impresarios of the avant-garde in all the arts' between the wars. The picture was taken during a*

house party at their family home, *Renishaw Hall in Derbyshire. Georgia's Borzoi Feo, who sets off her languid grace, was 'smuggled in secretly,' Beaton recalled, 'and had to be kept in the stables*

*so that Osbert should not find out.' Lady Diana Cooper (right), seen here in fancy dress posing as the figure of Charity, was one of the beauties of her age. The daughter of the Duke of Rutland,*

*she had been an actress; her husband, the anti-appeasement politician Sir Alfred Duff Cooper, was later ambassador to France.* [PHOTO, FAR LEFT: SASHA]
[PHOTO, CENTRE: CECIL BEATON]

scandal they sought. Nancy Cunard was the 'modern girl supreme'; her boyish beauty was sculpted by Brancusi and painted by Oskar Kokoschka; she was a poet who set out to shock; she succeeded, taking a black lover and publishing a 900-page anthology of black culture called *Negro*. As to the modern girl's brother, he was 'weary, anaemic, feminine, bloodless, dolled up like a girl and an exquisite without masculinity... a silk-coated lapdog...'

It was a time of lost certainties. 'I stand mid-way between youth and age like a man who has missed his train: too late for the last one and too early for the next,' George Bernard Shaw had a character say of the times. 'I have no Bible, no creed: the war has shot both out of my hands...' Some dabbled in Buddhism and the exotic mysteries of the East. They crossed the Channel to adore Jiddu Krishnamurti, who held 'holiday preaching-camps' for his disciples in Holland. He was an Indian who was pronounced the Messiah in 1925 by Annie Besant, the priestess of the theosophy movement, which claimed an intuitive insight into divine nature, based on the sacred writings of Brahmaism and Buddhism. Besant herself had an extraordinary career – she was elected president of Gandhi's Indian National Congress, for an Englishwoman who preached the virtues of

dresses filled out with angled shoulders and pleated skirts. Dark glasses, and sun visors for tennis and driving, arrived.

Memories of the trenches were blotted out with pranks and hoaxes and extravagance. At Cambridge, they played tiddly-winks in the streets; at Oxford, they climbed the Martyrs' Memorial and put chamber pots on top of it, china ones at first and, when the police shot them down with rook rifles, metal ones that had to be removed with elaborate scaffolding. The Oxford Railway Club was founded for drinking on night expresses; in full evening dress, its members joined the Aberdeen-Penzance express to drink and dine and make speeches. Brian Howard and his Oxford writer friends, Evelyn Waugh, Harold Acton, played leapfrog through Selfridges, set the Thames on fire (with petrol) and carried out elaborate hoaxes, inventing a modernist painter called Bruno Hat and staging an exhibition of his work painted by Howard, with catalogue notes by Waugh. Blacks were in fashion; Howard and his set made a cult of the revue *The Blackbirds* and its cast; it ran for over a year in London, and the Prince of Wales saw it twenty times. They invited the Blackbirds to their fancy dress parties; they dressed up as Queen Victoria, as cowboys, as stokers and sailors, taking over the swimming baths in Buckingham Palace Road, floating rubber horses and flowers on it and dancing to a black orchestra; the juxtaposition of black musicians and white girls in bathing costumes caused the

**Big noises:** *George Bernard Shaw (top left), the dramatist, critic, vegetarian, essayist, pamphleteer and fellow traveller on the beach, wearing little more than his beard. The sculptor Jacob Epstein (left below), with his great nude sculptures,* Genesis, Ecce Homo *and* Adam, *caused uproar and accusations of indecency and* blasphemy. *The painter Augustus John is seen (above) on a visit to Italy with the literary hostess Lady Ottoline Morrell. She fell violently in love with him but her extraordinary looks were too much even for the inveterate womaniser.*

[PHOTO, NEAR LEFT: MALCOLM ARBOTHNOT]

abandoning narrow notions of race and religion was a good stick with which to beat the colour-conscious and Anglican Raj: Krishnamurti himself was said to be the most famous man in Holland after the ex-Kaiser. T. S. Eliot, American-born and Harvard-educated but who for eight years measured out his life with coffee spoons as an employee of Lloyds Bank in London, used Buddhist imagery, amongst much else, in *The Waste Land*, the most famous poem of the mid-Twenties.

If nothing had yet been found to replace it, Victorian morality was still mocked by the moderns. The Bloomsbury Group of writers and artists shocked – deliberately so, for it was consciously avant-garde in its morals as well as its creations – and could be ruthless. Lytton Strachey had published his *Eminent Victorians* in 1918, killing off various nineteenth-century heroes and heroines with wit and irony, unconstrained by any tiresome considerations about the truth or fairness of his portraits.

The contempt for Victorian morals was underscored by Strachey's homosexuality, and the bisexuality of other members of the group like the artist Duncan Grant, Virginia Woolf and the economist John Maynard Keynes. The pioneer of the theory of full employment, he resigned as a Treasury adviser in protest against the harsh reparations imposed on Germany at Versailles; he was equally opposed to Churchill's restoration of the gold standard in 1925, and his insights about planned economies did much to influence Roosevelt's New Deal in America.

Virginia Woolf's manifesto, *A Room of One's Own* – 'a woman must have money and a room of her own if she is to write fiction' – was later seen by feminists as a turning point. In her nervous, haunting novels, such as *To the Lighthouse* and *The Waves*, she was too exotic, a modernist too driven by an inner ear, for real popularity. Only her lyrical fantasy *Orlando* caught a big audience, perhaps because of its hints of disturbed sexuality and vivid historical backdrop.

Outside the Bloomsbury Group, who were still 'essentially gentlefolks' as E. M. Forster detected, the miner's son D. H. Lawrence had a corner in naked and emotional heterosexuality; mixing submissive women and thrusting worker-lovers with ramblings about blood and earth made for a heady brew that

**The Bloomsbury Group** *centred on the Hogarth Press in the basement of Leonard and Virginia Woolf's house in Tavistock Square. It was founded with money Leonard Woolf had won in the Calcutta Sweep whilst a civil servant in Ceylon. The Group's contempt for Victorian morals was underscored by the homosexuality of Lytton Strachey (bottom left, with Ralph Partridge) and the novelist E. M. Forster (top left). Strachey appears again with Eddy Sackville-West and Virginia Woolf (right top). Aldous Huxley (centre), writer of* Crome Yellow *and* Brave New World, *was on the fringes of Bloomsbury. So was D. H. Lawrence; the gamekeeper in his banned novel,* Lady Chatterley's Lover, *was thought to be based on Lionel (above right), stonemason to Lady Ottoline Morrell (above left), and the last of her great loves.*

[PHOTO, CENTRE: CECIL BEATON]

[PHOTO, BOTTOM LEFT: FRANCES PARTRIDGE]

[ALL OTHER PHOTOS: LADY OTTOLINE MORRELL]

ramblings about blood and earth made for a heady brew that attracted both readers and the censors. He was without the wit of Aldous Huxley, the consciously clever author of *Crome Yellow* and *Antic Hay*. E. M. Forster himself took a scalpel to the uneasy relations between the Raj and its subjects in *A Passage to India*. The Sitwells – Osbert the satirist, Sacheverell the champion of Baroque and Rococo, Edith whose verse was read to William Walton's music in *Façade* – showed where a modicum of talent combined with aristocratic arrogance could still get you.

Respectable Britain had other interests, other heroes, mountaineers, pilots and speed freaks. Alcock and Brown were the first men to fly the Atlantic, from west to east, in 1919, winning £10,000 from the *Daily Mail* and earning themselves knighthoods; the feat was shortly repeated from east to west by the crew of the airship R34, one of whom celebrated his arrival in New York by parachuting to the ground to give instructions to the ground crew. Mount Everest replaced the South Pole as a British objective, and brought its own fresh tragedy in 1924 when Mallory and Irvine, using oxygen for the first time, disappeared into the clouds less than 2,000 feet below its summit. Vengeance of a sort was had when a British pilot dropped a Union Jack on the 29,039-foot peak from his biplane. The 'Triple Crown', for the fastest speed on land and sea and in the air, was won by the British. Sir Henry Segrave had broken both the speedboat and racing car records when he was killed in his boat *Miss England III* on Lake Windermere.

Middle England took the Prince of Wales as its beacon of manly behaviour. It noted the check on his suits, the shorts he wore beagling in Norfolk, the way he knotted his tie. When he broke his collarbone steeplechasing, it asked anxiously whether his riding should not be stopped 'in the national interest'. It enjoyed its little crazes – pogo sticks, the newly invented crossword puzzle (newspapers offered huge prizes for solutions, but were careful that no reader won by ensuring there were alternative answers), ice-skating and everything ancient Egyptian, following the discovery of the tomb of Tutankhamun.

**Fastest by land, sea and air.** *Engineering skill, and a ready supply of daring young men, led to a string of world records between the wars. Here (right) Captain Malcolm Campbell attempts to break the land speed record on Pendine Sands in 1927. The sands were waterlogged and he can be seen losing time by wiping his windscreen. In 1935, on the arid Bonneville Salt Flats in Utah, he became the first man to break 300 mph on land. He also held the world water speed record; his son Donald was killed at Coniston Water in another record attempt in 1967.*

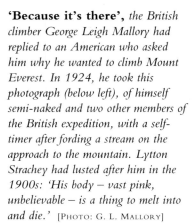

**'Because it's there'**, *the British climber George Leigh Mallory had replied to an American who asked him why he wanted to climb Mount Everest. In 1924, he took this photograph (below left), of himself semi-naked and two other members of the British expedition, with a self-timer after fording a stream on the approach to the mountain. Lytton Strachey had lusted after him in the 1900s: 'His body – vast pink, unbelievable – is a thing to melt into and die.'* [PHOTO: G. L. MALLORY]

It proposed, solemnly, that the Tube line that ran between Tooting and Camden should be called the Tootancamden, following the example of the Bakerloo.

When not listening to the new radio, it watched Mary Pickford and Charlie Chaplin in vast, cathedral-like cinemas equipped with elaborate, pre-talkie organs. Its taste in plays was for the light and amusing; Noël Coward had four running simultaneously in the West End in 1927. It read the detective stories of Agatha Christie, and the thrillers that Edgar Wallace, pacing about in his dressing gown, drinking sweet tea and chain-smoking, dictated to a chain of stenographers. It worshipped Lawrence of Arabia, though he fled from its attentions to join the RAF as an aircraftman under an assumed name. It nursed a passion for vitamin pills and potions. 'The secret of Napoleon's power was his immense vitality,' it was told. 'The same is true of most great men – Julius Caesar, Michelangelo, Gladstone, Cecil Rhodes – they were successful because they never got tired. Don't get tired... drink Bovril.'

Above all, it was besotted with cricket. In 1925, all England –

was obsessed with whether Jack Hobbs would beat W. G. Grace's long-standing record of 126 centuries in first-class cricket. Early in the season, he made 266 not out at Scarborough, the highest-ever innings in a Gentlemen versus Players match; Hobbs was a Player, a fact made clear by the omission of his initials on the scorecard. He followed it with 215 for Surrey against Warwickshire. There was a lull in his scoring in July and early August. Then his eye returned at Taunton against Somerset. 'Will Hobbs do it?' the commentators asked. His 101 in the first innings meant he was equal with Grace; in his second innings, he made another 101. The King wrote to congratulate him on the new record.

The government lifted the subsidy from coal as he was doing so. Prices fell, and the employers demanded wage cuts. 'Not a minute on the day,' the miners responded, 'not a penny off the pay.' A skilled miner made good money – £4 a week, as much as the driver of an express train – but he paid for it with his body. The pits were badly ventilated and hot; a doctor found that each man on a shift registered over 100 in both temperature and pulse rate. The men worked in semi-darkness and suffered from miners' nystagmus, a rapid and involuntary oscillation of the eyes. Roof falls were a constant peril; as many as 1,300 miners were killed and 160,000 injured in a year. If they avoided accidents, the dust still got in their lungs and gave them pneumoconiosis, which shortened their lives. There were no pithead baths. The men trudged home to their squalid terraces in filthy, wet clothes to wash in a tub of water. Sanitation in some company-owned houses stretched no further than a privy in an outdoor shed shared with other families. 'We would provide baths tomorrow if the people would use them,' the chairman of the Powell Duffryn Steam Coal Company and employer of 18,000 men, loftily declared to a parliamentary commission. 'You often find cocks and hens in the bathroom.'

There were hundreds of coal companies, many struggling to survive on thin, mean seams. Whoever owned the land on the surface owned the coal beneath it, and the landowners struck

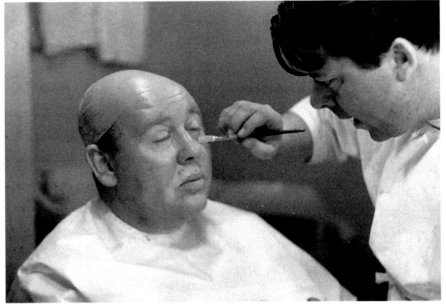

**All the world was a stage** *for British talent. A long tradition, the apprenticeship provided by provincial repertory companies, Shakespeare and other native playwrights, and the English language itself were useful props for a rich crop of actors. John Gielgud (right below) makes up for the opening performance of* The Tempest *at the Old Vic theatre in 1930. Noël Coward, actor, dramatist and composer, had four plays running simultaneously in the West End in 1927. He is seen on stage with Gertrude Lawrence (main picture) in* Tonight at 8.30. *Charles Laughton (right above), son of a Scarborough hotelier, was one of the first British actors to transfer successfully to Hollywood. A memorable screen Henry VIII, Captain Bligh and Quasimodo, he is here being made up as an 18th-century squire in* Jamaica Inn, *in which he appeared with Maureen O'Hara. The English always had a weakness for dressing up in drag, like the photographer Cecil Beaton (top left) for the sketch* All the Vogue.

[PHOTO, ABOVE: DOROTHY WILDING]   [PHOTO, TOP RIGHT: KURT HUTTON]
[PHOTO, NEAR AND FAR RIGHT: SASHA]

hard bargains with the coal companies. The Church was a big coal-owner; the Duke of Hamilton made £113,000 a year from the coal beneath his estates in Lanarkshire and Stirling, meaning that, without lifting a finger, he made more than 500 miners toiling down there. The men looked to the Trades Union Congress for support. The dockers, too, had a harsh life, and the militants wanted labour to show its immense power in a general strike to support the miners. 'They pick out the strongest men and discourage the old ones and the cripples,' Ernest Bevin said of the dockers' employers, 'and as long as these men can work hard they will keep them on, but they ruin them very quickly.' If they were not called at 8 am, they had to wait in the open for the next call. Baldwin was a conciliatory man – his most famous phrase, muttered in a Commons debate, was 'Give peace in our time, O Lord' – but the government had little option except to resist in a head-on confrontation with unions.

Creating an industrial Armageddon was a risky affair. The middle class had no time for flirtation with the working class; their great fear was of descending into it. In his bestselling novel of 1925, *Sorrell and Son*, Warwick Deeping described the trauma of a boy from a white-collar family who was sent to a council school. 'For the boy it had meant contact with common children, and Kit was not a common child,' he wrote. 'He had all the fastidious nauseas of a boy who has learnt to wash and to use a handkerchief, and not yell "Cheat" at everybody in the heat of a game...' As the strike threat escalated early in 1926, the *Daily Mail* capitalised on its readers' fears. 'The pistol to the nation's head,' it ran on the front page, with an editorial urging resistance 'for King and Country'. It was soon quoting Wordsworth: 'We must be free or die, who spake the tongue That Shakespeare spake...'

Perhaps from a guilty sense of having let the miners down in 1921, with much agonising and little strategy, the TUC called out 1.5 million energy and transport workers at midnight on 3 May. The government was ready for it. Hyde Park was cordoned off as a mass depot for food supplies. So many car owners answered the call to give office workers a lift to work on the first morning that London had its worst-ever traffic jam. The London stock exchange offered 1,400 special constables to keep order. The strikers loathed the baton-wielding 'specials', in their colonial hats, hacking jackets and breeches. Volunteer truck drivers included the Duchesses of Sutherland and Westminster; Lady Louis Mountbatten helped out as a telephonist at the *Daily Express* when print union members walked out. The *Daily Mail* flew in editions printed in Paris, whilst Winston Churchill abandoned the Treasury to edit the

official *British Gazette*. 'The laws are in your hands,' Baldwin told its readers. 'You have made Parliament their guardian. The general strike is a challenge to Parliament and is the road to ruin and anarchy.'

A TUC despatch rider sent back a stream of exhilarated messages from the West Country. 'Reading streets full of strikers,' he reported. 'Swindon: like a dead city except for workers standing around... Bath: not a tram. Few buses. Huge meetings... Plymouth: no trams, few buses. Pickets everywhere...' In truth, it was strike-breakers who were everywhere. Skeleton train services were maintained; in one legendary incident, an amateur driver who was having difficulty in stopping in the right position was told by a passenger: 'Hang on a minute, old chap, and I'll jump out and move the platform for you.' Undergraduates joined in the fun. 'We set out from Oxford in the evening in a vintage Bentley,' one recalled, 'and drove at great speed through the lovely English countryside. At Doncaster our driver stood us dinner and a bottle of champagne... From Doncaster onwards groups of strikers unsuccessfully tried to interrupt our progress by throwing stones or trying to puncture our tyres. However, our driver remained unperturbed, and merely accelerated when he saw a hostile crowd... Those of us who were to work on the [Tyneside] docks received our marching orders, while others went to drive trams or work the cranes.' The student blacklegs, supervised by a future librarian of Windsor Castle, worked from dawn to dusk, protected by sentries and a light cruiser

**Lucky chaps.** *These miners (left) at Tilmanstone colliery in Kent are fortunate to be standing up. In many thin, mean seams, the men worked on their knees in the heat, dust and semi-darkness. With the solidarity and discipline of soldiers marching to the front, South Wales miners (right) come out on strike against wage cuts. They failed, and many left for jobs in light industry in England.*

[PHOTO, LEFT: SASHA]

[PHOTO, RIGHT: EDITH TUDOR HART]

moored on the river. 'Some of the old hands who drifted back to work were surprised at the speed with which we unloaded the ships,' the student noted, 'but we realised that it was a different story working for a few days as an adventure, compared to regular work over a period of years...'

After nine days, the TUC backed down. 'Surrender of the revolutionaries,' the *Daily Mail* exulted, claiming that Zinoviev had planned the strike and that it had been fomented by 500 Soviet agents. The shamefaced *British Worker*, the official strike news bulletin, claimed: 'TUC now satisfied that Miners will get a Fair Deal.' They did not; Churchill wished to be magnanimous in victory, but Baldwin would have none of it. The miners, reduced to 'home-grown lettuce and mutton stolen from the hills', kept out on strike until hunger forced them back into the pits at the end of the summer. Their pay was cut; many of the poorer mines closed and the first of

**In the depths** *of the slump, in 1931, the great Cammell Laird shipyard in Birkenhead had a solitary dredger on its order book. Then the recovery got under way. Orders for* aircraft carriers and capital ships increased in step with German naval building. The great liner Queen Mary (above) was built on the Clyde in 1934. The worst was over.*

250,000 men plodded from South Wales to England to look for work. An Act banned sympathetic strikes designed to coerce the government, but it was never invoked. The unions had had enough of taking on the country.

A more successful revolution was nearing completion. 'The cabinet went mad yesterday,' Lord Birkenhead, the India secretary, wrote to a friend in April 1927, 'and decided to give votes to women at the age of twenty-one.' They now had the same voting rights as men, whom, indeed, due to wartime losses and longer life expectancy, they outnumbered by more than two million votes. The electric self-starters now fitted to cars made it easy for them to drive. They were said to be dangerous, but more than ninety-five per cent of fatal accidents – and there were many of them, with 7,000 deaths a year commonplace – were caused by men. Amy Johnson, the daughter of a Hull fish merchant, paid for flying lessons out of her typist's wages and flew solo to Australia with enormous publicity. The first woman cabinet minister, Margaret Bondfield, was appointed in 1929. In villages as well as towns, thousands of Women's Institutes, the WI, were opened, providing outings, lectures on everything from politics to jam-making, and charity sales. The Women's League of Health and Beauty organised keep-fit classes, and members gave displays in fetching black silk shorts in the Albert Hall and Hyde Park. New women's magazines gave their readers romantic stories, problem pages and fashion and cooking tips.

On the coat-tails of the Wall Street crash, in 1929, came a slump worse than that of 1921. World trade evaporated; British exports fell by more than half in two years. By the end of 1931, there were almost three million unemployed, a fifth of the workforce. From 1931 to 1935 Ramsay MacDonald's National Government cooperated with Conservative leaders; it was accused of treachery to the working class as it cut pay, including that of servicemen. When ratings at the Invergordon naval base heard on the radio in September 1933 that their pay was to be reduced by up to twenty-five per cent, though admirals would lose but seven per cent, they refused to muster or to ready ships for exercises. The government backed down, limiting the cuts to ten per cent, the amount by which the cost of living had fallen. But twenty-four ratings were dismissed from the Service and a bungled attempt was made to keep the incident out of the press. Word duly got out – 'Mutiny in the Royal Navy!' the world headlines screamed – and this led to a run on that second symbol of British might and stability, the pound sterling. Bullion poured out of London bank vaults, and Britain came off the gold standard.

The price of corn fell to 20s 9d a quarter, the lowest since the Civil War three hundred years before. 'Here are some of the finest and largest farms in England, into which these men have put all their fortune and labour of mind,' the journalist Philip Gibbs wrote from East Anglia. 'On every acre of wheat they lose £5 at the least... they dropped four to five shillings a head on every sheep... For five years their capital had been withering away... while their land has fallen in value to a quarter of what they paid for it.' Fields were abandoned to 'coarse, matted grass, thistle, weeds and brambles.' Farmers demonstrated with banners – 'Wanted in 1914, Neglected in 1930' – to no purpose. The cities liked their cheap Australian corn and New Zealand mutton. Old families could no longer keep up their great houses; a few lucky ones sold to schools or cottage hospitals, but in some the families retreated from wing to wing, the roofs falling in behind them, the casements rotting. A third of the country houses in Shropshire disappeared.

Unemployment climbed above three million. The heavy industries, steelworks and mines of the north and of South Wales were devastated. The great Cammell Laird shipyard in Birkenhead had a solitary dredger on its order book in 1931. The government introduced a means test to cut unemployment pay for those who had savings to fall back on. This was bitterly resented; the dole money was enough to keep the body, if not the soul, in country districts where men could grow vegetables and keep rabbits in their gardens. In the towns, it was close to starvation level. A National Hunger March was organised to protest, with big rallies in Hyde Park. Extra relief was given to the most depressed areas, while Europe was giving way to extremism, with Reds battling against Hitler's Brownshirts in Germany.

British government and workers shied instinctively from confrontation, but there was a sharp and earnest reaction away from the specious Twenties. It began with a reassessment of the war, a subject until then so unfashionable that R. C. Sherriff's play *Journey's End*, with its shattered hero who kept himself in the trenches only with the help of a whisky bottle, had been turned down by a score of theatres. It became the unexpected smash hit of 1929 at the Savoy; a studio performance broadcast by the BBC on the evening of Armistice Day had the biggest audience of the year. A translation of Erich Maria Remarque's *All Quiet on the Western Front*, showing Fritz to be little different from Tommy, was the bestselling book of the year. Siegfried Sassoon's *Memoirs of an Infantry Officer*, and Robert Graves's *Goodbye to All That*, anti-heroic, anti-war, anti-senior officers, changed perceptions. *The Times* disapproved of the authors. 'Determined, like the old fresco painters when they pictured Hell,' it said of them, 'so to scare, horrify and revolt the reader that he shall never think of war again without trembling and nausea.' But *The Times* itself would come to favour appeasement, and the young men at the Oxford Union, in a famous debate in 1933, voted that 'This House will in no circumstances fight for its King and Country.'

Dandyism gave way to social concern. The new poets, W. H. Auden, Stephen Spender and Cecil Day Lewis, were said to 'get in touch with reality' in their verses on such subjects as electricity pylons, and had leftist sympathies. Walter Greenwood wrote *Love on the Dole*, and George Orwell *The Road to Wigan Pier*. Oxford undergraduates went to the Rhondda valley at weekends to seek out unemployed Welsh miners – not a difficult task given their numbers – and joined the Communist-inspired October Club. It agitated against the university Officer Training Corps and hung a large portrait of Lenin in the Oxford Labour Club. A Left Book Club was started by Victor Gollancz, most autocratic of publishers, sending a left-wing book to its members each week for 2s 6d; it soon had 60,000 members. Virginia Woolf began writing for the Communist *Daily Worker*. The poets John Cornford and Julian Bell, Virginia Woolf's nephew, were killed fighting for the Republicans in the Spanish civil war; Auden, who served as an ambulanceman, and George Orwell, survived, though what the latter saw there of Communist methods sowed the seeds of *Animal Farm*.

Some students played with treason. Kim Philby, son of an eccentric Arabist, went up to Trinity College, Cambridge, in 1929. He was followed there by Guy Burgess, Donald Maclean and Anthony Blunt. Like Philby, they were public schoolboys; unlike him, they were also homosexuals, Burgess so promiscuous that he said that he could never travel by train because he would feel himself obliged to seduce the engine

**The Prince of Wales** *is seen here (right), in a picture from his private album, punting whilst an undergraduate at Magdalen College, Oxford, in 1914. Another photograph from his collection shows his future sister-in-law, Lady Elizabeth Bowes-Lyon, puffing at a pipe (above) to amuse royal princes at Glamis Castle in Scotland before she married the younger Windsor to become Duchess of York in 1923. She had no inkling that she would one day become Queen.*

**After abdication** *Edward and Wallis left for France (above) and permanent exile. The Duke of York, shy, stammering, reluctant, became George VI; his courage, and his brother's flaky attitude to Nazis and Fascists, showed the nation to have got the better of the bargain.* [PHOTO, ABOVE: CECIL BEATON]

**Two Windsor brothers,** *the younger, George, Duke of York (foreground left), and Edward, Prince of Wales, are seen at Glamis Castle, the home of the Bowes-Lyon family. After the death of George V, the elder brother became Edward VIII. He had, however, fallen in love with Wallis Simpson. She was a divorcee; he would not leave her, the Church of England would not accept her as Queen. Children in South Wales sang as they skipped:*

*Look what's coming down the street!*
*Mrs Simpson, ain't she sweet?*
*She's been married twice before*
*Now she's knocking on Edward's door.*

161

driver, though he sneered of Maclean that sleeping with him 'would be like going to bed with Dame Nellie Melba'. It was at Cambridge that they first flirted with Soviet Communism, though the extent of their treachery was not to be known for many years. Tiring of the jazz age – 'O O O that Shakespearian rag/It's so elegant so intelligent' – T. S. Eliot turned in another direction, to Anglo-Catholicism and his play *Murder in the Cathedral*. Graham Greene and Evelyn Waugh, the most gifted novelist of the new Disillusion, travelled further, to Roman Catholicism; many university aesthetes and Mayfair society people 'embraced the Scarlet Woman', as Rome was known.

Churchill's young nephew Esmond Romilly ran away from school at sixteen to publish a magazine for public schoolboys called *Out of Bounds*; it urged its readers to rise against Fascism, Militarism and Reaction. Romilly went to Spain to report on the civil war and when he returned, he eloped to the Continent with Jessica Mitford, daughter of Lord Redesdale. He was seventeen and she eighteen. Jessica progressed to Communism, and of her sisters, Unity Mitford, perhaps doomed by her second name, Valkyrie, fell in love with Adolf Hitler; while Diana Mitford married the fascist Oswald Mosley. Born on a country estate that employed thirty gardeners, to a line of

squires with a passion for boxing, holding bouts in the ballroom, Mosley had seemed in 1918 to be the most brilliant young MP in the House. Beatrice Webb thought so, and so did Churchill. He was suave – nicknamed 'the Sheikh' – hard-working and clever; he had 'made an art of himself'. He was, however, politically unstable. In ten years, he had been a Tory, an independent, a socialist and then a fascist. His Black Shirts made much noise and broke a few heads; their unpleasant bark, however, was much worse than their bite. The Communists, too, made little enough progress; the British party started the decade with 1,300 members and had barely ten times that number at its close. Whilst the extremists shadow-boxed above them, the great mass of the British kept their heads down and trusted to parliament.

The 'devil's decade' was far from being all doom and depression. It had its amusements, of which the Loch Ness Monster was one. Following a claimed sighting in 1933, thousands of tourists flocked to the Scottish lake in the hope of spotting it. The Reverend Harold Davidson, the rector of Stiffkey in Norfolk, also kept the nation laughing. Accused of seducing young girls, he was found guilty by a Church court and unfrocked.

**The Prince of Wales** *was a figure of fashion; the country noted the check he had spun for his tweeds, the shorts he wore to a beagle meet, the way he tied his tie, and copied him. Here (left) he bestows royal patronage on Cochran's Cabaret at Grosvenor House in London. The presence of Wallis Simpson at his side in 1935 adds to* *the sense of the risqué. The sparse outfits of Cochran's Young Ladies, seen here appearing in* Streamline *at the Palace Theatre in 1934 (right), show that, if London could not compete with French cabaret, it could bump and grind with the best of them.*
[PHOTO, LEFT: JAMES JARCHE]
[PHOTO, RIGHT: SASHA]

Maintaining his innocence, he kept himself in funds and publicity by fasting in a barrel on Blackpool beach. The police arrested him for attempted suicide by starvation; he successfully sued Blackpool Corporation for damages. He next appeared on Hampstead Heath with a dead whale, before joining a circus and posing with lions in a threepenny sideshow. At Skegness, fate caught up with him when he was mauled to death.

The abdication crisis certainly qualified as a diversion, if not an amusement. The Prince of Wales, the heir, was good-looking, blond, slim, elegant but slight and fragile, with a melancholy cast to his eyes and a set to his mouth revealing that, though he sought pleasure, he did not find it. He danced, he visited out-of-work miners in South Wales, he was enjoying an affair with a married woman, Wallis Simpson. In January 1936, his father died and he became King. The press knew well that he had a mistress since he made no secret of it, and photographs of the couple on holiday on a chartered yacht in the Mediterranean were published. Otherwise, the British newspapers stayed mum. It was etiquette that, since royals could not reply, their foibles should not be mentioned. The last time this rule had been broken, according to Robert Graves, had been by a sporting paper in the 1880s which said, out of the blue, that there was 'nothing whatever between the Prince of Wales and Lillie Langtry.' It followed that up a week later: 'Not even a sheet.'

Americans knew from their press that the King was contemplating marriage, which would provoke a constitutional crisis. The *News Chronicle* in Britain announced on its front page in the autumn that Mrs Simpson was going to Ipswich to get a divorce; why an obscure American lady and her husband, Ernest Simpson, a broker on the Baltic Exchange, merited this publicity was not explained. At the court in Ipswich, the judge was astonished to find crowds of American reporters in the public gallery, and plainclothes detectives, for an anodyne and uncontested divorce. He granted a decree nisi. By now the cabinet – Baldwin had replaced Ramsay MacDonald at the head of a second National Government the year before – was alarmed.

The Bishop of Bradford, Dr Blunt, finally broke the story from the pulpit, urging the King to behave like his Christian father. Sanctioned by a man of the cloth, the story now burst out: the King was to marry Mrs Simpson after making her Duchess of Lancaster. Baldwin discussed the matter in cabinet. The dominion governments were sounded out; the King was the only formal political link between the Empire and Britain. A twice-divorced woman, a commoner and a foreigner to boot, was unacceptable. 'Most ordinary people were for the King,' said Graves. 'Most important people were against him.'

Churchill and Beaverbrook supported the King; but as much to get rid of Baldwin, or so it was said, as from personal loyalty. The King dreamt up a compromise; the British were very good at them, but this was more complicated than most. Special legislation would be passed so that he could marry Mrs Simpson, but without making her Queen and with any children dropping their claims to the throne. Baldwin would not accept this; the King's wife must be Queen and her offspring heirs to the throne. Crowds shouted: 'God save the King from Mr Baldwin!'

The 'grey men' at the palace – of whom much would be heard sixty years later – were implacably opposed to Mrs Simpson. Knowing him better than most, they were not too keen on the King, either; he rarely went to church, he was bored by protocol and sometimes showed it, he had replaced some of them with younger men, he had even removed the herd of royal goats from Windsor Great Park, where they had munched contentedly for generations, and suffered them to undergo the indignity of the common gaze at the Zoo. The situation slipped into farce. Mrs Simpson removed herself to France. The King was going to join her, the rumour mills had it; then he was not, next he was so drunk he had to be stomach-pumped. The word Abdication was mentioned by the *Daily Mail*. A Yorkshire pickle manufacturer ran a daring advertisement in the *Bradford Telegraph and Argus*: 'The King may abdicate, but with the love for Dixon's jams and pickles the family sticks together like the Empire.' On the political fringes, the Communists and the Fascists found common ground. The Communist Harry Pollitt said loftily: 'There is no crisis in all this business for the working class. Let the King marry whom he likes. That is his personal business.' Oswald Mosley put his Blackshirts full square behind the King – the King was said to be soft on Hitler, and Mosley's support did him little good.

On 10 December, it was over. Baldwin read the King's message of Abdication to the Commons. He himself gave a farewell address to the nation on radio. He was succeeded by his younger brother the Duke of York – an excuse for more Shakespeare, 'Now is the winter of our discontent made glorious summer by this sun of York'.

Recovery from the slump itself was patchy but steady. By 1936 output was climbing, wages were stable and unemployment had fallen to under two million. Even in Glasgow, the writer Thomas Jones found that the drunken Saturday nights and fights on Argyll Street had disappeared together with barefoot women and children. Shawls were replaced by hats, and working girls 'are now always neatly dressed and are careful of their hair and teeth and fingernails – a great change.' There was money to spend on 'pools, perms and pints, on cigarettes and singles-and-splashes; on turnstiles, totalisers and... all manner of twopennyworth of this and that.' In depressed Wigan, George Orwell thought it 'quite likely that fish and chips, artificial silk stockings, tinned salmon, cut-price chocolate... the movies, the radio, strong tea and the football pools have between them averted revolution.'

Travellers from the moribund counties of the north were bemused to find the Midlands and south flowing with milk and honey. A hunger marcher from South Wales in 1936 found the streets of Slough awash with Welshmen looking for work in the booming light industries of the Home Counties. 'Thousands lined the streets,' he said, 'the accents were so thick I thought we were in the Rhondda, with this difference, instead of silent pits, massive factories all lit up were in full go.' A Liverpudlian was astonished to find Midlands factories advertising 'Vacancies'; he thought those days had gone for ever.

For those in work, white collar and skilled men, life was something close to bliss. They bought their own houses, at £450 or so for a pebble-dash and mock Tudor semi-detached, with a bathroom, a garage and a garden, in the new suburbs that sprang up along new arterial roads. Mortgages were cheap enough, at 4.5 per cent interest, for many to afford this middle-class symbol. Taxes were low at the £500 a year income level, with less than ten per cent in direct tax. A Morris Cowley cost £150, and many families acquired one, and a vacuum-cleaner, radio, gramophone, refrigerator, electric fire, washing-machine and other undreamt-of luxuries. 'You need money in this England,' J. B. Priestley wrote in 1934, 'but you do not need much money. It is a large-scale, mass production job, with cut

prices...' One household in five had at least one live-in domestic – of whom there were more now than in 1911 – and others employed a 'daily woman' to come in to cook and clean. Servants were in such demand in the south-east that thousands of girls from depressed areas were trained and transferred there under a government scheme. Families were smaller, leaving more spending money; the birth rate almost halved from pre-war levels with new contraceptives and birth control clinics. The population still grew, however; the pace of emigration slowed, whilst there was a stream of incomers from Ireland, and Continental Jews as Nazi racial policies bit.

Paid holidays were becoming universal. Youth hostels were introduced at the beginning of the decade; rambling and hiking became the rage. Holiday camps brought a week at the beach, with entertainment thrown in, to families who had had to make do with day outings. Foreign travel, to impoverished France and Germany and beyond, was a bargain.

Electricity – the country had the most developed national grid of high-voltage transmission lines in the world by the mid-Thirties – brought clean industry to new areas. There were 730,000 electricity consumers in 1920; in the Thirties that climbed to 9 million, and the industry was employing 325,000, whilst factories boomed with the demand for electrical appliances. Half a million motor cars were being made, bringing a wave of prosperity to Coventry, Birmingham, Luton, Oxford, Dagenham. Bakelite and plastics were coming in. The chemical industry was producing new artificial fibres like rayon, synthetic dyes, drugs and fertiliser. There were unprecedented advances in productivity. Huge industrial giants formed: ICI, EMI, Unilever, Royal Dutch Shell, Courtaulds. New jobs opened in distribution, loading and driving vans and trucks. Chain stores multiplied; Boots and Marks and Spencer were opening dozens of new branches each year. Hire purchase made the three-piece suite affordable for families to whom it had been a bourgeois vision. On the farms, free trade was replaced by protection, subsidies and anti-dumping. A Milk Marketing Board, stabilising prices and improving distribution, worked well enough to be followed by boards for eggs, potatoes, bacon and hops. New machinery arrived on the farms – tractors, the first combine harvesters, milking machines that a man and boy could operate.

And then there were arms. The government spent £1.2 billion on them between 1933 and 1938. They underpinned the recovery, but a human price was to be paid for them. Dark shapes were breaking surface in Europe.

**The last summer** *of the peace. These holidaymakers (right) are enjoying two new pastimes, sunbathing and the Sunday spin by car to the coast. Much of Britain was booming by 1939; its consumer and car industries were unmatched anywhere but America; the suburbs – with their cinemas and swift electric commuter trains – were enjoying a golden age. Paid holidays were* *universal, cars were cheap and, on the labour market, factories had 'Vacancies' signs. The Empire had grown, not diminished, since 1918; in place of the Continental extremes, fascism and communism, British politics muddled through with compromise coalition governments. The British had more to lose from war than any other people in Europe.*

[PHOTO, RIGHT: EDITH TUDOR HART]

## CHAPTER SIX

# FINEST HOUR

'THE CLEVER HOPES EXPIRE', W. H. AUDEN WROTE famously, 'of a low dishonest decade,' as peace collapsed into war like a punctured lung. It was fashionable to feel that Britain disgraced itself in the Thirties; that, through selfishness and appeasement, it and the world sleepwalked to disaster. Auden's phrase applied more accurately to himself – he coined it in the safety of New York – but it stuck. So did the notion of a country morally and materially unprepared for war.

Other countries did, at least in part, succumb in the Thirties – the French to self-loathing, the Americans to isolationism, Italy to vainglory, Spain to civil war, Germany and Japan and the Soviet Union to race or class hatred. The British had few ailments. Average incomes had risen by more than a third since the last war; average life expectancy was up by fifteen years, infant mortality halved. They were socially cohesive. The number of days lost to strikes, 162 million in the General Strike year of 1926, was down to 1.8 million in 1938. The fifty-four-hour week was reduced to forty-eight, even for exploited mill girls and shop assistants. Eleven million workers, proportionately the most in any major country, enjoyed paid annual holidays. They were healthier, taller and heavier than ever before. The crime rate was minuscule; in the 1930s, an average of fifty-six people a year were committed to trial for murder. Violence accounted for less than one per cent of crimes. Seebohm Rowntree was astonished to find that 'one may pass through working-class streets every evening for weeks and not see a drunken person.' They were furious smokers – four in five men and four in ten women – but no harm was seen in that. Unemployment, the worst ill, was falling rapidly.

'This is not the age of pamphleteers,' Professor Lancelot Hogben wrote. 'It is the age of engineers. The spark-plug is mightier than the pen...' The British had engineers in abundance. They were manufacturing more cars and aircraft than anyone but the Americans. The BBC had nine million radio licence-holders and its television service led the world. A Scottish physicist, Robert Watson-Watt, had demonstrated in 1935 that moving aircraft could be detected by radio waves. A transmitter sent a pulse of energy; if it hit an aircraft it was bounced back and appeared as a blip on a cathode tube. By measuring the time the pulse took to return, range could be estimated. Direction could be found by plotting the range from two adjacent radar stations, a technique known as 'range cutting'. The potential of this invention was not well enough appreciated to counter a feeling that air power had diminished Britain's island status – Stanley Baldwin assured parliament that 'the bomber will always get through' – and people feared war as never before. They expected the Germans to launch immediate and terrible air raids in which 600,000 civilians would die in the first few days, with double that number wounded. Bertrand Russell, the pacifist-philosopher, predicted

'**German aircraft** *again raided London and more bombs were dropped,' ran the original caption to this picture on 10 October 1940. 'Photo shows – A milkman carries on through the debris this morning.' The 'Blitz', the name given to the Nazi bombing, was the first time that foreigners had seriously inconvenienced the British in their islands since the Normans had arrived from France 874 years before. Many expected that 600,000 would die in the first few days of all-out bombing, and that national morale would shatter like a broken building. 'The homeless will shreik for peace,' the philosopher Bertrand Russell predicted of London, 'the city will be a pandemonium.' Had that happened, Europe would have been lost to dictatorships.*

*It did not, and this picture represents one of the great psychological turning points of modern history. Hitler could do his worst, but ordinary working men and women made up their minds they would not surrender and they would not panic. They would, like the milkman, 'carry on'. The Russians were to come to the same conclusion, and to pay a higher price for it; so, indeed, were the Germans when their turn came to face defeat. The significance of the British decision was not that it came first, though it changed all that came after; it lay in its being the only one to be taken by a free people, in whose lives concentration camps and gulags played no part. It kept alive democracy, 'the worst form of government,' as Churchill put it, 'except all those other forms that have been tried from time to time.'*

that London would become 'one vast raving bedlam, the hospitals will be stormed, traffic will cease, the homeless will shriek for peace, the city will be a pandemonium.'

In better moral and material shape than any potential Continental ally or adversary, the British thus had more to lose by going to war. They had no territorial ambitions; their empire, expanded with ex-German colonies and new Middle East responsibilities, was bloated enough. In 1937, Neville Chamberlain became Prime Minister, almost seventy, less strident than his famous father, the empire-mongering Joseph, a reforming health minister and capable chancellor with old-fashioned, wing-collared ways. He inherited a huge parliamentary majority, as committed to non-intervention as himself and with a like-minded electorate behind it, encourag-ing in him the dry arrogance and moral superiority with which he treated cabinet colleagues and opponents. Austria was annexed in the spring of 1938. Czechoslovakia was next on Hitler's agenda. The foreign secretary, Anthony Eden, resigned in protest at British appeasement and joined Winston Churchill on the back benches; they cried 'Wolf!' from the wilderness.

On 15 September 1938, Chamberlain flew to Germany. By now a majority of men thought he should defy Hitler, a majority of women that he should continue to appease him. He flew to Bad Godesberg on 22 September and the public swung back to him, the fear of bombing larger than the shame of selling out the Czechs. On 25 September the air raid services were mobilised, trenches and barrage balloons were prepared. Plans were published for evacuating two million from

**Fascists and appeasers.** *Unity Mitford (left) with her sister Diana chatting to Hitler's confidant 'Putzi' Hanfstangl in Munich in the 1930s. Unity returned to Britain in 1940, suffering from a mysterious gunshot wound. Diana was married to Sir Oswald Mosley (centre, giving salute), seen here at a meeting of his* British Union of Fascists in London's East End in 1938. Mosley's Blackshirts made no electoral impact; appeasers were of far more importance, like the Prime Minister, Neville Chamberlain (right), seen on his return from meeting Hitler in Munich in September 1938.

[PHOTO, FAR LEFT: JAMES ABBE]

London. 'How horrible, fantastic, incredible it is,' Chamberlain said, 'that we should be digging trenches and trying on gas masks because of a quarrel in a far away country between people of whom we know nothing…' As he spoke in Parliament on 28 September, he was handed a note; Hitler, he said, had invited him to visit Germany once more. He sped to Munich and persuaded the Czechs to surrender the Sudetenland; by 2.30 pm on 30 September, the crisis was over. On 1 October, he stepped from his aircraft with a piece of paper. 'I believe it is peace for our time,' he told cheering crowds in Downing Street that evening. 'No conqueror returning from a victory on the battlefield,' *The Times* eulogised next morning, 'has come home adorned with nobler laurels,' and only one member of the government resigned. The Czechs bought the British no peace; they did buy time. At Munich, the army could have sent no more than two divisions to France; the first monoplane fighters had only just started being delivered to the squadrons. After Munich, the army

Soviet Union signed a non-aggression pact with Germany. Europe's two great repositories of hatred agreed not to vent their spite upon each other; no more talk, for the moment at least, of Red swine or Nazi scum, instead a sweetheart deal secretly to dismember eastern Europe. Two days later, a bomb exploded in the main street of Coventry and five were killed in flying debris; it was dropped, not by a German aircraft, but by an IRA man into the basket of a tradesman's bicycle. On 31 August, the corpse of a murdered concentration camp inmate was dressed in a Polish army uniform and dumped in the German radio station at Gleiwitz on the Polish border as 'evidence' of a Polish attack.

In the pre-dawn of 1 September, the Germans invaded Poland. In the afternoon, BBC television was showing a Mickey Mouse cartoon to its 20,000 subscribers when the service was taken off the air. German bombers were over Warsaw; it was feared that they would use the BBC signals to home in on London, too. Chamberlain announced war, his voice dry and metallic on radio, at 11.15 am on 3 September. There were no crowds and no cheering, with only twenty people sightseeing outside 10 Downing Street; war was too familiar an acquaintance to merit an elaborate greeting. So slight was the hatred that the newspapers continued to refer to 'Herr' Hitler. At 11.27 am, the first air raid siren went off in London. Beardmore heard it with a 'sense of utter panic… We pictured St Paul's in ruins and a hole in the ground where the Houses of Parliament had stood. But nothing happened.' It was a false alarm; the 'raider' was a light liaison aircraft carrying a French military attaché. The first air combat took place on 6 September. A squadron of Spitfires from Hornchurch shot down two Hurricanes from North Weald after a radar identification error. It was not a good start.

Within a week, 1.3 million had been evacuated from the cities without mishap. Many came from the poorest slums and their

began expanding towards a planned thirty-two divisions, and the building of warplanes outstripped that in Germany. Volunteer and auxiliary units expanded rapidly.

Appeasement was, quietly, ruined in mid-March 1939 when the Germans marched into the rump of Czechoslovakia. Hitler 'now stands armed giving ultimatums on the Rumanian border,' a clerk, George Beardmore, noted in his diary. 'In this and similar circumstances a chappy like myself, only too happy to be left alone, begins to notice indignation rising within himself… Here, I tell myself, is the point where the tyrant must be stopped.' The British and French governments grudgingly agreed; they guaranteed Polish security, whilst Hitler vowed to 'cook them a stew they'll choke on.' Conscription was introduced in mainland Britain on 1 April. Fitful negotiations were undertaken with Moscow, with the aim of reproducing the same two-front threat the Germans had faced in 1914. Civilians began to carry their gas masks and were urged to sniff among the summer scents for the smells of poison, geraniums, pear drops, musty hay. On 23 August, with Anglo-French negotiators still in Moscow, the

condition shocked the rural middle classes who received them. Some children had to be kept in bed whilst their new hosts washed or burnt their verminous clothes, and others 'arrived sewn into a piece of calico with a coat on top and no other clothes at all.' Patients were moved to country houses converted into hospitals as city wards were cleared for the expected mass casualties of air raids.

The rich, and many foreigners, also abandoned London; almost half the great private houses in Belgrave Square were put up for sale, but there were few takers. The banks' central clearing house was moved to a stately home near Stoke-on-Trent, and the Prudential insurance company lived up to its name by taking its staff to Torquay. Suspected enemy sympathisers were rounded up and sent to a camp on a Surrey racecourse. 'Enemy aliens' – some fifty thousand mostly Jewish refugees with every reason to despise Nazis – were taken in front of tribunals, which had the power to intern or to place restrictions on movement. The whole of Scotland Yard was employed for a time on this task. Poisonous snakes and spiders were killed with chloroform at the London Zoo, and riflemen patrolled the cages when the sirens sounded lest dangerous animals escape. The aquarium was drained and the fish eaten. Almost a quarter of London's two million cats and dogs were killed in the first few days; a plague of rats and mice followed.

The first German aircraft did not appear over the capital until 20 November and turned back as soon as it was fired on. Almost a million men had been called up, on pay of two shillings a day for a private soldier; four divisions had sailed for France to hold the gap between the end of the fortified French Maginot Line and the Channel coast. The Germans had shown what they were capable of in Poland; Blitzkrieg – breakthroughs by armoured pincers of tanks, with divebombers above for mobile artillery, the infantry following to mop up – and terror. On the western front, the British remained almost

**Leaving town.** *Some 50,000 'enemy aliens' – many of them fervently anti-Nazi Jews – were rounded up (left). Most were sent to camps on racecourses and on the Isle of Man. It was not difficult to find them. In Hampstead, a London suburb with a heavy concentration of refugee intellectuals, a local policeman went to the public library and asked those who could read German to step outside. Many were soon released and were invaluable to the war effort. The cities lost their children, too, like this little girl (left above) waiting to be evacuated to the countryside. A few mothers refused to let their children go. This girl (right) helps the parson at Stepney in London to sort out the clothes of a friend from what is left of her house.*

[PHOTO, FAR LEFT: GEORGE RODGER]
[PHOTO, RIGHT: BERT HARDY]

motionless. They called it 'Sitzkrieg'. At sea, U-boat captains sank the battleship *Royal Oak* inside the 'impregnable' anchorage at Scapa Flow, and the aircraft carrier *Courageous*; in the South Atlantic, the Royal Navy retaliated by hunting down the German battleship *Graf Spee* and forcing her crew to scuttle her. In the air, British bomber crews dropped millions of anti-Nazi leaflets over German cities. The first British bombs to fall on German soil did so by accident; on 3 December, an aircraft attacking shipping suffered a malfunction in its bomb bay and its stick fell on Heligoland.

Great evil was abroad – the reports of Soviet as well as German atrocities in Poland and Stalin's winter attack on Finland left no doubt of that – but in London, stores sold build-it-yourself models of the Maginot Line for Christmas and cinemas re-opened. Over half the evacuees, appalled at the bleak midwinter in the countryside, poured back into the cities. It was the coldest winter of the century – under wartime censorship no weather forecasts could be published but the frozen Thames was evidence enough – and this combined with

a slump in construction to drive unemployment up to 1.6 million, despite the call-up. Food rationing was introduced in January; four ounces of butter and four ounces of bacon or uncooked ham a week and twelve ounces of sugar per adult. It was more than the German ration, but it rankled since the public was not told of the growing success of U-boats in imposing a blockade on British merchant shipping. A bomb exploded outside a London department store on 2 March, the capital's first of the war; it, too, was left by the IRA.

On 4 April, Chamberlain said that Hitler had 'missed the bus'. He tempted fate. On 9 April, the Germans invaded Scandinavia. Denmark was occupied within twenty-four hours; British and French troops were landed in Norway but had evacuated the central part of the country within a fortnight. 'We have in fact been heavily beaten – routed,' Beardmore noted in his diary. 'All that people like me can understand is that Germany has collected every country she has wanted.' In the Commons on 8 May, the Tory MP Leo Amery quoted Oliver Cromwell at the Prime Minister: 'I say, let us have done with you. In the name of God, go!'

He went. Churchill made his first speech as premier on 13 May, the growling humanity underpinning a flow of language both solemn and dancing. Physically, he offered his people nothing 'but blood, toil, tears and sweat'; morally, he gave them purpose: 'to wage war, by sea, by land and air, with all the strength God can give us... against a monstrous tyranny, never surpassed in the dark, lamentable catalogues of human crime.' He set the aim: 'Victory – victory at all costs, victory in spite of all terror, victory, however long and hard the road may be, for without victory, there is no survival. Let that be realised...'

He was a man of many parts – Beardmore called him 'soldier-statesman-historian', and to that he could have added renegade, aristocrat, journalist, watercolourist and even bricklayer, for he relieved his boredom whilst out of office with fits of wall-building – and as many emotions. At rest, he was 'pink and white, round-faced', short and delicate, with 'wispy hair, frail artistic hands'. The bulldog look, which came when he was animated, was part of a repertoire of expressions that, a Cabinet Office civil servant recalled, included 'the sulky look of a pouting child, the angry violent look of an animal at bay, the tearful look of a compassionate woman and the sudden· spontaneous smiling look of a boy.' Lord Halifax, the foreign secretary whom he pipped in the contest for the premiership, found his brain the most extraordinary he had encountered – 'a most curious mixture of a child's emotion and a man's reason.' He suffered the 'black dog' of depression, and wild

enthusiasms, for aircraft carriers fashioned from icebergs and aerial minefields and the like. He was sixty-six, and gave Hitler fifteen years in age, but nothing in energy – he slept for an hour in the early afternoon, and worked through until 2 am before rising again by 9 am. His adversary was a non-smoking teetotal vegetarian. Churchill was famously none of these.

It was a curious time for him to speak of victory. The following day, Holland surrendered and seven German armoured divisions tore through the tight wooded hills of the 'impassable' Ardennes to maul the light French cavalry screen holding the line. But the speech awoke in the British, tight-knit in their islands, a collective conviction that they would have to be killed outright to be beaten; stunning would not be enough. 'It is a fact that should Britain lose, it will not be in the accepted, historical manner in which nations lose – in which, for example, the Dutch (no blame to them) laid down their arms,' George Beardmore wrote on 16 May. 'I myself know as a fact that the country would be laid waste before we gave in – I mean I am sure of it as I am sure that I sit here...' He was an unmartial figure, an asthmatic North London clerk in his thirties; he felt swamped by 'horrible conjectures', but the die was cast and that was an end of it.

On 17 May, Brussels fell and the US embassy in London urged the 4,000-odd Americans in Britain to return home. The Germans reached the Channel coast at Abbeville three days later. The British Expeditionary Force fell back on Dunkirk, most of its heavy weapons gone, blear-eyed, exhausted and surrounded by tank forces that, in a 'miracle' caused by German caution, temporarily halted their advance on 24 May. The British expected to retrieve no more than a fifth of their quarter-million men. On 26 May, as the Germans were about to resume their advance, the evacuation began. It continued for nine days under heavy attack; it was an awful deliverance.

No breath of air, in that perfect summer, dissipated the odour of the dead as the men waited in long lines on the beaches. 'We might have been walking through a slaughterhouse on a hot day,' an artillery officer wrote of the last night. 'The darkness, which hid some of the sights of horror from our eyes, seemed to thicken this dreadful stench... No assistance that availed anything could be given to the dying men. The living themselves had nothing to offer to them. They just pressed forward to the sea, hoping that the same fate would not be theirs...' Trawlers, sleek yachts and motorcruisers, lifeboats, paddle-steamers – 665 civilian craft – joined the navy in a continuous line across the Channel. Men on destroyers were carried 'in the stokehole, engine room, mess decks, everywhere...' Commander Lightoller, the senior surviving officer from the *Titanic* disaster twenty-eight years before, took his yacht *Sundowner* across. He crammed 130 aboard – 'like the proverbial sardines, even one in the bath and another on the WC so that all the poor devils could do was sit and be sick' – whilst he and his son fought to prevent the overloaded yacht from foundering in the wash of the big Channel steamers and destroyers as it wallowed back to Ramsgate.

When it was over, 224,585 British and 112,546 French and Belgian troops had been saved from the prison cages. It was, as Churchill said, another miracle, but he added that it was also 'a

**The master builder.** *Winston Churchill does some pre-war bricklaying at his country home. The schoolboy dunce had fought the dervishes at Omdurman and escaped from the Boers; he had served as Home Secretary, First Lord of the Admiralty, as scapegoat for Gallipoli, and Chancellor of the Exchequer;*

*from 1929, he was out of office, earning his living by his pen. All his earlier life, he said, was preparation for his 'walk with destiny' from 1940. 'It was the nation and the race dwelling all round the globe that had the lion's heart,' he recalled in 1954. 'I had the luck to be called on to give the roar.' Some roar. Some luck.*

**Outgeneralled and outfought,** the British were driven back on Dunkirk in May 1940. Unaccountably, the Germans did not finish them off. A giant evacuation, which included French and Belgian troops, got under way across the English Channel. The men (main picture) waited their turn for the boats in lines stretching to the water's edge. Crammed on the decks (above) and in the stokeholds, they were vulnerable at sea – these Frenchmen (above) were rescued after their destroyer hit a mine – but Dunkirk (right) was worse, 'like a slaughterhouse on a hot day…' Ultimately, 337,000 safely regained British soil (far right).

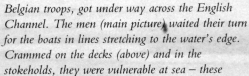

colossal military disaster'. Wars are not won by evacuations. Civilian Britain rejoiced in relief and triumph. The rescued soldiers, defeated, weapons abandoned often without a shot fired, were less grateful to the commanders and the officers who had shamed them. 'These dismayed men, savagely wounded in their pride,' wrote an observer who spent an evening in a Dorset pub with them, 'were seeking relief in bitter criticism of those set over them. We promised each other that whilst the war lasted we would never speak of what we had seen and heard that night...'

The Germans raced on through France; there were further Dunkirks as 135,000 more French and British troops were sealifted from the western French ports. Italy declared war on the Allies and the Soviets invaded Lithuania; like 'jackals from ambush', the other dictatorships feasted on democratic prey. Paris fell on 14 June; the armistice followed eight days later. In Regent's Park, the novelist Rebecca West found Londoners looking at the roses in a special way, smelling their scent, as if to say: 'That is what roses are like, that is how they smell. We must remember that, down in the darkness...' On 30 June, Guernsey fell, white sheets flying from its windows, followed next day by

Jersey. The Germans gave their surrender orders casually, in canvas bags dropped from aircraft. The Channel Islands seemed unlikely to be the only British soil they would take; Churchill had warned that the Battle of Britain was about to commence.

With Mussolini in the war, there were isolated attacks on Italian ice-cream parlours and restaurants. Italian waiters were suspended in mid-shift at the Ritz Hotel. Spaghetti houses put up signs saying 'British Food Shop'. New internees were sent to the Isle of Man, a pre-war holiday resort that proved congenial enough. They set up their own university and arranged concerts; three of the four members of the Amadeus Quartet, later the most famous chamber music group in the country, met there. Not all was so civilised, however. Three of the army escort of a batch of 2,700 internees sailing to Australia were court-martialled for keeping them in squalid conditions. Since many internees were highly educated, such treatment was harmful to the war effort as well as inhumane. 'Frankly,' a young Tory MP told the Commons, 'I shall not feel happy, either as an Englishman or as a supporter of this Government, until this bespattered page of our history has been cleaned up and rewritten.' It was; by 1943 ninety per cent of employable aliens were at work for a victory they desired quite as intensely as their hosts. Only 486, less than one per cent, were detained through the war. Some members of the Peace Pledge Union were prosecuted for encouraging the public not to fight. 'This is a free country,' a magistrate said dismissing the case. 'We are fighting to keep it a free country and these gentlemen, fortunately for them in my opinion, are living in a country where they can express their pacifism, or their non-pacifism, with perfect freedom.' Two spies who did land on the Scottish coast were instantly caught because they did not understand pounds, shillings and pence; another was seen coming ashore in hat and trench coat with a green suitcase. He might as well have labelled it 'Spy'.

'Personally,' George VI wrote in his diary, 'I feel happier now we have no allies to be polite to and to pamper.' The colonies and the dominions had been in the war from the first day and remained so, but they were family, not allies. 'We do not seek our independence out of Britain's ruin,' Gandhi confirmed, though he still strove to end British rule. 'Britain will die hard and heroically, even if she has to...' There were southern Irish volunteers, eighty thousand of them, too, and Dutch, Poles, Free French, Norwegians, Czechs and Danes as well as Canadian units. The British also had the increasing goodwill of the United States, but in the essential, the British were alone and, like their King, strangely happy to be so. They would, as they put it, be 'the home side' for the first time since the Norman conquest in 1066; their attitude to the Nazis was,

Beardmore wrote, the 'retort of the second-former to the school bully: "Come on and try."'

People were ordered to 'Stay Put' when 'Cromwell', the codeword for invasion, was announced, lest refugee columns swamp soldiers as they had in France. Security was sometimes mindless; one censor deleted *HMS Pinafore* from a theatre review because it was forbidden to mention HM ships. The sea, glistening in the clarity of high summer, was an incomparable barrier, immobilising on its far shore the strength of German armour and defusing the brilliance of German generals. Their hastily drawn-up invasion plan, Operation Sea Lion, envisaged landings at points along a 200-mile stretch of coast from Ramsgate to Lyme Regis. A first wave of thirteen divisions was to move inland to establish a line from Gloucester to Colchester; at this stage, if not before, they anticipated surrender. The British expected a concentration against London; an anti-tank ring in the outer suburbs was to fall back on a second, closer line, with a third along the Thames to be held by experienced regulars; a final inner redoubt around Westminster was to be defended to the last by crack Marines and Guardsmen.

In truth, the only defence was the sea. Had they crossed it, the Germans would have found little to stop them except flesh. By 1 July, the army had grown to 1.25 million, but new recruits drilled with broomsticks; one platoon had scarcely caught its first glimpse of a rare rifle when a runner asked their sergeant if he could have it back, as another platoon had never seen one either. The tank and glider traps they were preparing – old carts and bedsteads, broken-down cars, gunless pill boxes

disguised as tea stalls and haystacks – would not have caused a self-respecting panzer to pause in its tracks. Much effort was expended on removing road signs, station names and the destination boards on buses; the automobile associations refused to produce route maps for members and camouflaged the familiar yellow and blue motorcycles of their road patrols. It caused much irritation and confusion among the natives, but it would scarcely have inconvenienced invaders who had navigated their way across half Europe.

A million men had joined the Local Defence Volunteers, soon to be the Home Guard. They had no uniforms or ranks at first and the Germans answered the question of whether they would qualify as irregular forces under the Geneva Convention with a radio announcement that they would be shot as 'jackal snipers and murder bands'. Many were pensioners; the oldest was a former Regimental Sergeant Major who had seen action in the Egyptian campaign of 1884. One London company drilled with pikes borrowed from the Drury Lane theatre, whilst a platoon in docklands made hand grenades of raw potatoes with bits of razor blade stuck into them. John Astor, the proprietor of *The Times* and commander of the London Press battalion, converted his Rolls-Royce into an armoured car.

When a stick of parachutists was reported to have landed in Croydon, the local platoon commander found that he had only one man available; he rounded up fifteen others after they returned from work, and set off armed with a rifle and ten rounds of ammunition to do battle with the fortunately fictitious foe. To come in force, however, the Germans had to

**Preparing for battle.** *In June 1940, the cities were preparing to become the front line. Waitresses at a Lyons Corner House (left), one of the nationwide chain of restaurants that kept the country in tea, coffee and sandwiches, put up the wooden shutters against bomb blast from an expected air raid. These women were affectionately known as 'nippies' because of the speed at which they served their tables. In the crypt of Christ Church, the 18th-century masterpiece of the architect Nicholas Hawksmoor at Spitalfields in the London slums, a canny local (right) gives himself additional protection against the German Luftwaffe by sleeping in a solid stone sarcophagus.*

*The blackout was so effective that many pedestrians were knocked down by cars in the night streets until white lines were painted along the edge of pavements. The removal of signposts, and destination boards from buses, to confuse invaders was a double-edged precaution. It also confused the native British, who were sometimes taken for spies by their compatriots when they asked for directions. 'May we as civilians have immediate instructions as to how we are to act when stopped by people asking the way to places?' Miss Violet Oates complained in a letter to* The Times *from Gestingthorpe Hall, her country house in Essex. 'Both my gardener and his son have been questioned in this manner... As we are three miles from a police station it is impossible to notify the police of such persons before they are well away on their possible nefarious intentions.'*

[PHOTO, LEFT: GEORGE RODGER]
[PHOTO, RIGHT: BILL BRANDT]

come by sea, and this they could not do with any prospect of success until they had won command of the air. Only when they had defeated the RAF fighter strength could they protect their invasion fleet and the landing beaches from the Royal Navy and RAF bombers. They had little time to do so; by autumn, the seas would be too rough for their hastily assembled barges.

The Battle of Britain was among the most decisive conflicts in history, yet it was a very small battle. The total number of RAF pilots involved over the summer was less than 3,000; on some days, fewer than 600 were available for operations. The casualties, though grievous for so small a group, were less than five per cent of those suffered on the first day of the Somme. The German leadership never accorded it any climactic significance. Churchill sensed how vital it was – 'never in the field of human conflict,' he said, 'has so much been owed by so many to so few' – but his pilots joked that he was referring to their mess bills, and their two greatest commanders were sacked as soon as it was over. To most it was decisive only with

hindsight and the application of an 'if'; if the battle had been lost, so would the war.

Aircraft and pilot strengths fluctuated with the fortunes of combat and the arrival of new machines from the factories and new pilots from the Operational Training Units. With Lord Beaverbrook in charge, the British factories consistently beat targets for aircraft supply. The shortage of men, however, became so critical that the six months new pilots had spent at OTUs was slashed to a fortnight, so that with as little as ten hours' experience of flying fighters they were committed to combat. On 20 July, with the battle underway, the three Luftwaffe air fleets attacking Britain had 864 operational twin-engined bombers, 248 divebombers, 200 Messerschmitt 110 heavy fighters and 656 single-seat Messerschmitt 109 fighters. RAF Fighter Command had 531 single-seat fighters, Hurricanes and Spitfires. It was inferior by 3.7 to 1 in quantity, but not in quality. The divebombers and 110s proved easy meat. The critical struggle was between the single-seat fighters.

No machine had a decisive advantage. The Messerschmitt 109 had a marginal advantage in speed and turning circle. Its fuel injection engine allowed it to dive abruptly from level flight, where the British Merlin engines cut out momentarily with the negative G-force. Its wings could break up if overstressed, however; the visibility from its cockpit was poor, the narrow undercarriage unforgiving, and its range so limited that any pilot flying over England for more than thirty minutes risked running out of fuel over the sea on his return. The Hawker Hurricane was the mainstay of Fighter Command, slower than the 109 but able to withstand heavier punishment and easier to repair; with a powerful cone of fire and good sights, it was an ideal bomber-destroyer. The Spitfire was the work of R. J. Mitchell, a brilliant designer of record-breaking seaplanes in the 1920s. Convalescing after a lung operation in 1933, he had met young German airmen. Convinced that war would come, he drove himself against medical advice to perfect his fighter. The prototype flew in March 1936. Next year, at forty-two, he was dead, little known or honoured. His Spitfire – he thought it 'just the sort of bloody silly name they would give it' – had immense strength from its trademark elliptical wings and superb visibility from its bubble canopy. The Spitfire rarely broke up in the air and confidence in this enabled its pilots to dive it more deeply and turn it harder than the theoretically superior 109.

The pilot needed exceptional eyesight, extremely fast reactions, strength to handle unpowered controls, the endurance to fly several sorties a day, and the skill and courage to get very close to the enemy. An RAF pilot had only fourteen seconds' worth of ammunition, the German nine seconds'; this scarce resource was best used at a range of 100 yards or less. Height and the sun were of mortal importance; the classic attack was the dive out of the sun onto an unsuspecting prey, pulling out behind and slightly below the tail, and raking him from this blind spot. Above all, the pilots feared fire. 'Imagine how they feel,' said Archibald MacIndoe, the plastic surgeon who remodelled their faces and limbs at a special hospital in East Grinstead. 'On Friday night they are dancing in a night club with a beautiful girl and by Saturday afternoon they are a burnt cinder.'

Both sides, in general, fought with chivalry. 'You never even thought of it as killing men,' the British pilot Peter Townsend wrote. When he shot up a Heinkel bomber over the North Sea, he saw the gunner, fair hair streaming in the slipstream of a shattered window, mutilated beyond recognition, and the young pilot bent over the controls trying to keep his doomed aircraft from the waves. 'Through the window panels the other two members of the crew regarded me in silent despair,' he wrote. 'I pushed back my hood and signalled them to turn towards the coast. These men were no longer enemies but airmen in distress. If only we could have borne up their doomed aircraft with our own wings…' German float planes rescued RAF pilots from the sea, though normally the British had the great advantage of fighting over their own soil. When Townsend was himself shot down, he found himself being stood pints of beer in a nearby pub within a few minutes.

The RAF pilots, in image and often enough in fact, were young and puppyishly extrovert, an intimate brotherhood with their own understated language. They did not crash, they 'pranged'; they did not die, they 'went for a Burton', slipped

**Achtung, Spitfire!** *The helmeted head of the air gunner on a Heinkel bomber is in the foreground of this German picture (right). He is seen trying to bring the ring sight of his machinegun to bear on a Spitfire which has attacked his aircraft and is breaking away for another pass. RAF pilots avoided the German fighter escorts where possible, and concentrated their attacks on the slower and more vulnerable bomber streams. The Spitfire had a reflector sight that glowed between the pilot's eyes and the windscreen.*

**A Spitfire cost £6,000,** *a pittance for so fine a machine, and individuals could and did sponsor individual aircraft. An Indian maharajah paid for a squadron. The general public (left) was invited to contribute its sixpences and shillings to the Spitfire Fund.* [Photo: George Rodger]

away for a Burton ale. Few were more than twenty-six; half were ex-amateurs with a love for machinery and the air who had learned to fly with voluntary reserve and university air squadrons. Old class distinctions survived; some of them were NCOs, segregated on the ground from the officers in sergeants' messes. Four in five were British, though pilots from the dominions were among the best, and suffered terrible casualties; of twenty-two Australians, fourteen were killed, of the same number of South Africans, nine. The Poles were the best pilots of all, averaging 10.5 German planes destroyed for each Polish pilot killed, compared to 4.9 for the RAF.

The commander-in-chief, Hugh Dowding, was their antithesis. He had been an athlete, a ski champion and a decorated First World War pilot, but he was withdrawn and abstemious, a widower, a man who suffered fools curtly. They called him 'Stuffy'. His strategy was constant. It was to keep Fighter Command in being until autumn weather made seaborne invasion impossible. To do so, he had already prevented squadrons from being frittered away in France. Troops on the Dunkirk beaches had railed at the lack of air cover, but he cared little for that. His tactics, too, were designed to

husband his scant resources. Wherever possible, his fighters were to avoid the German fighter escorts and attack the bombers. Against this dour professional was ranged Herman Goering, the only German Reichsmarschal, himself a former First War flying ace, but seduced now by easy victories and raddled by drugs, obesity and evil – he was the arranger of political assassinations and concentration camps. He had options – lobotomising the RAF by destroying its radar sites and control centres and airfields, grinding it away by attrition in the air, terror-bombing cities – and he vacillated between them.

The battle started in July with German attacks on British coastal convoys and air combat over the sea. Virginia Cowles reported, 'To the right you see a plane falling like a bullet into the sea leaving a long black line of smoke against the sky; so to the left one of the great silver balloons in flames; directly above a fighter diving down on one of the bombers and suddenly a tiny fluttering parachute.' By early August, nevertheless, the Dover straits had become so dangerous that the Royal Navy was forced to withdraw its destroyers from them. The Germans prepared for an all-out assault for 13 August, *Adlertag*, by bombing the radar stations which they knew to be an essential

**'The Few'**, *Churchill called the RAF fighter pilots, among them Flying Officer R. F. Rimmer, resting at a flight dispersal prior to being 'scrambled' for take-off at the fighter airfield at Duxford near Cambridge. He was killed in action on 27 September 1940 as the battle was being won.*

**These shot-down** *German airmen are being escorted through Victoria Station in London on their way to a PoW camp on 7 September 1940, the critical day when the warning codeword for invasion, 'Cromwell', was issued to British forces. Attacks on airfields had reduced the RAF fighter control system to near-chaos and the pilot losses were becoming unsustainable. On that day, however, the Germans switched to the mass bombing of London.*
[PHOTO: GEORGE RODGER]

part of the RAF control system. On Eagle Day itself, the Germans flew almost 1,500 sorties. They lost forty-six aircraft and shot down thirteen. Two days later, they attacked from airfields in Norway and Denmark as well as France; in combat raging from Scotland to Devon, they lost seventy-six aircraft to thirty-four RAF fighters shot down. They called it *Schwarze Donnerstag*, Black Thursday. The lesson was not lost on the Americans, whose eventual participation the British knew was of more mortal consequence to them in this conflict than in the last. 'The Hitler war machine has run for the first time into an opposition that is tough and strong,' the New York *Herald Tribune* wrote. 'The British need help badly; they need every form of help we can give them, and they need it now; but they have shown that they know how to use it…'

The loss rate of unescorted bombers on daylight raids was unacceptably high. From now, they would have fighter protection and that, given the short range of the 109, dictated that the battle would focus on southeastern England. Here they met the RAF's 11 Group, commanded by the New Zealander Keith Park. Goering, so shocked at officer casualties that he ordered that no bomber was to fly with more than one officer in its crew, concluded that the attacks on the radar stations were ineffective: it was a colossal error. On 24 August, as Park had feared, the Germans began to concentrate their attacks on his airfields in the southeast. The battle entered its critical stage: in the fortnight that followed, 231 of the RAF's 1,000 available fighter pilots were killed or wounded; of 85 Squadron's eighteen pilots at Croydon, fourteen were shot down, two of them twice. On the opening night, a German bomber group that had been briefed to attack targets in Rochester bombed London by mistake. Goering was furious; he threatened to transfer the group commanders to the infantry, for Hitler, who had curious nostalgia and admiration for the British, fellow Aryans, had prohibited attacks on London. In retaliation, Churchill authorised the RAF to bomb Berlin the following night. They did almost no physical damage – they killed some cows in the outer suburbs – but they pricked Nazi vanity.

In the last two days of August, the Luftwaffe flew 2,800 sorties in an all-out effort against the airfields. Activity was such that the St Mellons Golf Club amended its rules. 'A player whose stroke is affected by the simultaneous explosion of a bomb or by machinegun fire may play another ball,' it decreed. 'Penalty one stroke.' On 31 August, the RAF lost thirty-nine fighters; in a week, 115 pilots were killed or wounded. This was almost double the output of the OTUs, and it was worse than it looked, for the experienced dead were replaced by fledglings, so that a quarter of the pilots had less than two weeks of squadron experience. On 1 September, Fighter Command lost fifteen to the Luftwaffe's fourteen. One of the Germans shot down, under armed escort on a train at Chatham station, was so confident of victory that, when a waitress ran out of the station buffet and rattled a Spitfire Fund collecting box under his nose, he laughed and put a five-mark note in it.

The ratio next day remained at a critical thirty-one to thirty-five. 'Our losses became so heavy that newly arriving squadrons were run down more quickly than resting squadrons could take their place,' Dowding recollected. The RAF control system was a near-chaos of cut telephone wires, power outages and bombed operations rooms; its brain was going. Pilots, flying several sorties a day, were exhausted; those who parachuted safely were instantly returned to combat. A pilot sat slumped in his fighter after landing it. The ground crew thought him dead or wounded. He was asleep. By 6 September, six of 11 Group's seven sector airfields were seriously damaged. The British knew that they had begun to lose; the Germans, seeing Hurricanes and Spitfires still rising where their intelligence officers had assured them they would meet only ghosts by now, were not so sure.

On 7 September, invasion seemed so imminent that the warning codeword, 'Cromwell', was issued. As Keith Park flew his Hurricane over London in the afternoon, he saw the great city burning in oily black and red. Blazing paint and rum settled in a fiery scum on the Thames. 'Send all the pumps you've got,' a fire officer pleaded. 'The whole bloody world's on fire.' There had been a *Zielwechsel*, a target switch; the Germans had sent a huge formation of almost 1,000 aircraft to bomb the capital. 'I said "Thank God",' Park recollected. Hitler, in fury over the RAF bombing of Berlin, had pledged to 'raze their cities to the ground.'

It was a fateful decision. It opened a box of horrors for civilians on both sides, and, with the cities now taking the punishment in place of the battered airfields, it shifted the air balance to the British. Reserves, fed into battle with such parsimony by Park and Dowding, began to swell. Losses fell.

On 17 September, Operation Sea Lion was postponed indefinitely. Confirmation that the battle was won came ten days later, when the German bombing streams were broken up before they could reach London. 'The Luftwaffe was bled almost to death,' a German officer said, 'and suffered losses which would never again be made good.' Pilots suffered *Kanalkrankheit*, 'Channel sickness', a combination of stress and chronic fatigue, with stomach cramps, vomiting, loss of appetite and acute irritability. It was too common for medical officers to ground them all; instead, with severe cases, they diagnosed and treated appendicitis, a minor operation that gave an excuse to rest a pilot for two or three weeks. It was a matter of honour for the fighter pilots to stay with the bombers; sometimes they did so for too long. On 3 October, nineteen of them drowned when they ditched in the Channel: 'wild water dotted with parachutes, pilots floating in their lifejackets, and greasy oil slicks where another 109 had ended its last dive...'

They developed 'Spitfire snobbery', claiming always to have shot down a Spitfire or to have been its victim, when three in five British fighters were Hurricanes. They believed, too, that

the Spitfires were being fitted with new engines. 'The other day we tangled with these newer Spitfires and had three losses against one success,' one of them, Ulrich Steinhilper, wrote on 19 October. 'Sooner or later one side had to run out of aircraft and young men to fly them... London was invariably the target, necessitating maximum range penetrations... Time was now against us and time was running out...' In the dawn of 27 October, Steinhilper woke in his cold and musty tent and went to the washstand. 'As I shaved I examined my hollow cheeks and sunken eyes. When would my time come?' He was shot down and taken prisoner later in the day. Goering, shaken, called off mass daylight bombing. The victors were dealt with swiftly by men with different tactical ideas and better versed in office politics than they. Dowding was given twenty-four hours to vacate his office, to become a humble representative of the aircraft production ministry posted to the USA; Park was downgraded to Training Command. It was, Park said, a 'base intrigue' for which he would feel bitter 'to my dying day'.

The great U-bend of the Thames below Tower Bridge was unmistakable. The German bomber pilots rarely had difficulty

in finding their target. They came night after night as the Blitz of Britain replaced the Battle from September 1940 until its full fury abated, but did not cease, the following May. At first, they concentrated on the docks and the East End slums that surrounded them. When they crept over the city as a whole, the government was relieved. 'If only the Germans had had the sense not to bomb west of London Bridge,' said Clement Attlee, 'there might have been a revolution in this country. As it is, they have smashed about Bond Street and Park Lane and readjusted the balance.' They bombed Buckingham Palace, and the Queen was pleased: 'Now I feel we can look the East End in the face.' The BBC could do the same. On 15 October, Bruce Belfrage was reading the news from Broadcasting House when there was a muffled explosion and a voice asked: 'Are you all right?' A bomb had exploded on another floor, killing seven; Belfrage continued reading unruffled.

Other cities were savaged – Plymouth was raided so often that at night it became a silent 'tomb of darkness', many of its people spilling out to sleep in country barns and churches. Every city with substantial docks was visited and revisited – Liverpool burned for a week after one raid; an ammunition ship exploded in the docks, taking six other ships with it and hurling riveted steel for two miles. On 14 November 1940, the airspace over Coventry was saturated with 449 bombers. The medieval heart of the city and its great cathedral were destroyed, at a cost of only one aircraft. The British were reading Luftwaffe signals traffic; they knew a great operation was planned – they even knew its codename, Moonlight Sonata – but they did not know where and their night fighters were not yet efficient. More than five hundred were killed. In Scotland, Clydebank was devastated in two nights of bombing so severe that almost every house was damaged and its night-time population fell from 47,000 to 2,000 as its people sought safety on the moors.

It was London that suffered most, absorbing into its much greater size 19,000 tons of bombs where no other city suffered more than a tenth of that. The Anderson shelter saved many lives. It was made of two curved pieces of corrugated steel sunk into the ground, the entrance protected by a steel shield and earth embankment, with more earth on top, on which some grew flowers. Others thought the Andersons flimsy and made for the tube stations at night, but even deep below ground they were not wholly safe. Water from a burst main submerged them in sand and sludge in one incident; at Bank station, 111 were killed by the blast of a bomb that threw them in front of an incoming train; later, more than 150 were crushed to death when someone slipped on a packed escalator. Spent shrapnel from anti-aircraft guns killed more on the ground than enemy aircrew above, but the noise of the guns did marvels for morale.

St Paul's survived, a symbol amid the flames. A bomb powerful enough to have blown its face off landed in front of the steps, but failed to explode; the team who extricated it amid tangled gas mains and electrical cables twenty-six feet below the surface won the newly instituted George Cross, given for heroism away from the battlefront, though in truth London was the battlefront. In a great fire raid of 29 December, twenty-eight incendiaries fell on the cathedral; one seemed certain to set the dome afire until it fell onto the parapet and went out. Some thought it a miracle, but eight other Wren churches went that night, together with the Guildhall; there was almost a firestorm, for the Thames was at a low ebb and the fireboats often helpless, with two great conflagrations in the City. 'I said out loud as we turned away from the scene,' wrote Arthur Harris, later head of RAF Bomber Command, 'Well, they are sowing the wind.' He would ensure that they reaped it.

The Café de Paris was sliced open early in 1941, crowded with society girls in evening dress and officers on leave. The band leader 'Snakehips' Johnson was killed along with thirty-three others, and a hundred wounded, the girls tearing strips from their evening dresses for bandages. The ambulances were swamped and casualties were ferried to hospital by taxis.

Looters prowled the wreckage, ripping open handbags and stealing rings from the dead, and helping themselves to the 25,000 bottles of champagne the night club had in stock. Overall, however, crime fell sharply during 1940 and 1941.

Morale creaked in the smaller provincial targets, where the damage and dangers were more concentrated, but the capital was, Churchill said, 'like some huge prehistoric animal, capable of enduring terrible injuries, mangled and bleeding from many wounds, and yet preserving its life and movement…' It was the focal point of world attention – American radio reporters filed their nightly stories to the crump of bombs – and it knew it. It took a grim and collective pride in proving that it could, as the phrase went, 'take it'. The novelist Virginia Woolf, soon to drown herself, examined the smouldering ruins of Mecklenburgh Square. 'Who lived there?' she wondered. 'I suppose the casual young men and women I used to see from the window; the flat dwellers who used to have flower pots and sit in the balcony. All blown to bits.' She came across a neighbour. 'They actually have the impertinence to say this will make us accept peace…!' he told her. Then he ambled off; 'he watches raids from his flat roof and sleeps like a hog.' George Beardmore wrote in his diary, 'No question of not surviving the bombing, which is regarded not with heroism or wringing of hands but as a colossal nuisance which must soon end.' The only sign of hysteria he saw was a chalked notice board at a tube station which said "Positively No Admittance". '"No Entrance" would have been quite sufficient,' he wrote.

A number of psychiatric clinics were prepared for victims of stress; one had a single patient in two weeks, and only twenty-three patients after more than two months. Another was disbanded after a month, patientless. Hospital admissions for neurotic illnesses fell; there were fewer suicides, too, and less drunkenness. Church attendance increased in 1940 and stayed high in 1941, before the newcomers departed with the bombers. Those who had faith found it deepened, the unofficial survey Mass Opinion concluded, and in those who had little it was weakened further. At the London Zoo, it was found that the chimpanzees ignored both bombs and guns, but were frightened by sirens; camels were the most phlegmatic, and continued to chew the cud even when a bomb fell a few yards from their enclosure.

Football matches continued. Police were booed when they stopped a Tottenham Hotspur game during an air raid alarm; the wail of the siren had been deliberately drowned out by the persistent cheering of the crowd who did not want their sport interfered with. The favourite song of the Blitz was the haunting 'A Nightingale Sang in Berkeley Square', and Vera Lynn, a plumber's daughter from East Ham, sang her plaintive 'We'll Meet Again'. Dame Myra Hess gave shilling concerts in the National Gallery; by the end of the war, almost a million people had listened to chamber music in the bombed gallery. Joseph

Kennedy, the US ambassador and father of John F. Kennedy, was driven every evening to Windsor Great Park before, to the intense relief of his hosts, leaving altogether in December 1940 to assure the *Boston Globe* that 'Democracy in Britain is finished'. His successor, John G. Winant, was loved because he said on arrival that there was no place he would rather be. He was greeted by George VI at Victoria Station; it was the first time that any monarch had gone to meet a foreign ambassador, and it showed the overriding importance set on relations with Washington. Winant followed the local example and slept each night in his apartment in Grosvenor Square, like the six in seven Londoners who simply stayed at home during the bombing.

The last raid was the worst. It came on 10 May 1941, Cup Final day, as, far to the north in Scotland, the Deputy Führer, Rudolf Hess, was parachuting from a Messerschmitt close to the estate of the Duke of Hamilton, on a bizarre personal mission to conclude a peace deal. The moon was full and the Thames had a low ebb tide, a favourite bombers' combination. Big Ben had a bomb through its tower, though it continued to chime; Churchill wept over the gutted House of Commons, while Westminster Abbey, the Law Courts, and the Tower of London were seriously damaged. Every main railway station was put out of action. A quarter of a million books burned in the British Museum and paper shards floated beneath the half-obliterated sun the next day for thirty miles. The bomber pilots could see the red glow from Rouen, 160 miles away. The city smelt of burning soap from the ruined Palmolive factory. The raid killed 1,436, more than the San Francisco earthquake. There was never anything so bad again. People waited for the bombers, but they did not return in force to Britain. In eight months, 39,678 had been killed, 20,000 of them in London. The deaths were far below pre-war expectation – the million cardboard coffins that had been prepared were left unused – but the number of homeless was much worse, with one in six Londoners bombed out. They now gained a respite because the bombers were being transferred elsewhere, to the East, for the invasion of Russia.

The intimacy and solitude of the British war – what Churchill called the 'finest hour' – was over. Others were involved now, and the battlefields became distant, the plains of Russia, the North African desert, the Atlantic wastes. Urgent exhilaration gave way to lengthy anti-climax. The country had had Churchill's blood and tears; now was the time for toil and sweat, British women's in particular. The great bulk of young single ones, and a majority of married women, served in the auxiliary forces or worked in industry. At nineteen, Princess Elizabeth, the future Queen, joined the Auxiliary Territorial Service as a trainee driver. Amy Johnson, the 1930s record-breaker, was lost when she baled out of an aircraft she was ferrying over the Thames Estuary. Unmarried women under thirty were conscripted into the labour force or the services in 1941; in 1943, this was extended to all under fifty. Married women up to the age of forty had to register as labour which could be directed to industry. They made up forty per cent of those in engineering, as welders, fitters, inspectors, including the huge, 1.6 million strong aircraft industry that produced more than 25,000 aircraft a year. In steelworks, women fed the blast

**Bookworms, undaunted** *by their surroundings, look for volumes in the ruins of Holland House after a raid on London. The home of the Earl of Ilchester, it had been built in 1607, and in the first half of the 19th century was the social centre of the Whig party.*

furnaces and controlled rolling mills. They were a majority in the munitions factories; they replaced men on the farms.

Ernest Bevin, son of a Somerset farm labourer put out to work at eleven, the trade union leader who became labour minister, poacher turned gamekeeper, proved a driving and no-nonsense taskmaster. Powerful and squat, sitting next to the patrician Churchill in the Commons he seemed to J. B. Priestley to embody 'the other half of the English people'. He used his labour well, extracting from it concessions he would never have tolerated in his previous pugnacious life. Seventy-hour weeks were common in 1940, the crisis year, but by 1943 this was seen as damaging, and the norm became fifty-five hours for men and fifty for women. They worked a six-day week, with a week's paid holiday a year. More than a million men and women who had passed the retirement age of sixty-five stayed on at work. Much thought went into encouraging high productivity. The BBC broadcast *Music While You Work* twice daily for the factories, raising production by fifteen per cent in the following hour.

The overall effort was immense. All save 60,000 of the pre-war unemployed found work, joined by more than two million who had not sought it before. At its height, war production was absorbing almost half of gross national product, the highest ratio reached by any combatant country. The production of small arms

and shells increased tenfold in the first three years of war, artillery sevenfold, wheeled vehicles by 350 per cent. Six million tons of merchant shipping, and a million tons of warships, were built.

Pay, at least when compared to the 3s 6d a day now given to army privates, was good. The aircraft industry was particularly generous. A skilled aero-engine fitter could make £20 a week, as much as many doctors. Women, however, were discriminated against. In engineering, they averaged half what men earned. Sixteen thousand came out at the Rolls-Royce aero-engine plant in Glasgow over unequal pay for women. There were other strikes, too, in places familiar from the Twenties and Thirties, the Kent and Lanarkshire coalfields, Liverpool docks, shipyards at Barrow-in-Furness. Bevin reacted angrily. Under a new regulation, those inciting strikes or lock-outs faced five years in prison. This applied whether or not the cause of the stoppage was legally a 'trade dispute'.

The country had learned from the Great War, however, that it was dangerous to delay social progress to a nebulous post-war age. A committee was appointed in June 1941 to examine social insurance. It was headed by William Beveridge, a veteran specialist in unemployment, former director of the London School of Economics, dry and overweening, part academic and part visionary. He set out to kill 'the five giants' of want, ignorance, squalor, idleness and disease. 'A revolutionary moment in the world's history,' Beveridge said, 'is a time for revolution, not patching.' The Report was, in fact, more pink than Red. It was based on cooperation between voluntary and public action, and individuals and the state. The government was to provide family allowances, a comprehensive health service and high employment. Beveridge planned, quite literally, for cradle to grave security; the Report embraced both maternity benefits and a funeral allowance set at £20. A single flat-rate contribution by workers and employers, topped up by the state, was to provide benefit for unemployment, sickness and disability, with old age, widows' and orphans' pensions and benefits. A system of 'national assistance' was to provide for those who fell outside other benefits. It was all to be run by a new ministry of social security.

At a time when, in fiction, many readers were finding comfortable solace in the peaceful and ordered novels of Trollope and Jane Austen, the Report was an extraordinary bestseller. It had total sales of 630,000 copies, including an American edition of 50,000. A shortened version was distributed to resistance groups in Europe, to show them the post-war world for which the British, at least, were fighting. It was no more than a report, not legislation; Churchill, in particular, was leery of its promises, but could not ignore the enthusiasm it aroused. The Christian Socialist William Temple, Archbishop of Canterbury, who made famous the phrase, 'The Welfare State', was for it. So, less predictably, were younger Conservative ministers, Harold Macmillan, R. A. Butler, names for the future, and the established Anthony Eden at the Foreign Office. Quintin Hogg thought it 'above all an opportunity to re-establish a social conscience in the Tory Party.' It was followed by a series of government white papers, on a National Health Service, on the Keynesian means of disarming cyclical unemployment through public expenditure, on social insurance. The Butler Education Act of 1944 was the most radical of the century; family allowances were introduced.

The Russians held the Germans outside Moscow in December 1941; in the same month the Japanese bombed Pearl Harbor; as an added bonus Hitler declared war on the USA. 'Thank God America must be fully committed,' George Beardmore wrote the day after, 'for now we can't lose.' It was different from winning, though; times were bleak. A new war, with Japan, was added to the burden, and Hong Kong fell after eighteen days of fighting. The great ships *Prince of Wales* and *Repulse* were sunk in a few minutes off the coast of Malaya. The German Afrika Korps under Erwin Rommel broke through Libya and threatened the British in Egypt. In mid-February 1942, Singapore fell and 130,000 British and Imperial troops were taken prisoner. Churchill admitted that it was 'a heavy and far-reaching defeat', for it exposed British prestige in Asia to the humiliation of mass surrender. There were soon reports of the beheading of Australian and Indian soldiers; 50,000 prisoners were crammed half-starved into four barracks in the Changi military base in Singapore. The German warships *Scharnhorst* and *Gneisenau* slipped through the Channel. Tobruk fell to Rommel, the Japanese advanced through Burma and down the Pacific islands towards Australia. The British felt themselves

incompetent; only the Russians seemed to be putting up a fight.

At home, from mid-1941 clothes had been rationed as well as food. Women could buy no more than three woollen dresses, two pairs of shoes, four blouses and a raincoat. Instead of stockings they painted their legs with suntan lotion or onion skins, and then drew in a seam with eyeliner. Turn-ups disappeared from trousers; skirts and shirt tails were shorter and double-breasted jackets disappeared. All, children and adults, were allowed a maximum of half a pound of sweets a month. Beer was not rationed; instead, the alcohol level was halved.

Supplies were dependent on the Battle of the Atlantic, as German submarines, the U-boats, stalked the convoys of freighters from American and Canadian ports. From 1941 British codebreakers at Bletchley Park began to be able to read the signals traffic transmitted to the Enigma code machines on the U-boats. It was an achievement of huge significance kept secret until well after the war; another was centimetric radar, which enabled surfaced U-boats to be detected and attacked at night. The Germans operated in wolf packs of up to a dozen U-boats; the codebreakers knew where to find them. There was, however, a gap devoid of RAF Coastal Command and RCAF air cover south of Greenland, known as the 'black pit', and exploited by long-range Type IX U-boats; and, when the Germans improved their Enigma machines in early 1942,

**The Cruel Sea.** *Without the Atlantic lifeline to America, Britain would have been crippled. The Battle of the Atlantic was long and bitter. The convoy system (top left) gave some protection against the 'wolf packs' of*

German submarines, 'U-boats', but for months losses in merchant ships far outstripped the shipyards' capacity to launch new tonnage. This picture, taken from the deck of a tanker, shows the barrage balloons which were hoisted from some ships to deter air attacks. The losses were high; a British merchantman is seen (above) in its death throes and four survivors of another torpedoed ship (left) grasp a line and a lifebuoy thrown by the crew of a Royal Navy warship in mid-Atlantic. The balance swung against the U-boats when codebreakers at Bletchley Park learnt to read German signals traffic in the greatest intelligence operation of the war.

**Disaster at Dieppe.** *Six thousand troops, mainly Canadian and British but including Americans and Free French, made a 'reconnaissance in force' on the French coast at Dieppe in August 1942. They were routed. In nine hours, 1,000 were killed and twice that number were taken prisoner. The German picture (right) shows wounded troops marching into captivity a few moments after their surrender. All their tanks and equipment were abandoned; the Royal Navy lost a destroyer and thirty-three landing craft, and the RAF lost more than a hundred aircraft flying support missions. It proved the immense dangers of amphibious assault. It had its value, however, as Hitler realised. 'We must realise that we are not alone in learning a lesson from Dieppe,' he told his commanders. 'The British have also learned.'*

*To show their displeasure at the landing in 'Fortress Europe', guards in the distant Stalag VIIB prisoner of war camp at Lambsdorf in Germany manacled British PoWs. This picture (top) was taken by a prisoner with an illegal home-made camera.*

months of heavy losses followed before the code was again broken. In March 1942, 834,184 tons of shipping were lost; the total for the first three months of the year was 1.93 million tons, far outstripping building capacity. To these perils were added, for the seamen on the Arctic convoys supplying Russia, freezing seas and the indifference of those they were helping. When a freighter arrived in Murmansk, a Scottish crewman led a cheer. The faces on the pier were 'blank, indifferent'. Into the silence, the Scot shouted: 'All right, go to hell then.' The dockers were prison labourers under guard. In July 1942, twenty-three of the thirty-six merchantmen in convoy PQ-17 were sunk when the convoy was ordered to scatter and its Royal Navy escort steamed off to meet the German pocket battleship *Tirpitz*, wrongly thought to be at sea.

The tide of war was seen to turn in October and November 1942, far off, in the North African desert. Under General Bernard Montgomery, the 8th Army pounded its way through Rommel's lines at El Alamein. The battle was not won by brilliant generalship – Rommel wrote of his enemy's 'astonishing hesitancy and caution' – but by attrition. Montgomery outnumbered Rommel by 195,000 men to 104,000, and by 1,000 tanks to 489, and he lost more of both than his adversary. It was, nevertheless, a victory, the first of any consequence over German troops since 1918. It was well-timed; it came as the adult milk ration at home was being cut to 2.5 pints a week and the public – and Churchill – were desperate for a success. Montgomery, jaunty, prickly if crossed, no brasshat (he wore a beret), with a gift for handling men and for public relations, exploited it well.

The Germans were considerably more concerned with 'Bomber' Harris than with 'Monty'. North Africa was a sideshow compared with the destruction the RAF was visiting on their cities. 'We shall be coming every night, every day, rain, blow or snow,' Harris told them in a broadcast. The campaign was hugely expensive. A Lancaster cost £42,000 against the £6,000 for a Spitfire; each of its engines required the same manufacturing input as forty car engines. It cost £10,000 to train each of the five-man crew. Each bomber represented a total investment of £120,000 but, before any landings on Hitler's 'Fortress Europe', it was the only direct way for the islanders to get at their foe.

They carried 500-pound general purpose bombs, heavy steel cases with a small explosive charge, and then great 8,000-pound canisters, crude dustbin shapes without nose or tail fins, crammed with enough explosive to destroy a street. They mixed in containers packed with ninety sticks of magnesium to ignite anything flammable. Marker bombs came in reds, yellows and greens, and 'pink pansies', 4,000-pound bombs filled with benzol, rubber and phosphorus that burned with a pinkish flash visible for miles. Great effort went into marking a target but it was an illusion to think that a bomber stream up to ten miles broad and 4,000 or 6,000 feet thick could attack with precision at night; they bombed built-up areas and sometimes each other – a bomb from an aircraft above, one pilot recalled, 'went through the port wing and the engine started to fall out... another bomb must have gone between the cabin and the mid

upper gunner... I shouted to bail out and the plane began to fall.' Specialist units could pinpoint targets – 617 Squadron flew one of the most precise missions of the whole war when it breached the Moehne and Eder dams – but the big bomber fleets needed a large town to aim at.

It was a cruel and dangerous business. The aircraft were bitterly cold, the temperature falling 2.5 degrees Centigrade for every thousand feet of height; they vibrated continually and the unpowered controls were exhausting for the pilots. Some of the older aircraft could not get above 10,000 feet, where they were highly vulnerable to ground fire; even a Lancaster at 21,000 feet was a target for flak as well as night fighters.

The first thousand-bomber raid was made on Cologne on 31 May 1942. It was followed by ones on Essen and Bremen. Firestorms were created, where the heat from individual fires was so great that they sucked in air from around them to create a burning blanket with temperatures of 1,000 degrees Centigrade. During a thousand-bomber raid on Hamburg in July 1943, 'Trees three feet thick were broken off or uprooted, human beings were thrown to the ground or flung alive into the flames by winds which exceeded 150 miles an hour,' according to a secret German report. 'The fortunate were those who jumped into the canals and waterways and remained swimming or standing up to their necks for hours until the heat should die down.' Forty thousand were killed in a night, as many as in the whole Blitz. 'Terror, terror, terror,' a German commentator said. 'Pure, naked bloody terror.' Harris claimed that he would 'produce in Germany a state of devastation in which surrender is inevitable.' He failed; the Germans cracked under onslaught no more than had the British. It was said the German war effort would be wrecked. It was not; even in ruined Hamburg, production was back to normal within fifty days. In Germany as a whole, it increased; tank and aircraft production doubled in 1943.

**Waiting was the worst.** *An RAF station commander (left) catnaps in the small hours before counting his crews back as they return from night operations.*
[PHOTO: GEORGE RODGER]

**Yanks.** *British troops sang a sour little ditty about their better paid, better fed and better clothed American allies:*

*I've just returned to England from*
*    somewhere overseas*
*Instead of love and kisses, the girls*
*    give me the breeze;*
*Said they preferred the Yanks and*
*    gum,*
*A little jeep, a country run,*
*My good-time English sweetheart,*
*My faithless English rose.*

*The British were puzzled by the racial discrimination in the American forces. Like this girl at a dance in Lancashire (right), they got on well with black GIs. One of these, stationed in the West Country, wrote home: 'The more I see of the English, the more disgusted I am with Americans. After the war, with the eager and enthusiastic support of every negro who will have served in Europe, I shall start a movement to send white Americans back to England and bring the English to America.'*
[PHOTO: BERT HARDY]

'Men and women have been overwhelmed in a tornado of smoke and flame,' Dr George Bell, the Bishop of Chichester, said in the House of Lords after an 800-bomber raid on Berlin in February 1944. 'It is said that 74,000 persons were killed. The policy is obliteration openly acknowledged. This is not a justifiable act of war.' The statistic was inflated, but only for the moment. Harris ignored the bishop, but an uneasy national conscience, stirred by the near-obliteration of harmless Dresden in the last days of the war, was to deny him the peerage that should, by right, have rewarded so senior a figure and honoured the men who flew for him. 'The knife', the historian Angus Calder wrote, 'was blamed for the meat.' Harris's own

casualties were grievous. Between 18 November 1943 and 31 March 1944, 1,117 RAF bombers and their crews were lost over Germany; it was the equivalent to Bomber Command's entire front-line strength. Many aircrew were under twenty. In all, 46,000 of them were killed in the campaign against Germany. Of every 100 joining the squadrons, fifty-one died on operations, nine died in training and other crashes, three were badly wounded, twelve became prisoners and one evaded capture after being shot down. Only a quarter remained free and physically unscathed. By May 1944, when fifty aircrew who tunnelled their way out of the Sagan PoW camp in Silesia were shot by the Gestapo, air bombing was switching from

Germany to targets in France. The bomber crews operated over enemy territory; plans were advanced for a landing on it.

The British could not hope to land in France unaided, despite the Russian successes against German ground forces. The first Americans had arrived in London in April 1942, filling a small office block with staff. By mid-1944, they needed 2.5 million square feet. The streets around Grosvenor Square were a Little America, where the journalist Ernie Pyle reported, 'an Englishman stood out as incongruously as he would in North Platte, Nebraska'. The officers' mess was in the ballroom of the Grosvenor House hotel. Other ranks went to Rainbow Corner on Piccadilly Circus, which could seat and feed 2,000 at a time. Open twenty-four hours a day, its key was symbolically thrown away as it welcomed its first customers.

They were 'overpaid, oversexed and over here' (to which their retort was that the natives were 'underpaid, undersexed and under Eisenhower'). A private earned more than an RAF Flight Lieutenant; they could afford the best tables in restaurants, taxis made beelines for them; they had supplies of nylons and chewing gum. As to sex, they were blamed for a general decline in morals. Illegitimate births almost doubled during the war. In London, there were many deserters, living feral lives without ration books and outside the law, for whom theft was often a necessity. But the feeling of general immorality was not justified; as Philip Ziegler, the historian of wartime London, noted, there was no crime wave, merely a 'crime ripple'.

The Americans were not popular with Londoners, Mass Observation found; three quarters of Londoners liked the Dutch, two thirds the Czechs and half the Free French; they adored the Russians – the Red Flag flew over Selfridges store and Ivan Maisky was the most fashionable ambassador in town – but only a third liked the Yanks. Many of those were girls. Evelyn Waugh remarked on, 'Multitudes of drab, ill-favoured adolescent girls and their aunts and mothers, never before seen in the squares of Mayfair and Belgravia. There they passionately embrace [GIs], in the blackout and at high noon, and are rewarded with chewing-gum, razor blades and other rare trade goods.'

Londoners liked black GIs, however, who made up seven per cent of American forces in Britain; they said they found them better mannered and more pleasant than the whites. The friction between the two was soon clear. Restaurants and hotels turned blacks away for fear of losing white American custom. Learie Constantine, the great West Indian cricket all-rounder, was asked to leave the Imperial Hotel when white Americans threatened to cancel reservations. He sued. The judge fined the hotel £5.50 and deplored the technicality that prevented him from imposing a much stiffer sentence.

The average GI was paid three times more than his British counterpart. Cigarettes in the PX were a tenth of the price of those in the NAAFI; razor blades were cheaper and better; the Tommy had to pay for his tea and bun whereas the Americans got free coffee and donuts. The GIs were better dressed, so much so that Tommies at first mistook them for officers and saluted them. The two sides met mainly off-duty, in a pub or dance-hall where American spending and girl-pulling power were resented. Some 50,000 girls got engaged to or married

American servicemen, and it took six months to ship the 'GI brides' and their children to New York after the war.

For their part, the Americans found the British army class-ridden. They noted that even tanks showed up the class divide; the heavy, slow infantry tanks were the preserve of the more bourgeois Royal Tank Corps, where lighter tanks were with the dashing Royal Armoured Corps, ex-cavalry units officered by the 'most mentally inert, unprofessional and reactionary group in the British army'. One American was astonished to be warned in a British officers' mess that he must never mention girls, religion or money, on pain of buying drinks all round, which 'limits the discourse to polo, cricket, dogs and the war'. The British relied much more on NCOs, a separate caste, with their own mess and quarters, who did many things that officers did in the US army, in which almost half the men were noncoms.

The British flattered the Americans to their face but, behind their backs, did not think them martial. General Sir Harold Alexander, commanding all Allied troops in North Africa, wrote in secret that 'they simply do not know their job as soldiers, and this is the case from the highest to the lowest... a few bombs and they all go to ground and call for air support...' Harold Macmillan, British political adviser at Allied Force Headquarters, said to a new arrival: 'You will always permit your American colleague not only to have a superior rank to yourself and much higher pay, but also the feeling that he is running the show. This will enable you to run it yourself.' The

British thought themselves Greeks to American Romans. Montgomery, back in Britain to serve under General Eisenhower in the landings in France, was snide in his assessment of the American, most of whose career had been as a pen-pushing staff officer. Monty allowed that 'Ike' was 'a very nice chap. I should say he is probably quite good on the political side. But I can also say, quite definitely, that he knows nothing whatever about how to make war or to fight battles; he should be kept right away from all that business if we want to win the war.' Eisenhower kept his view of Montgomery to himself. 'God damn all British,' the less inhibited General Patton fumed, 'and all so-called Americans who have their legs pulled by them. I would rather be commanded by an Arab.'

Yet these tetchy allies were about to embark together on the largest and most complex amphibious assault in history. The Russians were so cynical about the claims that the Allies would open a 'second front' that they gave the name to their cans of American-supplied Spam, as if that was all they could expect of the capitalists. The British, tired of waiting, called it the 'Secondhand Front'. The tell-tales could hardly be hidden; there were 3.5 million men under arms in Britain in the spring of 1944, a million of them Americans. The south of England was a gigantic military camp. Shipping in Southampton was berthed eight abreast. In April, diplomats were no longer allowed to leave London and diplomatic bags were held up; only the Free French complained.

Paratroops dropped on Normandy on the night of 5 June. At dawn on 6 June, the first wave of 72,215 British and Canadians, and 57,000 Americans, landed on the beaches. D-Day was later described as 'the longest day', but a corporal in the Royal Hampshires described it with commendable brevity in his diary. 'Sea very rough,' G. E. Hughes wrote. 'Hit the beach at 7.20 hours. Murderous fire, losses high. I was lucky T God. Cleared three villages. Terrible fighting and ghastly sights.' The losses were severe, particularly among the Americans on Omaha beach; the British and Canadians had almost 4,000 casualties, the Americans 6,603. They held, however, and by the end of June 850,000 men and 150,000 vehicles had been landed in France.

Coincidentally with D-Day came V-bombs; V for *Vergeltungswaffe*, Reprisal Weapon. The V1 rocket had a ramjet that propelled it at up to 400 mph, its compass pre-set with the bearing for London, and a log to determine distance. When it had flown the required distance, the engine cut out. It left a small crater but its blast was deadly. One fell on the Guards Chapel close by Buckingham Palace during morning service, killing 119. In the first two weeks more than 1,700 were killed;

**Operation Overlord.** *The D-Day landing in Normandy on 6 June 1944 was the biggest amphibious assault in history. Royal Marine commandos wade ashore (left), whilst others clamber down (right) from their landing craft lugging a small motor scooter. The 72,000 British and Canadian troops outnumbered the Americans, and they were more fortunate in the beaches assigned to them.*

there was a second evacuation of children and mothers; a million left London. 'It was as impersonal as a plague,' Evelyn Waugh wrote of the assault, 'as though the city was infested with enormous, venomous insects.' Their measure was soon got – fighters patrolling over the Channel flipped their wings over or shot them down and anti-aircraft fire on the coast got the survivors – and their launch sites in France were overrun.

The U-boat war was won, British and Indian troops broke the siege of Imphal and started to drive the Japanese back into Burma; the 'dim out' replaced the blackout, the Home Guard was disbanded. It was, however, the Russians and the Americans who made the running in the final stages of the European war, and who picked up the trophy liberations and conquests – Rome, Paris, Budapest, Vienna, Berlin itself. The British made do with Brussels. They were involved in slogging and unglamorous fighting in the Low Countries, and in Italy, where the comic genius Spike Milligan heard the scraping shovels that marked a group of London Scottish burying their dead as a piper played the Skye Boat Song, a low-key affair, 'the men's groundsheets glistening in the half-light and the silhouette of the lone piper against the sky.'

Montgomery was criticised for the slow British break-out from Normandy, and the lack of the dash that saw the Americans reach German soil in September 1944. He gambled on a glider and airborne assault to bypass the Siegfried Line and to rip into Germany through Holland. It was a bold move to capture bridges over the Dutch rivers close to the German

**'They fought like lions'**, *the Germans said of the paras at Arnhem (right), and the British also praised German conduct. 'They allowed our doctors to go on working and to evacuate our wounded into their own hospital,' General Urquhart, the commander, told war correspondents.*

*The end was not in doubt. Less than a quarter of the 10,000 who took part escaped, in boats or by swimming across the Rhine; 1,200 were killed and the rest captured. Like Dieppe, another disaster, Arnhem entered the national legend; the British have a feeling for heroic failure.*

border; Montgomery claimed it could end the war by Christmas. British paratroops were to seize the furthest bridge, at Arnhem over the Rhine. The advance guard of the British 1st Airborne Division dropped safely west of Arnhem on the far side of the Rhine on 17 September; the rail bridge over the river was blown up, but they moved onto the northern end of the road bridge leading into the town. Press reports claimed the operation was 'going like clockwork'; it was not, though two other river crossings were secured, on the Maas and the Waal. The weather was bad, with driving rain that hampered air support.

The paratroopers had landed close to the headquarters of General Model, who commanded the defence of the town, and

there were two Panzer SS divisions in the area. The Germans had dug themselves in at the southern end of the bridge, with artillery and tank support; the men of the 2nd Parachute Battalion had none. For four days, they held their end of the bridge against furious assaults whilst a Guards division ran into heavy resistance as it tried to fight its way through to Arnhem from Nijmegen in the south. The Paras were overwhelmed. The rest of the division were battered within a shrinking perimeter west of the town. For the last three days they were without water and food; despite the courage of the pilots, supply drops landed in the German lines. Montgomery ordered them to withdraw across the mile-wide river on the night of

25 September. Only 2,400 of the ten thousand who took part in the operation got away in boats or by swimming across the river; 1,200 were killed and the rest captured.

Though the Allies now reverted to Eisenhower's broad-front strategy, Arnhem entered that part of the national heart reserved for gallant failures. The beaten men praised the victors for their humanity after they overran the main dressing station. The crew of a dug-in German tank allowed a medical orderly to pass their position to bring in a wounded man, asking him not to reveal their position. The Germans equally flattered their adversaries. 'The most highly qualified material we have encountered during the whole invasion battle,' a German war correspondent quoted officers and men of the unit he was with. The paratroops 'fought like lions against the ever tightening ring. Many groups which were split up fought on for five days without any supplies of food or ammunition. Towards the end they defended themselves with jack knives and pistols...'

A new rocket, the V2, gave Londoners a harsh reminder of the less gentlemanly war being waged over German cities. The V2 travelled at 3,600 mph reaching an altitude of 100,000 feet with a ton of amatol explosive in the nose, a mixture of TNT and ammonium nitrate. It came without warning since it travelled too fast for its engine to be heard. In eighty days, V2s killed 5,475 and destroyed 25,000 houses. On 25 November

many were lost in 1944 as in 1939, and the new year saw fresh outbreaks in the mines and engineering shops. 'We are – all of us, at the office, in the shops, and at home – weary of war and its effects,' Beardmore wrote. 'Intense cold has arrived with snow, ice, hail and sudden clashes of cold that go to make the illusion that we are on the Russian front. The V2 rockets also help the illusion. Even obtaining an everyday thing like soap has its problems, let alone the replacement of identity cards, ration books…'

The last rocket to be fired at Britain was shot down by gunners over the Suffolk coast on 27 March 1945. Victory was little more than a month away, but it was incomplete. The British were still fighting the Japanese in Burma; in May, the victory month, the bacon ration was cut from four ounces to three, confirmation of further hardships ahead; and they were aware, if dimly, that, in terms of the grandeur of nations, they had lost. The Russians had snapped the spine of the Wehrmacht, the Americans had made the invasion of Europe possible. For the first time in centuries, there were other powers in whose presence the British felt abashed.

Churchill was the symbol of their grandeur. When he stood for election, amid the victors' talks at Potsdam outside Berlin, it was assumed that he would win handsomely. George

**Cheering their hearts out,** *more than 3,000 British PoWs (main picture) rush from a German camp towards their American liberators in April 1945. Most were fit and well; they received Red Cross parcels and often had more luxuries – chocolate, jam, cigarettes – than their German guards, with whom in general they got on.*

*A horrifying contrast was revealed when British and Indian troops in Burma liberated a Japanese prison camp in Rangoon (below). The British PoWs were emaciated and listless, some too shocked to smile. They had no medical supplies and no food but rice; the guards treated them 'as animals'. Worse would be found before the Japanese war was won.*

one hit the Woolworth's store at New Cross in London, killing 160. 'Things were still falling out of the sky, bits of things and bits of people,' a girl said. 'A horse's head was lying in the gutter. There was a pram hood all twisted and bent and there was a little baby's hand still in its woollen sleeve… Where Woolworth's had been, there was nothing, just an enormous gap covered by clouds of dust. No building, just piles of rubble and bricks and underneath it all, people screaming.'

The boat-train service from London Victoria to the Continent resumed in January 1945 after a five-year break. Elation was mute, however; it was an ill-tempered time. More days were being lost to strikes than in peacetime; three times as

**VE Day.** *The celebrations of Victory in Europe in May 1945 were restrained and introspective. Some were cheerful enough (top), but the general mood was thoughtful (right). Terrible things had been discovered in the German concentration camps. The war in the Far East continued and evidence of Japanese atrocities was mounting. Rationing did not ease* *with the peace; it got worse, as the British now accepted responsibility for defeated Germans and Austrians, and prepared temporarily to administer the French and Dutch empires in Asia, as well as their own. They also had a guilty private secret; they were not going to re-elect Churchill, the man who had brought them through.*

[PHOTO, RIGHT: WOLF SUSCHITSKY]

Beardmore was not so sure. He heard two workmen, plumbers or gasmen, discussing the election campaign. One said: 'Don't want him again.' He gave the other a long look. 'Enough battles for one lifetime,' he replied. After a long pause and a sip of tea, the first man said: 'Bloody Russia', and gazed at a drop of tea on his donkey-jacket. The second man said: 'The old cock's just aching to wave us up and at 'em again,' to which the first man replied, having waited to see if the other was of the same opinion: 'Catch me.' They were talking about Churchill.

No more warriors, no glory; no more up and at 'em, whoever they were, Russians or Indian nationalists. Vote for the quiet life. A fundamental instinct was giving way.

## CHAPTER SEVEN

# 'MY CLASS IS ON THE UP AND YOURS IS ON THE DOWN'

**Soaking the rich.** *A couple in formal dress catch a post-war train at London's Waterloo Station for the races at Royal Ascot. The corporal gazes at them curiously, as if they are an endangered species. The Labour government, elected in the 1945 landslide, indeed seemed set on the 'euthanasia' of the rich. Surtax, the 'supertax' applied to large incomes, reached 97.5 per cent. The real income of the wealthiest 100,000 in the country fell by almost two thirds between 1938 and 1949. The tax increases – which hurt the middle classes as well as Ascot-going 'toffs' – were needed in part to pay the soldiers seen here; the new Cold War made immense demands on a country weakened and impoverished by the six-year struggle against Germany and Japan.*

*There was also, however, an air of triumphalism and social revenge as the Socialists set about nationalising industry and redistributing wealth. Aneurin Bevan, the Health Minister, bragged that his class – he was the son of a Welsh miner – was climbing, whereas that of the Tory grandee he was speaking to was 'on the down'. More notoriously, the Labour Attorney-General, Sir Hartley Shawcross, exulted in 1946 that: 'We are the masters now.' In fact, he said 'for the moment' rather than 'now'; since he added 'and not only for the moment but for a very long time to come', the misquotation had little effect on his meaning.*

[PHOTO: HENRI CARTIER-BRESSON]

A VIOLENT THUNDERSTORM GREETED VICTORY IN Europe, in symmetry with the one that had seen off the peace six years before. No guns or sirens challenged it, lest they reawaken recent fears; instead, church bells were pealed and tugboats on the Thames whistled the dot, dot, dot, dash of the 'V' sign. The royal family were bathed in cheers when they appeared on the balcony of Buckingham Palace. They had shared London's perils – 'the children won't leave without me,' the Queen had explained, 'I won't leave without the King, and the King will never leave' – and its shortages. When Eleanor Roosevelt stayed with them she found them eating the same meagre fare that could be found in any canteen.

When Churchill appeared, however, the applause deepened into a 'full-throated, almost reverential roar'. The crowds shouted affectionately his 'absurd little nurserymaid name' – 'Winnie, Winnie!' – and held babies high in the air to see him. Two happily drunk and dirty Cockneys, dancing in a slow shuffle 'like a couple of Shakespearean clowns', bellowed: 'That's 'im, that's 'is little old lovely bald 'ead!'

It was calculated that it would take at least a year to finish off Japan. The British and Indian troops of General Slim's 'Forgotten Army' had got no further than Rangoon, and the Australians were preparing to land on Borneo. Churchill had expected to remain in command until this unfinished business was completed, but a Labour party conference voted against any continuation of the coalition. An election was called for 5 July 1945.

The new-fangled opinion polls suggested a heavy Conservative defeat; such an act of lese-majesty against Churchill seemed impossible. The old warrior was out of sorts, however. He anticipated that the Red Army's conquest of eastern Europe could lead to fresh war, hot or cold; Labour resolutions calling for public ownership of 'the land, large-scale building, heavy industry and all forms of banking, transport and fuel and power' smacked to him of Bolshevism. His alarm showed. 'I declare to you from the bottom of my heart,' he said on radio, 'that no socialist system can be established without a political police.' He claimed that the Labour leadership, his ex-coalition colleagues, would 'fall back on some form of Gestapo, no doubt very humanely directed in the first instance…'

Churchill's fears ran counter to the mood of the country. Sweeping social change was in the air, better health services and education; the younger Tories accepted it; the troops felt it was what they had fought for. A Guards sergeant in Holland was astonished to find flush toilets and pleasant gardens in the houses of ordinary people. 'We owned two thirds of the world,'

he said, 'and we were worse off than them.' They knew that Clement Attlee, the Labour leader, dry and restrained, clipped in moustache and manner, was no secret policeman; it was said that if he declared a revolution it would sound no more than a 'change in the regional railway timetable'. The result, delayed for three weeks whilst the votes of far-flung servicemen were collected, was a Labour landslide. An unknown farmer took a quarter of the poll in Churchill's own seat, which Labour and the Liberals had declined to contest. His doctor found Churchill in deep gloom as the size of his defeat sank home, but he was interrupted when he started speaking of the people's ingratitude. 'Oh, no,' Churchill said. 'I wouldn't call it that. They have had a very hard time.'

Within three weeks, the nuclear strikes on Hiroshima and Nagasaki brought Japanese resistance to a sudden end. By 9 September, British troops were ashore in Malaya; three days later, Singapore was retaken without a fight. The new government had many deficits to offset this sudden bonus. British losses were much lower than in the Great War, 270,000 servicemen and merchant seamen, and 60,000 civilians, were killed together with 100,000 Canadians, Indians, Australians, New Zealanders and South Africans.

The material damage was far greater. Four million homes had been damaged, and 500,000 destroyed. Shipping losses, at 13.5 million tons, were equivalent to two thirds of the peacetime merchant fleet. The country had been beggared; the cost of the war was put at £28 billion. A third of the gold reserves and $4 billion in overseas assets had gone. Huge sterling and dollar debts had been run up. Direct taxation had increased threefold, and indirect by more than 150 per cent. The new American president, Harry Truman, clarified the brutal truth by unilaterally and unexpectedly ending Lease-Lend a week after the Japanese surrender. No more American imports would arrive without down payments in cash; Lord Keynes, still a Treasury adviser, called it a 'financial Dunkirk'. He was soon in Washington to negotiate a $3.75 billion loan. It came with strings; as proof of the new subservience to the Americans, the British had to undertake to make sterling convertible with the dollar by the summer of 1947.

Labour had inherited a near-bankrupt country, yet it was committed to high employment and a hugely expensive welfare system, and to extending State ownership to a fifth of the national economy. Simultaneously, the British reached the high water mark of their global responsibilities. They now administered almost a third of humanity. The empire was restored intact; to it was added temporary sway over the empire of others. British and Indian troops landed in Indo-China and secured Saigon. They used released Japanese prisoners to fight against Communist Viet Minh guerrillas set on preventing a French return to Vietnam. They played a similar part in Java and Sumatra, where resistance was mounting against the re-imposition of Dutch rule. The Mediterranean was more than ever a British lake; the North African coast and the Levant were subject to British arms, which also aided Greek royalists

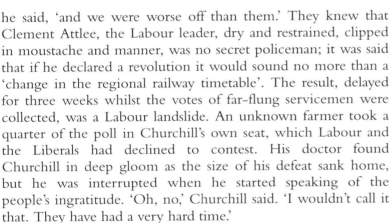

in their anti-Communist campaign. Southern Persia was occupied. The British shared, too, in the governing of Germany, Austria and Italy. The Royal Navy was at its historic peak with almost a thousand warships; the RAF disposed of 50,000 aircraft; for all that, the Americans were superior in the air and at sea, and the Russians on land.

'We are a great nation,' the government's chief scientific adviser, Sir Henry Tizard, warned, 'but if we continue to behave like a Great Power we shall soon cease to be a great nation.' The pleasures of peace were subsumed by the strain of socialising a weakened and over-extended country. The rich were savaged by death duties and a new 'surtax' that reached 97.5 per cent of income; the poor remained unhoused and all were subject to rationing more draconian than anything seen in the war. 'A bus conductor, two women and three schoolchildren, driven desperate for somewhere to live, camp out in a large dilapidated room without light, water and without fuel for a fire,' George Beardmore noted. 'Sullen and dirty faces swollen with colds, an orange-box scraped dry of all but coke-dust, two saucepans on an unmade bed, a spirit-stove on which bacon was frying, and a green teapot shaped like a racing-car on a strip of newspaper many times ringed…'

Such were the early spoils of war.

'We come from different classes,' the Labour firebrand Aneurin Bevan told a prominent Tory. 'My class is on the up and yours is on the down.' It seemed so, a war on capitalists, as the government nationalised in quick order the Bank of England, the mines, the railways, civil aviation, long-distance road transport and, at its last gasp, iron and steel. Bevan himself drove the medical profession and its unwilling hospital consultants into the National Health Service. With a florid, fleshy face to frighten the bourgeoisie, he was one of thirteen children brought up in a squalid terrace at Tredegar in Wales, a pit worker at thirteen and leader of the South Wales miners in the General Strike, searing in his oratory and in his contempt for Tories he labelled as 'lower than vermin'.

He was, however, the rough diamond in an altogether more genteel cabinet. The three ministers who led the assault on the 'commanding heights' of the economy had enjoyed the most classic of British upbringings, at public school and Oxbridge; the country was radicalised by, and with the tacit acceptance of, the middle class, not Bevan's workers. Clement Attlee, the prime minister, was quiet and prosaic, a product of the pleasant Thames-side suburb of Putney, typical of those middle-class socialists who had turned left out of moral conviction whilst working in the slums. He had served as a major, and been wounded, in the Great War. He was a vigorous reformer, but no Red; 'Little Clem' had no time for Soviet Russia.

In finance, the new Chancellor was an Eton and Cambridge man, easy meat for cries of 'class traitor'. Hugh Dalton was the son of a Canon of St George's Chapel at Windsor, a tutor to

**'She was poor'**, *the old song ran, 'but she was honest.' It applied, in general terms at least, to post-war Britain. The picture of the Salvation Army (right) in a Sunday city street catches a respectful innocence. Black marketeers – 'spivs' in back-formation slang from 'VIPs' – flourished; crime was otherwise low, crimes of violence negligible.*

*His policies might be radical, but Clement Attlee (far left), the Labour premier, was no Red; seen adjusting a cold frame, he was that most patient and reassuring of national symbols, the amateur gardener. The Foreign Secretary, Ernest Bevin (left), was the orphaned son of a Somerset farm labourer, put to work as a carter's boy at eleven; this harsh background strengthened the former union leader's contempt for extremists. 'Molotov, Stalin,' he said of the Soviet leadership, 'they are evil men.' He faced them down over the Berlin blockade, and helped lock the Americans into Western Europe through Nato. At home he brooked no appeasers.*

[PHOTOS, LEFT: FELIX MANN]

[PHOTO, RIGHT: BERT HARDY]

barrister in the country. He was married to an Eno's Fruit Salts heiress – ironically he suffered chronic stomach ailments – and had made a fortune from patent law. When he helped to squeeze the rich, he squeezed himself. Before the war, he had founded the far-left paper *Tribune*, and had shouted so stridently for a Popular Front with the Communists that the Labour mainstream expelled him. With his small rimless glasses, erect and primly puritan, existing on nut cutlets and carrot juice, he seemed more than a mere disciple of the austerity he preached. 'There but for the grace of God goes God,' Churchill muttered, whilst a Tory MP in heated debate warned him not to 'shake his halo at me'.

They were clever men, but they had no experience of high finance and business. A City friend of Dalton found himself trying to explain the function of the Stock Exchange and Government securities to the new Chancellor. 'Here was one of the big men in the Labour party taking up high office,' he wrote, 'who seemed utterly ignorant of the workings of the monetary system.' As he was being driven to London for his first day at the Treasury, Dalton bragged that he would 'press the button for my new slaves' and tell them 'to put my ideas into practice'; his friend thought that the slaves would soon enough become his masters.

The reforms came thick and fast through Labour's first post-war term. Family allowances, of five shillings a week for the second and every subsequent child, had been introduced in the dying days of the Churchill administration; they were joined now by free school dinners and milk. The school leaving age was raised to fifteen. The first comprehensive schools were opened, catering for secondary-age pupils, regardless of age and ability, in an attempt to prevent brighter children being streamed into grammar schools when they passed the 'Eleven Plus' exam. The hated 'means test' was dropped from new unemployment and sickness benefits; contributions were still made by employees, employers and the State, but direct taxation was used to ensure that the benefits were universally available irrespective of previous contributions or personal savings. Free legal aid was provided in and out of court. The larger local authorities were required to prepare development plans and were given compulsory purchase powers for slum clearance and new housing. Almost a tenth of England and Wales was scheduled to become protected national parks.

Farmers were guaranteed minimum prices. Coal, electricity, gas and water were transferred to State ownership; a transport commission was set up to integrate the nationalised railways

the future George V. Dalton inherited his father's domineering manner and moral aloofness, his voice booming through the Treasury. He had been a wartime head of special operations, charged with bringing death and destruction to Nazi-occupied Europe; he now turned his interest to 'reactionaries, the elderly and the rich...'

The industrial overlord at the Board of Trade, and minister of economic affairs, Stafford Cripps, was the son of a Tory MP, a turncoat lawyer who had served in the Labour governments of 1924 and 1929 and who had been ennobled for his pains. Cripps had passed through Winchester and Oxford; after a first career as a research chemist, he had become the youngest

**The 'commanding heights'** *of the economy – the mines, steel, railways, power, long-distance trucking, civil aviation – were nationalised. The steel industry, like this Welsh works (below) at Port Talbot, became a political football with the Conservatives committed to reprivatising it. The coal industry, with the pit winding gear seen here (right) in the Rhondda Valley in South Wales, was run down and as much a liability as an asset. The miners, seen here celebrating at the Durham Miners' Gala (far right), remained a breed apart; with the dockers, they were the most militant group in the country and their relations with the National Coal Board were little better than they had been with the colliery owners.*

[PHOTOS: WOLF SUSCHITSKY]

and the long-distance road haulage of almost 4,000 trucking businesses. There was, to the anger of the Labour left, no question of worker control. Cripps said that, 'even if it were on the whole desirable', which he much doubted, the workforce was incapable of managing large concerns. The new captains of big industry were public servants, in theory non-partisan technocrats; in practice, they were more detached and Olympian than the privateers they replaced.

Nationalisation – Attlee preferred 'socialisation' – was a costly and complex affair. Shareholders had to be bought out of companies that were suffering from the wartime years of neglect and under-investment. With the railways came tracts of urban wasteland, the great ports of Southampton and Hull, decrepit railway hotels and the old imperial travel agents, Thomas Cook. Coal was a giant industry; the country was almost entirely dependent upon it for locomotion, electricity generation and gas, and domestic heat and cooking. Private

companies owned entire pit villages, cokeing ovens, railway spurs, wagons, barges, depots, farms and forests.

The rise in taxation needed to fund the programmes fell heavily on the very rich. The real incomes of the top 100,000 people fell by sixty-four per cent between 1938 and 1949, and that of the top half million by more than a third. Whilst they lived, the rich were subject to rates that left them with tenpence from a pre-tax pound, and when they died their estates and art collections were sold off to pay death duties. The middle classes were hard hit, too; their post-tax real incomes fell by seven per cent in the first years of peace, whilst those of the working class rose by nine per cent. Some Labour politicians had a confiscatory mindset, talking of bringing about a 'euthanasia of the rentier' with low interest rates. Those with unearned incomes, however, refused to buy 'Daltons', the 2.5 per cent Government stock of 1946–7, at anything approaching par, and it had to be dumped at a big discount.

Dollar shortages and enforced austerity affected the country at large. At the end of the war, the weekly ration stood at eight ounces each of sugar and fats, four ounces each of jam and bacon, three ounces of chocolate and sweets, two ounces each of tea and cheese, two pints of milk and one egg. In February 1946, the fats ration was cut. That May, bread was rationed for the first time; adults were restricted to nine ounces a week. It had been avoided in both wars; now, ironically, it was brought in so that the British could feed the 22 million Germans whom they were governing in the British Zone.

The worst year was 1947. On New Year's Day, large notices appeared outside every pit confirming that 'this colliery is now managed by the National Coal Board on behalf of the people'. Cabinet ministers met at the Board's headquarters to celebrate the realisation of an old dream. It was a disastrous start. A high-pressure area brought northeasterly winds from Siberia and the coldest winter in living memory. Kew Observatory recorded no sunshine whatever between 2 and 22 February. Old machinery and strike-happy miners had already lowered production; what coal was cut remained blocked by snowdrifts at the pithead. The Thames froze. Big Ben was silenced, its machinery frozen. Colliers with fuel for London were icebound in the northeastern ports. Emergency food and fodder for animals was airdropped by RAF transports. Unemployment quadrupled to almost two million in a few weeks as power cuts and empty furnaces brought industries to a halt.

Demobbed servicemen found 'nothing but queues and restrictions and forms and shortages and no food and cold...' They wished themselves anywhere but Britain; there were long queues outside Australia House and many sailed for Canada and New Zealand. Some 50,000 GI brides had already left for New York to join their husbands; a similar number of men now quit for Southern Rhodesia. After the freeze, in mid-March, came the thaw and floods. The Thames was three miles wide at Chertsey; floodwater contaminated London reservoirs.

In July, Princess Elizabeth became engaged to Lieutenant Philip Mountbatten. They married in November. In between, newspapers were reduced to as few as six pages to save on imported newsprint. Perhaps it was as well; they had little cheerful to report. The meat ration was cut further and the bacon ration halved. A seventy-five per cent levy was slapped on Hollywood films to save dollars. The basic petrol ration was abolished; taking the car out for a spin was forbidden. The foreign travel allowance went too, so that the British, having liberated the Continent, were unable to visit it on holiday. The convertibility of sterling, the price of the American loan, led to a run on the pound and was suspended. On 15 August, the British Raj ceased to rule and independent India was partitioned. South Yorkshire miners went on strike. An emergency budget increased profits taxes, sales tax and the duty on alcohol. Two slaps were given to the memory of Walter Raleigh, the colonising ex-favourite of the Princess's great namesake, Queen Elizabeth. Imports of American tobacco, which he had first made from Virginia, were suspended. Potatoes, another Raleigh discovery, went on ration.

There were, however, silver linings in these damp clouds. The royal wedding drew great crowds. The bride, escorted by the scarlet-and-blue Household Cavalry, arrived in an ivory dress with flowers of beads and pearls. Unable to leave the sterling area, the newlyweds left for a honeymoon in Hampshire. The groom was given the dukedom of Edinburgh.

Flagship of the welfare state, the National Health Service proved immensely popular. Free medical care was offered to all on the basis of need rather than the ability to pay. Drugs were prescribed free, and there was no charge for spectacles or dental work. Bevan, lisping in his flowing Welsh accent, fought a bitter battle with the medical establishment. To win it, he 'stuffed the consultants' mouths with gold', allowing

**Love lost.** *Princess Margaret fell in love with her father's air equerry, the Battle of Britain fighter pilot Peter Townsend. He is seen here (far left) in the front of the car during the royal tour of South Africa in 1947. The princess, then seventeen, sits next to her sister Elizabeth, with the King and Queen behind them. Townsend was divorced and in 1955, 'mindful of the Church's teaching that Christian marriage is indissoluble', the princess announced that the romance was at an end. Her eyes show her sadness as she returns to London (left) after a final country weekend at which Townsend was present.*

[PHOTO, FAR LEFT: IAN LLOYD]
[PHOTO, LEFT: DEREK BERWIN]

**Love won.** *Princess Elizabeth arrives with her father at Westminster Abbey (right) in 1947 for her marriage to her third cousin, Lieutenant Philip Mountbatten. It was the high point of a grim year. The winter was the worst since 1881; rationing was more severe than during the war. The foreign travel allowance was abolished to save currency, and the future Queen spent her honeymoon in Hampshire.*

[PHOTO, RIGHT: BERT HARDY]

**Richard Burton** *was a coming star. He made his stage reputation in Christopher Fry's* The Lady's Not for Burning *in 1949. It was a Broadway success; in 1952 he received the first of seven Academy Award nominations for his first Hollywood film,* My Cousin Rachel. *He is seen (left) walking with his coalminer father in Pontrhydfen, his Welsh birthplace. Elizabeth Taylor, to whom he was twice married, was emerging from child stardom to play adult roles.*
[Photo: Raymond Kleboe]

them to maintain pay beds in hospitals now taken over by the State. The NHS became one of the world's largest employers overnight; it required a vast and shambling bureaucracy, and costs escalated far beyond the most pessimistic forecasts; but it was the high point of post-war idealism and the people loved it.

Medicine was now free; little could be spent on food, and many luxuries were for export only; more than ninety per cent of cars were sold abroad. There was plenty of spare cash. The cinema reached its zenith, with 1,600 million tickets sold a year; many went three or four times a week to escape from austerity. Laurence Olivier's *Hamlet* won four Academy Awards; it was the first British film to win an Oscar for best movie, and Olivier was best actor. 'Ealing Comedy' became a genre. British stars, James Mason and Stewart Granger, Vivien Leigh and Margaret Lockwood, flourished.

All sports thrived. Denis Compton, the 'Brylcreem Boy', made 3,816 runs in the hot summer of 1947; there was 'no rationing in an innings by Compton,' the reporters wrote. He was a footballer, too, attracting crowds of 60,000 to the Arsenal ground. Forty million went through the turnstiles each year; in a non-violent, pre-hooligan age, they passed youngsters from hand to hand over their heads to the front. Speedway and pigeon racing flourished.

If foreign travel was barred, Billy Butlin's holiday camps boomed at home. He had built three of them during the war; the government paid part of the cost and used them as barracks for the duration. With peace, he got them back at bargain price and had no difficulty filling them. He had half a million customers in the summer of 1947, the campers handing in their ration books at the start of the week for his chefs to clip for them. Butlin was a great showman, staging opera and Shakespeare in the camps. The Arts Council was founded as part of this cultural idealism. It helped to fund new festivals at Aldeburgh, Cheltenham and Edinburgh and supported the opera at Covent Garden, the Old Vic, the big orchestras and the main provincial theatres.

**Escape from austerity.** *Knighted in 1947, Sir Laurence Olivier and his wife Vivien Leigh (right) were international stars, along with Stewart Granger, Huddersfield-born James Mason and Bristol's Cary Grant. The first international arts festival had been launched in Edinburgh in 1947, under Rudolf Bing. The cinema enjoyed a final pre-television boom, selling more than 1,500 million tickets a year. Olivier's* Hamlet *was the first British movie to win an Oscar for best film. Another British entry, the ballet drama* The Red Shoes, *won two more awards. Three classic 'Ealing comedies' were also made,* Passport to Pimlico, Whisky Galore! *and* Kind Hearts and Coronets, *starring Alec Guinness.*
[Photo: Graham Hales]

**Peers of the realm** *arrive at the House of Lords next to Westminster Abbey (opposite) for the coronation in 1953. The new Queen Elizabeth II posed for a ceremonial portrait by Cecil Beaton (left). Prince Charles (above), the new heir to the throne, looks unimpressed by pomp and circumstance as he holds his head next to his grandmother. In the second row, his other grandmother Princess Alice of Battenberg, the mother of Prince Philip, strikes an austere note among the glitter in her religious habit. The ceremonies were among the first great events of live television, a medium the House of Windsor would come to know all too well.*

[PHOTO, LEFT: CECIL BEATON]
[PHOTO, FAR LEFT: HARRY TODD]
[PHOTO, ABOVE: REG SPELLER]

219

**A glimpse of stocking.** *Nylons were the vogue (right), still rare in 1951 and eagerly tracked down. Christian Dior (left) launched his New Look spring collection in Paris in 1948 to immediate cross-Channel acclaim. Stockings were highlighted, either continuing the colour scheme of the dress from hem to ankle, or in contrast to it. The Secretary of the Housewives' League remembered, 'there was Christian Dior, lowering the hemlines almost to the ankle with enormously full skirts and little slim tops... and nothing that we had in the cupboard was any longer in fashion and an awful lot of us said, "Oh we can't afford it, and we can't buy it", but of course we did.'*
[PHOTO, RIGHT: ERNST HAAS]

Drab 'utility' dresses were replaced by Christian Dior's New Look. The hemline was lowered to the ankle with full skirts. The government disapproved; the skirts used too much scarce material and the hour-glass shape was held to promote immorality. The House of Lords was warned of a 'tidal wave of divorce' sweeping the country, reaching ten times the pre-war level. Many were of hasty wartime marriages, and the birth rate was sharply up in the 'baby boom', but the flood rattled Church leaders and the government increased its aid to the Marriage Guidance Council. For all that, it was an innocent and well-behaved era, soberly hatted and mackintoshed; there was little crime other than the black market, where 'spivs' sold bootleg petrol, nylons and perfume.

India was a prodigious loss. It took with it 1.5 million square miles of territory, and two thirds of the population of Empire, antagonistically divided between 225 million Hindus, almost 100 million Muslims, and 6 million apiece of Sikhs and Indian Christians. The country was already effectively Indian-run. The Viceroy, Field Marshal Wavell, had barely a thousand British administrators; he was almost entirely dependent on Indian officials. Attlee recognised that it could only be held by consent, and that had been withdrawn. Gandhi and Jawaharlal Nehru had run a vigorous 'Quit India' campaign during the war and had been arrested for their pains. Scores of post offices and police stations were attacked, with policemen burned alive inside them. A mutiny broke out aboard a Royal Indian Navy frigate early in 1946; the crew claimed that their British captain called them 'black buggers' and 'jungli Indians'. It spread to other RIN ships in Bombay before British and Mahratha troops put it down, but 223 were killed.

Wavell was a sensitive and cultured soldier, who had published a fine anthology of poetry, but Gandhi's charm made little impression on him. He found him 'a shrewd, obstinate, domineering, double-tongued, single-minded politician... an

the Viceroy, Nehru and Jinnah in December 1946 failed. Attlee lost patience with Wavell, finding him a 'curious, silent bird'. He replaced him in February 1947 with Lord Louis Mountbatten, the King's cousin and the dashing ex-destroyer captain who had accepted the Japanese surrender at Singapore.

Opinions of Mountbatten were mixed. The anglophobe American general 'Vinegar Joe' Stilwell called him 'the Glamour Boy… childish Louis, publicity crazy… fatuous ass.' Attlee thought him 'an extremely lively, exciting personality. He had an extraordinary capacity for getting on with people.' He added that he 'was also blessed with an unusual wife'; so unusual indeed, that she was rumoured to have had an affair with Nehru. Edwina Mountbatten spoke later of her feelings for Nehru and 'the strange relationship – most of it spiritual – that exists between us.' It was the non-spiritual part that intrigued the gossips. Mountbatten took little time to decide that partition was inevitable, and to bring forward the date of independence from mid-1948 to mid-August 1947. The killings urged speed. The two sides took to sending trains to each other full of the dead and dying. 'You could see them coming with fly swarms around them,' the BBC's Wynford Vaughan Thomas reported. 'And when the bodies were taken out and laid down, there would be about two thousand a time.'

In the final days, Sir Cyril Radcliffe, lawyer and

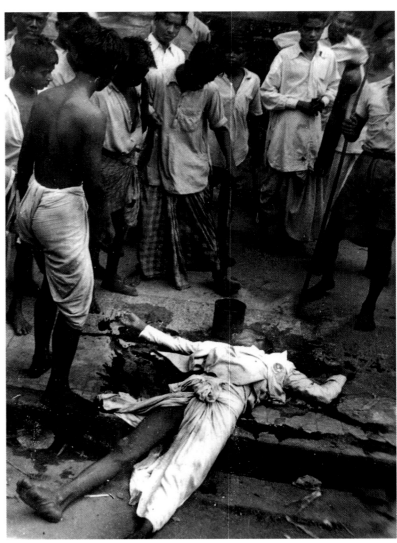

unscrupulous old hypocrite.' Mohammed Jinnah, the Muslim leader, and the Hindu pair of Gandhi and Nehru were products of Empire; all three were London-trained lawyers and Nehru had been at Harrow, Churchill's old school. It did not prevent their talks from breaking up in acrimony. 'The two great mountains have met and not even a ridiculous mouse has emerged,' Wavell complained. The only practical way to resolve Hindu-Muslim tensions, he concluded, was to divide the country into two sovereign parts, Hindustan and Pakistan.

In August, Muslim goondas, hooligans, ran amok in Calcutta. The looting and burning spread from the slums on the Hooghli river to the residential districts. The mobs opened the fire hydrants to impede the firemen, and dumped bodies at cross-roads to force army patrols to halt. Exhausted men of the York and Lancaster Regiment found the city centre looking as if 'an armoured division had swept through on the tail of a heavy bombardment.' Control was regained after two days, as British troops in gas clothing and masks worked to cleanse Calcutta of its shame, but Hindus fleeing to the countryside inflamed their co-religionists to embark upon the 'Bihar butchery' in which seven thousand Muslims were slaughtered.

Nehru was sworn in as the head of an interim government, accusing Wavell of divide and rule tactics. The Viceroy retorted that he was trying to 'unite and quit': the British had the responsibility and no power, whereas the Indians 'have the power but little or no responsibility.' Fresh talks held between

**Farewell to the Raj.** *India was the first British withdrawal from Empire, and incomparably the bloodiest, preceded by Hindu-Muslim massacres. In Calcutta, Muslims ran amok in 1946 and murdered more than 3,000 Hindus (below) before British troops restored order (left). The country was partitioned into India and Muslim Pakistan at independence in 1947. Lady Edwina Mountbatten, wife of Lord Mountbatten, the last Viceroy, bids adieu (right) to British India, and her friend Pandit Nehru, the new prime minister, with 7,000 guests in Delhi. Nehru had been given a biography of the Italian patriot Garibaldi when at school at Harrow in England in 1906. Here were the fruits of his reading. He had reason to look pensive.*

administrator, poring over maps and census returns in the Viceregal estate in Delhi, drew the distant boundaries of the two new states he was inventing. It was a thankless task. He had to decide, for example, into which country Calcutta would fall. The majority of the population were Hindu, but Muslim East Bengal was dependent on its jute mills and shipping; without it, the Muslims argued, they would become a 'rural slum'. Calcutta went to India; East Bengal, now Bangladesh, indeed slumped into squalor. General Ismay, who had joined the Indian Army forty years before, struggled sadly to dissect a 'living entity with one brain, one heart, one set of organs.' He carved apart the armed forces, the national debt, the railway rolling stock, old all-India associations like the Kennel Club.

Jinnah flew from Delhi to Karachi, his new capital, aboard the silver Viceregal Dakota on 7 August. 'I never expected to see Pakistan in my lifetime,' he said on his arrival. Mountbatten flew to Karachi on 13 August to wish Pakistan well. As he returned on 14 August high over the Punjab there were fires everywhere beneath his aircraft; they were not lit in celebration, but marks of atrocities. Below him, Sikhs and Hindus were fleeing east, and Muslims westward. The Hindus fleeing Lahore were so densely packed in the station that segments of the crowd fell onto the track, like icebergs calving from a glacier; when a train arrived, they squeezed through the doors and windows and onto the roof. As one pulled away, it reminded one RAF officer of a serpent covered with lice.

'At the stroke of the midnight hour,' Nehru said of the night of 14/15 August, 'when all the world sleeps, India will awake to a life of freedom!' He had spent nine years in prison to achieve it. On 15 August, Mountbatten, no longer Viceroy, was sworn in as Governor-General. In the evening, the Union Jack was lowered at Lucknow; it had flown since the Mutiny, a memorial to the two million British who had died in India over the centuries. British officers hauled it down, severing the flagpole at its base, and drank a last traditional toast: 'To the King-Emperor and the Sepoy'. A rainbow soared over Delhi, green, white and saffron, matching the new Indian flag.

The ex-Emperor of India 'took it without a murmur,' Attlee said. 'You can't imagine old Queen Victoria sacrificing the Imperial Crown without a struggle, not a bit of it. But George VI didn't mind at all.' He was no longer GRI, Georgius Rex Imperator. 'The first time he wrote me a letter with the I for Emperor of India left out,' his mother, Queen Mary, wrote, 'I felt very sad.' The King spent the day happily enough, shooting grouse on his Scottish estate at Balmoral.

In Calcutta, a crowd invaded Government House, breaking furniture, slashing Queen Victoria's picture, and making off with much of the silver. An RAF corporal watched Indians rip the fittings from his railway compartment: 'They're ours now,' they explained. Indian society made merry in Delhi's Government House, whilst mass murder took place at Connaught Circle nearby. In Amritsar, Sikhs celebrated by

rounding up Muslim girls and raping them. Muslims in Lahore fired a Sikh temple with the congregation inside. During the next nine months, some 14 million people – Sikh, Muslim, Hindu – were driven from their homes and hundreds of thousands were murdered. 'All the King's horses and all the King's men,' the former Governor of the Punjab, Evan Jenkins, said, 'could not have prevented communal violence in villages so widely scattered across the country…' The last British troops left to the strains of Auld Lang Syne at the beginning of 1948. By the end of the month, Gandhi had been murdered.

Some found the hasty handover unseemly. 'Do you mean that, after beating the Germans and the Japanese,' an astonished Pathan tribesman on the North West Frontier asked a British officer, 'you're going to be chased out of India by Hindu lawyers?' To Churchill, it had 'the taint and smear of shame'. He thought it 'appalling. "Scuttle" is the only word which applies.'

There was further scuttling in Palestine, where the British were caught between other Muslims, Arabs, and Jews. The Arabs objected that, since the arrival of the British in Jerusalem in 1917, the Jews had by immigration both legal and clandestine increased their share of the population from seven per cent to a third. Three tenths of the land was now Jewish-owned instead of one per cent. The self-effacing request to the British for a spiritual home had escalated into a demand for a Jewish state. During the war, Haj Amin, the Mufti of Jerusalem, had raised a Muslim Army of Liberation to fight Jews and British with Nazi help, whose main unit was an SS division, the 13th Handschar, recruited in Bosnia and wearing the SS Death Head emblems

on their fezes. For their part, Jewish terrorists had shot dead Lord Moyne, the Minister of State in Cairo and a personal friend of Churchill.

The Americans supported the Jews, though at a distance. 'We want to let as many as possible of the Jews into Palestine,' Truman said, adding: 'I have no desire to send 500,000 American soldiers there to make peace…' That task fell on the exhausted British. Jewish attacks on them multiplied, the Haganah radio calling them 'unclean sons of Titus' and their rule 'the Nazi-British regime'. This was centred in the King David Hotel in Jerusalem, whose kitchens Irgun terrorists dressed as Arabs entered with milk churns filled with explosives. Ninety-one were killed. 'If we had not stood alone against Hitler,' the Archbishop of York pointed out, 'there would be no Jews in Palestine or anywhere else.' Ernest Bevin, the foreign secretary, was personally incensed. 'I do not want any Jews killed either,' he told the Jewish leader Chaim Weizmann, 'but I love the British soldiers. They belong to my class. They are working people.' Terrorists sent him a letter bomb.

By the beginning of 1947, Irgun and the Stern Gang had murdered more than 350 people. The British evacuated their women and children from Palestine to Egypt; the Jews jeered at them, the Arabs threw stones. 'Nobody loved us any more,' one woman concluded. Officials and troops moved into special security zones, nicknamed 'Bevingrads'. A soldier wrote home to Lancashire: 'Dear Mum, I am in Bethlehem where Christ was born, but I wish to Christ I was in Wigan, where I was born…' Menachem Begin, later an Israeli prime minister, ordered the abduction of two young sergeants when three of his men were sentenced to death. A few days later, the *Exodus*, a ship crammed with 4,500 would-be illegal immigrants, was intercepted and turned back by the Royal Navy. The Irgun men were hanged; the following day the British sergeants were strangled and then hanged from a eucalyptus tree with mines sown around it. There were anti-Jewish riots in Liverpool, Manchester and Glasgow.

Security forces of 80,000 troops and 20,000 police were not enough. Bevin, massive, slouching, exhausted, half-carried into meetings, taking amyl nitrate for his failing heart, complained that 'everyone is kicking us around'. To the Jewish diplomat Abba Eban he seemed to symbolise 'the policy of a tired nation, weary of responsibilities beyond its power'. Attlee agreed that 'it was no longer any good our holding the baby'; handing the problem to the United Nations, he ordered a withdrawal. Almost a million 'protected people' of the British King were soon Palestinian refugees from the new state of Israel.

Not all the imperial peoples wished to turn their back on Britain. In June 1948, as the last British soldiers were quitting Palestine, the old troopship *Empire Windrush* moored on the Thames with 510 would-be immigrants from Jamaica aboard. They were not allowed ashore. The British Nationality Act was passing through parliament, however; under it, the citizens of any colony qualified as British subjects and were entitled to British passports. A Colonial Office spokesman described the 'unorganised rush' of Caribbean immigrants as a 'disaster', but little could be done. 'These people have British passports and they must be allowed to land,' the Colonial Secretary, Arthur Creech Jones, said. There was nothing to worry about, he added, 'because they won't last one winter in England.' But they did, the first of successive waves of coloured immigrants from the West Indies and, later, India and Pakistan. They were temporarily housed in a large air raid shelter on Clapham Common; from there they moved into houses in nearby Brixton, which became the core of Caribbean settlement in London.

Neither did the British themselves give up on Empire. Far from it; Bevin was as imperialist as Churchill. He was anxious to develop British Africa, for its men and minerals and food potential, and the Middle East for its oil. Attlee toyed with the idea of using Africa to replace India as a reservoir of imperial troops. He asked the Chief of the Imperial General Staff, Viscount Slim, how long it would take to create an African force of similar size and quality to the Indian army; Slim thought at least twenty years. The Colonial service expanded; where it had recruited seventy in 1932, in 1945 it took 1,700. They felt themselves an elite; where everyone else 'was chasing tea-leaves, in the Colonial Office you dealt with every aspect of government, no matter what it was, all over the world.' Their

**'Nobody loved us anymore.'**
*The British were caught between Arab and Jew in Palestine. Jewish terrorists bombed the King David Hotel in Jerusalem, the Army headquarters for Palestine, in July 1946. British soldiers are carrying a victim out of the hotel (left). The calculation that the British would weary of their United Nations mandate was correct. Outrage was followed two years later by withdrawal and the creation of the state of Israel.*

**The human traffic** *of Empire reversed. As the British returned home from overseas, they were joined in their islands by former colonial subjects. These West Indians (right) in London's Soho district were pioneers.*

[PHOTO: BERT HARDY]

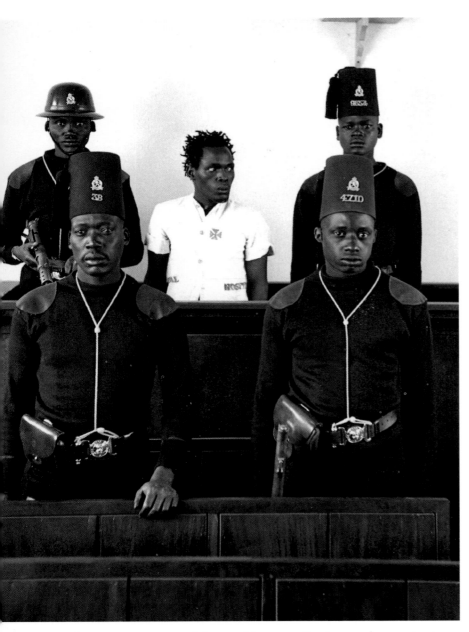

**'General China',** *the captured Mau Mau leader, faces trial in the courthouse at Nyeri in Kenya (left). Between 1952 and 1956, more than 11,000 Kikuyu Mau Mau were killed; the guerrilla movement was largely based on the tribe. The forces were continuously engaged in combat, large-scale in Korea, counter-terrorist in Malaya, Cyprus, Kenya, Aden.*

**A wounded** *Special Air Service soldier is carried through the Malayan jungle (right) for helicopter evacuation in 1953. In a long campaign, key to Asian stability, the British beat Communist insurgents. The price of all this was compulsory military service and forces that did not drop below 750,000 until 1957.*

[PHOTO, LEFT: GEORGE RODGER]

autobahns; a prodigious Anglo-American airlift got underway. The shape of the Cold War was confirmed in 1949. Bevin succeeded in locking the United States into Europe through NATO. A Federal Republic was established in West Germany and the Berlin blockade was broken.

With equal and less happy implications, the British chose to keep their distance from the Continent. Jean Monnet, the French 'father of Europe', was keen for close alliance with London. In three days of talks with Sir Edwin Plowden, a senior official, at his farmhouse near Rambouillet in April 1949, it was made clear to him that London 'had no desire to commit itself, however loosely, to an economic relationship which might have led to a closer union with France, or indeed, any other country...' The lion was tiring, a lion in winter, but it still roared alone. Monnet was saddened; his attempt to form a core around which a European Community might one day be formed met 'no response from the one great power in Europe which was then in a position to take on such a responsibility.' The French turned to Germany.

The British still thought of themselves as a great power, Plowden explained, standing between the US and the USSR. 'We'd kept out of Europe for centuries,' he said, 'and had no desire to join it in its down and out condition.' Grandeur came expensive, in lives and cash. In the Far East, British troops were fighting Communists in Korea and Malaya. Defence spending soared to more than ten per cent of national output. The new Chancellor, Hugh Gaitskell, piled up taxation to pay for it; the standard rate of income tax climbed to 47.5 per cent and surtax reached almost the 100 per cent mark. The political flashpoint was not this soaking of the rich, but his decision to charge for spectacles and false teeth. Aneurin Bevan resigned, enraged that the spell of a wholly free Health Service had been broken, and by another 'socialist' product of Winchester and Oxford at that.

Resources were poured into a programme to develop nuclear weapons, under the 'atomic knights', Penney, Hinton and Cockroft, for Attlee was concerned lest the Americans retreat into isolation. Though British scientific input had been vital to the development of their bomb, the Americans offered little cooperation. British intelligence had failed to detect the atom spy Klaus Fuchs, German-born but naturalised British, who had been passing secrets to Russians. He was arrested in 1950 only after an FBI tip-off. The same year, two diplomats who had served in sensitive posts in Washington disappeared. Donald Maclean and Guy Burgess defected to Russia, leaving behind them Kim Philby, a third and as yet undetected Soviet agent.

dreams were grand but seldom realised; a scheme to turn Tanganyika into a British larder with a gigantic groundnut scheme was a costly fiasco. The Colonial Secretary complained that Bevin 'thinks you develop Africa by putting Africans in lorries and letting them drive into the bush.'

Bevin needed no lessons from Churchill on the Soviet threat. 'Molotov, Stalin, they are evil men,' he said, and acted on it; Bevin, his nose jutting in an unmistakeable triangle of flesh beyond his horn-rimmed spectacles, was one of the great breakwaters on which Red aspirations in the West were dashed. As Communists overthrew democracy in Czechoslovakia, the Americans sent sixty Superfortresses to Britain to warn off the Russians. There was no formal agreement. 'We were just told to come over and "we shall be pleased to see you",' an American general said in astonishment. A permanent American presence was established, and it was soon to be nuclear. Stalin blockaded land routes to Berlin; if he was not challenged there, the British urged the Americans, the Allies would ultimately be driven from Germany. An RAF officer had the idea of supplying West Berlin entirely by air to avoid clashes on the railways and

'This is no time for despondency,' the King said in 1951 as he opened the Festival of Britain, a fantasy world built on twenty-seven acres of cleared bombsites in London. It was dominated by a Disney-like 'Dome of Discovery' and the 'Skylon', a pointed aluminium device suspended over the site and compared to the British economy, for it had no visible means of support. There were pavilions for 'fun, fantasy and colour', and 'contemporary' furniture moulded in bent shapes with spindly legs and ball feet. The Royal Festival Hall was opened and upriver there were funfairs and sculptures by Epstein and Henry Moore.

Labour had barely scraped through the election the year before. The Festival was intended to lift national spirits. It did that well enough, but it did not save the Socialists. Bevin died in harness the month before it opened. Attlee became ill while Bevan and Gaitskell fought. The government was tired and ailing. It fell in the autumn. Winnie was back, at seventy-seven. He had a majority of less than twenty seats, however, and his administration practised the consensus politics of what *The Economist* called 'Butskellism', half Tory left as in the new Chancellor, Butler, and half Labour right as in Gaitskell.

The Tories promised lower taxes, less red tape and more housing – 'set the people free' was their slogan – but there was

little radical change. Only iron and steel were denationalised. The economy continued its gentle expansion. By the end of 1954, rationing had disappeared. Labour's planned new towns, Basildon, Crawley, Stevenage, became real, to the anger of locals swamped by the decanting of the London slums. Pleasure motoring and weekend traffic jams resumed. People took 'package holidays' to the Spanish Costas; at £32 for a fortnight there were many takers and a large new industry was spawned. They shopped in equally newfangled supermarkets.

Empire grumbled on; the Communists in Malaya were beaten, but fresh troops were sent to Nairobi to stop Mau Mau terrorists slitting the throats of fellow blacks, and white farmers and their cattle, in a gruesome campaign for Kenyan independence. In technology, at least, the British retained their status. The codebreakers at Bletchley Park had produced the world's first electronic digital computer during the war. Its genius, Alan Turing, was to die a shabbily treated and unhonoured suicide; the British often confused greatness with self-promotion. A British company, Ferranti, nevertheless produced the world's first commercial computer in 1951. In 1952, the year that the King died, a Comet airliner started the world's first commercial jet service, and a British atomic bomb exploded on the Monte Bello islands in Australia.

With a great sense of theatre, Everest was climbed by a British expedition a few hours before the new Queen's coronation. It was a New Zealander and a Nepalese Sherpa who had made the summit, and it rained in London, but few cared. It was the grandest day since the end of the war. Television cameras were in the Abbey, prompting the start of a British obsession with the box. National coverage had been improved by transmitters in the Midlands and Manchester, and, just in time for the coronation, Belfast; a buoyant industry was producing more than 250,000 sets a year. It was a sentimental year; the footballer Stanley Matthews at last finished on the winning side in a Cup Final, and Sir Gordon Richards, the most loved jockey in a race-mad country, won the Derby at his twenty-eighth attempt. England beat Australia to regain the 'Ashes' at cricket (though Hungary beat the national soccer side by 6–3, its first home defeat) and Winston Churchill, who had suffered a stroke, won the Nobel Prize for literature.

Physicists led in nuclear power and ICI chemists in artificial fibres; medical breakthroughs were made in antibiotics and immunology; Francis Crick, with his American colleague James Watson, identified the genetic material DNA. The British were good pioneers, with more than their share of Nobel laureates in the sciences to prove it. They held world land and water speed records, and the air speed record for a time; their aircraft, the shapely V-bombers and Hunter fighters, were elegant as well as fast. There were, however, worrying signs that they lagged in commercial exploitation. The Americans overhauled the British in jet airliners after three Comets crashed with metal fatigue; a monster, eight-engined transport, the Brabazon, was a fiasco. Whilst Germany and Japan were in ruins, the Midlands car plants could sell anything they made. An officer in the occupation force in Germany had suggested that the British take over the Volkswagen plant; it took only 130 hours to build a saloon, an undreamt-of figure at

**Festival of Britain.** *A century after the Victorians' Great Exhibition of 1851, the south bank of the Thames was devoted to a national celebration. The Royal Festival Hall was opened; a sculpture entitled 'The Islanders' (left) showed the natives as sturdy fisherfolk, but looks indebted to Continental totalitarian 'social realist'*

*statuary. The strange aluminium device beyond it is the 'Skylon'.*

**Denis Compton** *(right) in a cricket Test against Australia at the Oval in 1953. 'There is no rationing in an innings by Compton,' reporters noted; the great cricketer was also an Arsenal footballer.*

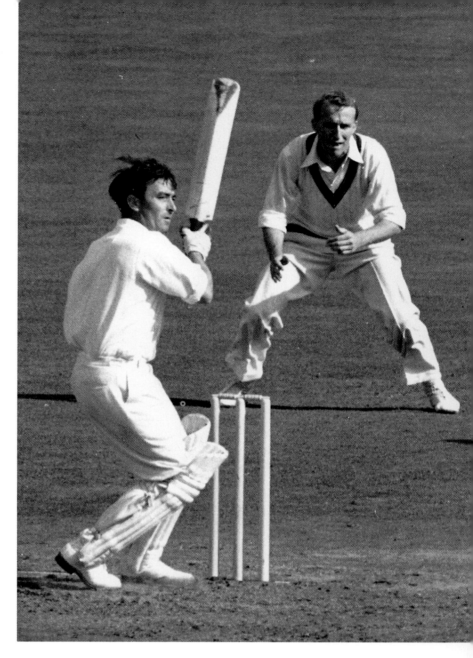

home. He had test driven the car and thought it would be a winner. He was ignored. Ten years later, spearheaded by the world-beating Beetle, the West Germans had overtaken the British as the world's leading car exporters.

In 1955, Sir Anthony Eden replaced Churchill as Prime Minister, winning a solid majority of fifty-eight seats despite continuing industrial unrest marked by rail and dock strikes. He was dogged by Empire. British troops in Cyprus faced another struggle for independence led by Archbishop Makarios, continuing after the troublesome prelate was exiled to the Seychelles. In June 1956, the 38,000 British troops quit the Canal Zone in Egypt, another momentous withdrawal after eighty years. The next month, the Egyptian leader Colonel Nasser took advantage of their absence to nationalise the Anglo-French Suez canal company. Eden, comparing Nasser to Hitler and haunted by memories of Munich, intervened with force and Israeli collusion. An Anglo-French invasion started on 31 October.

Militarily, it was a brilliant success; the Egyptian air force was largely destroyed on the ground and Egyptian army units brushed aside by British and French paratroopers. It was a political disaster. Two junior ministers resigned on the spot, and Butler was deeply disturbed. Labour joined with the Liberals and dissident Tories to demand 'Law not War'. The *Observer* and *Guardian* newspapers referred to British 'gangsterism'. The Foreign Office thought it adventurism; the Treasury was alarmed by intense American disapproval. Washington forced through a ceasefire resolution at the UN, where the Soviet invasion of Hungary slipped under the wire. President Eisenhower, outraged at the return to gunboat diplomacy, made it clear that sterling would be left to fend for itself. To prevent a devaluation, the Treasury needed a billion-dollar loan. No ceasefire, Washington made clear, no money.

Eden was exhausted; his wife said he was so obsessed with Suez that 'the canal seemed to be flowing through my drawing room.' Ten days after the ceasefire, and a humiliation carefully noted by the leaders of colonial independence movements, Eden absented himself and flew to Jamaica to rest. His ill-health – he had had jaundice and three gall-bladder operations – had undermined his judgement, some thought. It was the end of a brilliant career.

The Suez year was a social watershed, too. A play, *Look Back in Anger*, opened at the Royal Court theatre. It was written by a little-known actor, John Osborne, and it gave rise to the phrase 'Angry Young Man' for the new generation. Its hero, the ranting Jimmy Porter, was hailed by the critic Kenneth

Tynan as 'the completest young pup since Hamlet'. The old were driven to fury; compared to their own sacrifices, what had the young to be angry about? There was, indeed, very little; no great causes, just a steady growth in prosperity and the slow rot of a now unfashionable Empire. Osborne drew little distinction between reactionary blimps and welfare staters. He thought the monarchy was 'the gold filling in a mouth of decay'. He did not like the Conservatives; 'Tory is the rudest four-letter word I know,' he said. He had little time for Labour, either: 'I hate you, Gaitskell.' He was, in the main, simply angry. In his next play, *The Entertainer*, Laurence Olivier played Archie Rice, a seedy, gap-toothed music hall comedian, the embodiment of a class-ridden, ramshackle and moribund Establishment. Osborne called it a 'farewell to hope and dignity'.

Mannered and sophisticated wit, the theatre of Terence Rattigan and Noël Coward, slid from favour. Harold Pinter brought an air of menace with *The Birthday Party* and of claustrophobia with *The Caretaker*; the Kitchen Sink school of drama arrived with Arnold Wesker's *Chicken Soup* and *Roots*. John Braine's abrasive novel *Room at the Top*, with its angry, seducing anti-hero Joe Lampton, was a fresh blow to the

**The literati.** *Evelyn Waugh (above) had brought out* Brideshead Revisited *in 1945, a serious novel suffused with nostalgia for the pre-war English country house, before reverting to satire in* The Loved One *in 1948. He devoted the 1950s to the 'Sword of Honour' trilogy, the best fictional treatment of the war so far. Both he and the poet John Betjeman (far left below) were in revolt against the present, championing the Victorian age instead, as their props in these photos testify. Betjeman's affection for middle-class suburbia was not shared by John Osborne, whose play* Look Back in Anger *(left above) created the 'Angry Young Man' in 1956. The Welsh poet Dylan Thomas (left below), lyrical, rhythmic, lusty, died of drink in 1953, as did the ex-IRA bomber and borstal boy Brendan Behan (near left), after writing two good plays,* The Quare Fellow *and* The Hostage. *By now the poet W. H. Auden's best work was behind him, but his influence was still strong (far left middle). Graham Greene (far left top) inhabited an often seedy and sinister world of his own, Greeneland, pervading the exotic locations of his best novels.*

[PHOTO, CENTRE ABOVE: KURT HUTTON]
[PHOTO, CENTRE BELOW: LEE MILLER]
[PHOTO, NEAR LEFT: HENRI DAUMAN]

'Teenagers' *had existed before, of course, but, well behaved and with little money, no attention was paid to them. By the end of the 1950s, with full employment, they had colossal spending power. Milk bars (left) opened for their amusement, and jazz clubs challenged the old* palais de danse. *This one (right) is the 'Club Martinique' in Newcastle; with the Tyneside shipyards at full belt, the disposable income of these youngsters was more than the total wage of the old generation.*
[PHOTO, RIGHT: KURT HUTTON]

genteel. The working class was becoming fashionable; Shelagh Delaney set her *Taste of Honey* in a Salford slum and Allan Sillitoe's *Saturday Night and Sunday Morning* featured the terraces of Nottingham. Ian Fleming had started writing his James Bond fantasy-thrillers that – like the gold-plated Daimler limousine of the extravagant Lady Docker, much-married showgirl turned industrialist's wife – caught the public yearning for expensive knick-knacks and flashy living. An art exhibition at the Whitechapel Gallery displayed blow-ups of advertisements and film stills, and a painting with a comic book and neon cinema sign, precursors of pop art. Commercial television arrived, with an advertisement for Pepsodent toothpaste; it was sedate enough at first, but it hinted at a new world where marketing and image were as important as mere substance.

Old certainties frayed. Protesters singing folksongs marched to the Atomic Weapons Research Establishment at Aldermaston to call for unilateral disarmament; the Campaign for Nuclear Disarmament was a middle-class affair, of intellectuals, playwrights, philosophers and clerics, for British workers had little interest in radical politics. There were race riots in London's Notting Hill district. The monarchy still clung to old shibboleths; Princess Margaret announced that she would not marry Peter Townsend, the Battle of Britain pilot who had served as her father's equerry, since he was divorced. But it, too, was changing. The last debutantes were presented to the Queen.

The sweet ballads of Vera Lynn fell from grace; the young wanted raunchier, more explicit music. They got it, and the film *Rock Around the Clock* caused near-riots in cinemas. 'Teenagers' were a new phenomenon. Nobody had bothered to classify them as a group when they had short hair, good manners and little money. Now they had attitude and cash, spending £500 million a year on clothes and records. The film *Expresso Bongo* covered their strange fascination with coffee bars. Teddy Boys wore pseudo-Edwardian clothes, with greased hair, long draped coats with velvet collars and narrow drainpipe trousers. The 'Teds' liked to rumble, provoking fights in dancehalls and seaside resorts; 3,000 of them went on the rampage through south London in 1956, smashing shop windows and overturning cars. Tommy Hicks, a young merchant seaman, was discovered singing – in a coffee bar – in London's Soho. He changed his name to Tommy Steele, recorded 'Singing the Blues' and became a sensation. He might be a pale imitation of Elvis Presley but the BBC's cult rock show, *Six-Five Special*, was uncovering bands that would challenge the American domination of the English scene.

Eden was replaced by Harold Macmillan early in 1957. Hardline Tories held Butler's opposition to Suez against him in the leadership contest. Macmillan was, by nature, a trimmer skilled in dissimulation; he had first backed Suez, then turned against it. His habitat, assumed as much as natural, was the grouse moor; he affected the air of an Edwardian grandee – he was the Eton-educated grandson of a Scottish crofter who had made a fortune in publishing, and was married to the daughter of the Duke of Devonshire – thus disguising a shrewd and calculating mind beneath an affable and 'unflappable' exterior. He healed the party, neither side knowing which wing he stood on; nor, perhaps, did he himself, for he was an actor-manager who could slip into a role in a moment.

Prosperity was his stock-in-trade. He cut taxes, reduced troop strengths from 750,000 to under 300,000, and abolished conscription before his handsome win in the 1959 election. Television sets, washing machines and refrigerators appeared in working-class homes; motor scooters were within reach of the young, and cars of their parents. The British were learning to enjoy themselves. They were preparing for the Sixties.

## CHAPTER EIGHT

# SEX, SIN AND THE SIXTIES

THE SIXTIES WAS ONE OF THOSE SELF-AWARE decades that define themselves almost before they begin. It was a watershed in morals and much else and the stage was set in the first year, when Penguin Books was charged with obscenity in publishing the novel *Lady Chatterley's Lover*. The arbiter of public morals, the Lord Chamberlain, an earl and former Governor of Bombay, was pitted against the book's dead author, D. H. Lawrence, son of a Nottinghamshire miner. Not only the writing was said to be obscene. The prosecution suggested that the plot – which had the 'lady of a great house', Lady Chatterley, 'run off and copulate with her husband's gamekeeper' – was itself socially unnatural.

The trial had two famous high points. 'Is it a book', the prosecuting counsel asked the jury, 'that you would wish your wife or servants to read?' His case half-dissolved in the general merriment at the snobbery of the remark. It was lost when Richard Hoggart, a specialist in literacy and a defence witness, was asked whether the word 'fuck' – whose spelt-out appearance was central to the allegation of obscenity – gained anything by being printed as the conventional 'f★★★'. 'Yes,' said Hoggart in rapier reply, 'it gains a dirty suggestiveness.' The trial was the moment, the critic Kenneth Tynan said, when the Old England of the prosecution, and the novel's cuckolded baronet, a place of 'separation… control… death', met in real battle with the 'contact… freedom… love' of Lawrence's brave New Britain. The book, now agreed to be among the worst of Lawrence's novels, sold out its initial print-run of 200,000 copies the day it was cleared for publication. Sex, and class, were clearly on the national agenda.

The social goalposts were moving. In January 1960, Lady Pamela Mountbatten, daughter of the last Viceroy of India, married David Hicks. The groom was not a gamekeeper; he was an interior designer which, to many, was far worse. Five months later, Princess Margaret married a photographer in Westminster Abbey. Though Anthony Armstrong-Jones was soon ennobled as Earl of Snowdon, and was a man of talent, the coupling of the Queen's sister with a working commoner was a further blow to diehards. True, Macmillan's administration remained comfortingly traditional; it included a duke, the heir to a barony, a marquess and three earls. There were signs, however, that the new decade would not suffer its social superiors gladly. The *Daily Mirror* described the premier's appointment of the Earl of Home to the Foreign Office as 'the most reckless since the Roman Emperor Caligula made his favourite horse a consul'. Fears that such contempt would spread were confirmed when a critic – and a peer at that, Lord Altrincham – described the Queen as 'a priggish schoolgirl, captain of the hockey team, a prefect …'

**'Wait till you see the Stones!'** *the New York socialite 'Baby' Jane Holzer said in 1964. 'They're pure sex! They're divine… They're all young, and they're taking over, it's like a whole revolution…' The Rolling Stones are seen here promoting their album* Beggar's Banquet. *The British became the only real challengers to the American domination of global pop culture in the 1960s. The common language helped; so, too, did the world's wonder that a people long locked in a chrysalis of calm and deference should emerge as wanton butterflies.*

*When Mick Jagger was convicted for possessing amphetamines in 1967, legally bought in Italy, the editor of* The Times *wrote that it was 'precisely the same' as though the Archbishop of Canterbury had bought 'proprietary airsickness pills on Rome airport'. The comparison, like the country itself, was morally muddled and breathtakingly naive; two years later, the Stone Brian Jones was dead of drug abuse.*

[PHOTO: MICHAEL JOSEPH]

A new satire industry – the lustiest since the eighteenth century, and with the modern press and television to speed it on its way – was in the making. It was largely dominated by university graduates; this added to its appeal. The decade was infatuated by youth and the destruction of icons. 'What do you need to be of the Sixties?' asked one of its early creations, the *Sunday Times* Magazine. 'First, you should be under thirty. Second, you should be in tune with your times...' Who better, then, to savage their elders than the Oxbridge-educated heirs to the Establishment? A more worldly-wise nation would not have reacted so strongly to satire's first products, the revue *Beyond The Fringe*, the magazine *Private Eye*. The stars and writers – Peter Cook, Dudley Moore, Jonathan Miller, Alan Bennett – were cuddly and clean-living by the standards of the

decadents of Weimar Berlin, with whom they were extravagantly compared. The threshold of outrage was low enough for offence to be taken at the columnist Bernard Levin for dubbing Manningham-Buller, the Attorney-General, as Sir Reginald Bullying-Manner.

The British had preserved a particular guilelessness in their islands, for they had escaped the atrocities and political catastrophes that engulfed their neighbours. Like the Americans, with whom the French now lumped them as 'les Anglo-Saxons', they were unannealed. 'In an English girl's eyes,' a visitor wrote, 'is a starry innocence only possible in an island that has not been invaded for a thousand years...' This absence of cynicism led to the decade's great moral failing, its inability to distinguish the libertarian from the libertine. Other

ages had drawn a careful distinction between the two; those who laid siege to received morality in the Sixties, feeling themselves pioneers, did not. In truth, they were not new; very little in so ancient a society was. Even the division of the world into reactionary 'squares' and daring 'swingers' was old. In his book on the Sixties, *The Neophiliacs*, Christopher Booker, himself a founding editor of *Private Eye*, traced 'square' back to the 1770s, when it was coined to describe those who wore square-toed shoes after the fashion had passed. 'Swinger' and 'swinging' were older still; they dated back to plays in Restoration London. The polarity between the two, however, was real enough.

Inflation, high taxation and death duties were playing havoc with landowners, ex-officers, gentlefolk on fixed incomes; the National Trust saved what country houses it could, whilst those with the stateliest homes followed the lead of the Duke of Bedford, who, to make ends meet, had opened Woburn Abbey to the public, the aristocracy itself thus becoming an offshoot of the entertainment industry. This was the England of 'Disgusted, Tunbridge Wells', the mythical colonel who wrote angry letters to the *Daily Telegraph* from his retirement in genteel Kent, and he had much to be disgusted with. National service had ended; Britain, which still had troops stationed in more foreign postings than any other Nato power, was the first whose young men were no longer conscripted. The nuclear bomb, the ticket to Great Power status, was under threat. The Campaign for Nuclear Disarmament rally in Trafalgar Square at Easter in 1960 attracted a crowd of 100,000; tempers were frayed, arrests were made and the police were met with the first cries of 'pigs' and 'fascists'. The Labour party split over the issue. At its conference, the CND leader Canon Collins chanted 'Ban the Bomb' and 'Gaitskell Must Go' as trade union leaders combined with his supporters – 'pacifists, unilateralists and fellow travellers' Gaitskell called them – to pass a motion demanding that Britain disarm. 'There are some of us,' Gaitskell told a hostile hall, 'who will fight, fight and fight again to bring back honesty and sanity to the party we love.'

CND itself split, a self-appointed Committee of 100 declaring that it was prepared to break the law. Its tone was hysterical. In 1961, John Osborne wrote an open 'letter of hate' to 'the men with manic fingers leading the sightless, feeble, betrayed body of my country to its death... There is murder in my brain and I carry a knife in my heart for every one of you. Macmillan, and you, Gaitskell, you particularly.' A rally went ahead in Trafalgar Square despite being banned; anarchists, beatniks, ravers and those set on a police punch-up

mingled with the pacifists. The largest mass arrest in British history followed, those detained including Osborne and the actress Vanessa Redgrave. Bertrand Russell, at eighty-nine, was imprisoned for inciting a riot. 'Macmillan, Kennedy and Khrushchev,' he said of the leaders of the nuclear powers, 'are the wickedest people in the history of man.' If this suggested that the venerable pacifist had re-entered an adolescence that Osborne had not left, it was of little consolation to those still nostalgic for British might. The programme for a home-grown nuclear rocket, Blue Streak, was scrapped. Macmillan was to persuade a reluctant Kennedy to provide Britain with Polaris missiles. The warheads would be British, and the submarines from which they would be launched, but the claim of an independent nuclear force was wearing thin.

The empire was dissolving at accelerating pace. 'The wind of change is blowing through this continent,' Macmillan said on a visit to South Africa in 1960, 'and, whether we like it or not, this growth of national consciousness is a political fact.' Macmillan's real audience was in Britain, not Cape Town, and he was preparing it for rapid decolonisation in Africa. The dream of an African Army to replace the lost Indians was snuffed out. By the end of the 1950s, Ghana and Nigeria were independent, with Kenya and Tanganyika soon to follow, whilst South Africa was on the verge of leaving the Commonwealth. At the same time, immigration was escalating. Sixty thousand arrived in Britain in 1960. The following year, with 120,000 coming, the government published an immigration bill to a backdrop of race riots in Nottingham and London's Notting Hill Gate. As well as the West Indies, many now came from India and Pakistan, which had almost limitless reservoirs of people so poor that an immigrant's modest wage in a British hospital or textile mill represented a fortune; potential ghettoes were forming in Bradford's Manningham district, at St Paul's in Bristol, in inner Leeds as well as in Brixton and Southall in London. Sir Oswald Mosley had returned from his voluntary exile in France to stand as MP for North Kensington on behalf of the 'British Movement', a rival to the anti-immigrant National

Front. He polled less than eight per cent of the vote; British racism was more talked about than real. The bill provided the first modest restrictions on the inflow. 'Britain's Race Law', the *Daily Mirror* nevertheless headlined. 'This Is An Outrage.'

People sensed other outrages. Terrace streets, mean but homely, were bulldozed and their occupants decanted into soulless tower blocks. Birmingham pulled down its historic centre and redeveloped it as concrete precincts snared in a web of flyovers. The Sunday opening of cinemas and pubs in Wales was legalised. 'Swansea has bowed its head to Bacchus,' a nonconformist minister complained. A boom in gambling followed another relaxation in the law. Disused church halls were turned over to Bingo. Betting shops and gambling clubs flourished. So did striptease clubs. Paul Raymond, the owner of Raymond's Revue Bar in London's Soho, was fined £5,000 for keeping a disorderly house. He had, the magistrate said, attracted those who 'out of curiosity or lust' had come 'to see the filth portrayed in this establishment.' Revealingly, he added that they included 'members of all classes'. With a nation to tap, Raymond stayed open and prospered.

Though labour relations remained sour, the working class had, in Macmillan's phrase, 'never had it so good'. Many industries – steel, chemicals, textiles, white goods and, particularly, cars – were working near capacity. The millionth Morris Minor was produced in 1961; central heating, washing machines and refrigerators were also within the grasp of many families. Coal was starting its long decline as oil and nuclear power took its place, but miners laid off from the northern pits found ready work in the Midlands car plants. It was in comparison with others that the rust showed. Britain had the lowest growth rate of any major industrial country; its share of world exports was still huge, a fifth, but that had fallen from a quarter in seven years. Sterling was weak. The defence budget was proportionately the highest of any Western country; in addition to the large standing army on the Rhine, amphibious forces were still kept east of Suez. The economy was characterised by 'stop-go'; when the brakes came off, the imports that were sucked in soon produced a crisis in the balance of payments, leading to higher interest rates and wage freezes as the cycle was repeated. 'Britain', the US Secretary of State, Dean Acheson, said cruelly in 1962, 'has lost an Empire and has not found a role.' World power gone, the British went cap in hand to the Continent and requested permission to join the Common Market. The following year, they stumbled across their new role; they became global entertainers.

**Winds of change.** *Harold Macmillan warned an audience in Cape Town in 1960 that the forces of black nationalism were blowing through Africa. His hosts took little notice; the South Africans were busily constructing apartheid, and quit the Commonwealth the following year. The British were leaving their African colonies. Jomo Kenyatta (right), imprisoned in 1953 and then exiled for his leadership of the defeated Mau Mau insurgency, waves his ceremonial fly whisk as he is released. Kenya became independent at the end of 1963. In what was a familiar process, the former prisoner became his country's first president, remaining on good terms with his ex-gaolers and the capitalist West, so ensuring a good measure of prosperity for his people.*

[PHOTO, LEFT: MICHAEL JOSEPH]

[PHOTO, RIGHT: IAN BERRY]

**Concrete evidence** *that Sixties style did not extend to architecture or town planning abounded. Cities that could afford it — and most could, for generous grants were available for slum clearance — ripped out their Victorian terraced housing and Gothic office buildings. The occupants of a wasteland (above) point out, against appearances, their presence whilst beyond them the high-rise slabs in which they will soon be rehoused go up. Birmingham replaced its historic Bull Ring with circles and squares of concrete (right) and a road system which largely ignored the convenience of pedestrians. The new M1 motorway (far right) at least appears functional; in practice, large sections of it wore out and had to be relaid.*
[PHOTO, ABOVE AND NEAR RIGHT: NICK HEDGES] [PHOTO, FAR RIGHT: JOHN CHILLINGWORTH]

**Open house.** *American tourists pose (left) at Blenheim Palace. Birthplace of Winston Churchill, it had been given by a grateful nation to the 1st Duke of Marlborough for his victories over the French in the 1700s; now the nation's high taxes and death duties meant it must go commercial. The opening of stately homes to the public was an early example of 'theme park Britain'; soon enough they would be joined by themed coal mines and textile mills and other relics of the past.*

**Cliveden,** *a still functioning country house, was at the centre of the great scandal of the decade. Hysteria surrounded Mandy Rice-Davies and Christine Keeler (right, in centre of picture), and allegations of orgies at Lord Astor's Thames valley home.*

1963 was *the* climactic year of Tynan's war, in which the classless forces of the brave New Britain – satirists, hairdressers, photographers, models, designers and trendsetting clerics and criminals – ambushed and routed the old order. *Private Eye* lampooned the prime minister as Macmillian, a decadent emperor fanned by naked houris, whilst gossip columnists ate grapes by his side, ageing homosexuals danced under classical columns in togas and bowler hats and their more conventionally-minded colleagues sported with models in a marbled bath. It was the fall of Rome.

The times were indeed full of sound and fury; they did for Harold Macmillan, and introduced Harold Wilson, who, after Gaitskell's sudden death of a rare chest disease, became leader of the Labour party; the 'fab four', the Beatles pop group, were launched, Liverpudlian cosmonauts travelling into unexplored regions of adulation and fame. Quite what this signified was another matter. Form counted more than substance; it was the age of the adman, not the engineer. In a country which within recent memory had led in aviation, antibiotics, genetics, nuclear physics and a host of other fields, the engineering feat which most impressed it in 1963 was the start of passenger services by Hovercraft, a noisy and furious method of transport which promised much and delivered little.

The year started with a slap in the face. De Gaulle vetoed British membership of the EEC. The British had dallied long enough for Europe to discover that it could get on very well without them. The French had now joined the Germans in a sustained period of growth; in Britain, a distinct breed of economic critics, as waspish as their theatre counterparts, argued whether the blame for the recurrent sterling crises and falling productivity should fall on Luddite unionists or feeble managers. Rejected by the Continentals, humiliated by dependence on American rockets, the islanders looked inward.

In February, they happened upon the Beatles' first hit, 'Please Please Me'. The following month, it was the turn of a book called *Honest to God*. The author of the slender new volume was the Bishop of Woolwich, John Robinson. Most of the country nominally shared the bishop's Anglican faith; nine in ten of these went to church at best once or twice a year, and the great majority – weddings and funerals apart – never. In this apparently godless market, *Honest to God* sold 750,000 copies. Robinson was one of the few bishops of whom the public was aware. He had given evidence for the defence in the Lady Chatterley trial, during which he had described sexual intercourse as an act of 'holy communion'. His fame doubtless helped, but there was a further reason for the book's success. In it, the bishop took an axe to the view of God as 'a sort of celestial Big Brother' who, from his vantage point 'up there above the clouds', looked down disapprovingly on those who failed to attend church or to stand up to temptation.

The book itself, though true to its image-obsessed age in treating religion as 'a series of flash-light pictures', was not easy to decipher. 'Relativism, utilitarianism, evolutionary naturalism, existentialism,' a key passage read, 'have taken their stand, quite correctly, against any subordination of the concrete needs of the individual situation to an alien universal norm.' Readers dimly perceived that traditional Christianity was the 'alien' norm, over which their own needs should take precedence. Robinson was more specific in an article in the tabloid *Sunday Pictorial*. 'Regarded as a code of conduct, the Sermon on the Mount is quite impracticable,' he wrote, since it 'tears the individual loose from any horizontal nexus.' His audience might be puzzled by 'horizontal nexus', and his reference to God as an amoral 'ultimate reality', but it divined readily enough that a bishop was junking conventional notions of Christian conduct.

A new BBC satire show, *That Was The Week That Was*, or TW3, was soon mocking Robinson's self-service religion: 'This handy little faith… optional extras… if you want Transubstantiation you can have it, if you don't you don't have to…' The Church had now joined politics in the pillory, an ordeal the bishop himself was not sure it would survive. 'The next five years, I suspect, will tell which way the Church will die,' he concluded with an apocalyptic flourish. It staggered on, in fact, its 'ton-up vicars' with their motorbikes and rock masses and crypt coffee bars preaching to dwindling congregrations, frightening off the ageing faithful without making much progress with the young; by contrast, Roman Catholicism, which stuck to the old certainties of discipline and damnation, enjoyed a modest revival.

Bishops and actresses were the traditional centrepieces of English dirty stories. As *Honest to God* topped the bestseller lists, new stars – cabinet ministers and models – were unveiled. A trial opened at the Old Bailey in March. Three months before, a West Indian named John Edgecombe had fired shots outside a flat in London's Wimpole Mews. Two models were in the flat: Mandy Rice-Davies, an eighteen-year-old blonde, and Christine Keeler, dark-haired, leggy and barely twenty-one. The latter had been Edgecombe's lover; he fired twice at her when she looked out of the window, but missed. Keeler was a main prosecution witness at the trial, but she had fled abroad.

The following day, the *Daily Express* ran a large photograph of Christine Keeler on its front page. Close by was a story saying that John Profumo, Secretary of State for War, had offered his resignation to Macmillan for 'personal reasons', but had been asked to stay on. Journalists were well aware of a link between the model and the minister; their libel lawyers prevented them from publishing it, so they ran items on Profumo and Keeler close to each other as a wink to those also in the know. The story dated back to July 1961. Profumo and his actress wife, Valerie Hobson, were invited by Lord Astor to spend a weekend at his Cliveden estate in Buckinghamshire. Profumo was relaxing after sending 6,000 troops and two fighter squadrons to Kuwait, which had successfully defused the threat of an Iraqi invasion. A small cottage on the estate was rented by Stephen Ward, a London osteopath, amateur portrait painter and philanderer. The two parties met at the open-air swimming pool. Ward introduced Profumo and his wife to Christine Keeler, who was staying with him.

It was a casual meeting, and the sex that followed it was casual, too. Whether or not Christine Keeler charged for her favours, a question which later assumed some importance, she certainly bestowed them freely. Profumo, to whom Ward gave her telephone number, was a beneficiary over the next few months. He met her at Ward's flat in Wimpole Mews, and once in his own house when his wife was away. Among Keeler's other lovers, however, was Captain Eugene Ivanov, a Soviet naval attaché. There was no evidence that any pillow talk was passed on, but British intelligence arranged for the minister to be warned that his mistress posed a security risk. He dropped her, though doing so with wild indiscretion in a letter that began: 'Darling'.

Matters might have rested there but for the British

intervention in Kuwait. This had revealed shortcomings in military training, with many soldiers succumbing to heat exhaustion. Colonel George Wigg, a Labour MP and a defence expert, felt that Profumo had swept this under the carpet. His feelings towards the minister were not kindly. The shooting affray at Wimpole Mews caught his interest. He was told by intelligence contacts that Ivanov, now back in Russia, and Profumo had both been visitors at the flat. Spy fever, and talk of treason in high places, were already running high. The British did not merely write spy stories – John Le Carré's *The Spy Who Came In From The Cold* appeared in 1963 and James Bond made his screen debut in *Dr No* – they lived them. The print was still wet on the case of John Vassall, who had been blackmailed into giving secrets to the Russians after being photographed in a homosexual honey-trap whilst a clerk in the British embassy in Moscow. 'Entrapped by his lust,' the

Attorney General had said at his trial, 'he had neither the moral fibre nor the patriotism to alter his conduct.' That phrase – 'entrapped by lust' – had broader echoes. A country renowned for its sexual coyness now seemed to be talking of little else. 'Are We Going Sex Crazy?' the *Daily Herald* asked.

The press was hot on Wigg's heels. Keeler spoke to the *News of the World* and gave the 'Darling' letter to another Sunday paper. It was discovered that Mandy Rice-Davies had been the mistress of Peter Rachman, a notorious slum landlord who had, before his recent death, dropped severed chicken heads and excrement through the letter-boxes of sitting tenants to persuade them to flee from properties that quintupled in value once he had gained vacant possession. A new word, 'Rachmanism', had been coined to describe his activities; it was added to a story that already had a peer in Lord Astor, a cabinet minister in Profumo, a Soviet agent in Ivanov, a brace of photogenic good-time girls, and a procurer in Stephen Ward, who, as luck would have it, turned out to be a vicar's son.

On 21 March, the Commons debated the case of two journalists who had been gaoled for refusing to reveal sources to the tribunal set up to investigate the Vassall affair. The newspapers were in sour mood with the government; so was George Wigg. He rose in the late evening to say that waves of rumours were washing about the head of a member of the government front bench. He asked the Home Secretary to answer them. He did not name Profumo, who was at home in bed, from which he was urgently summoned at midnight to meet the Conservative Leader of the House and Chief Whip. Profumo denied any misconduct. The next morning, 'pale and taut, self-controlled but obviously under high emotional tension', he told the House that, although he and his wife had met Miss Keeler, and he had been 'on friendly terms', he had not seen her since December 1961, and that he had nothing to do with her non-appearance at the Old Bailey, both of which were true. He added that there had been 'no impropriety whatever' in his relations with her, which was not true. He said that he would sue 'if scandalous allegations are made or repeated outside this House'. With that, he left to spend the afternoon at Sandown Park races with his wife and the Queen Mother.

Five days later, the *Daily Express* tracked Keeler down in Madrid. The paper photographed her in black boots, mini-skirt and tight sweater. When she returned to London Airport, she was mobbed by reporters. She had told the *Express* that she had been Profumo's mistress; the paper's lawyers advised that her unsubstantiated word would not hold up against the minister's. Continental newspapers could, and did, run the Keeler version of the affair; as in the Abdication crisis, the British were left in a state of aroused ignorance. Thirty-two European periodicals

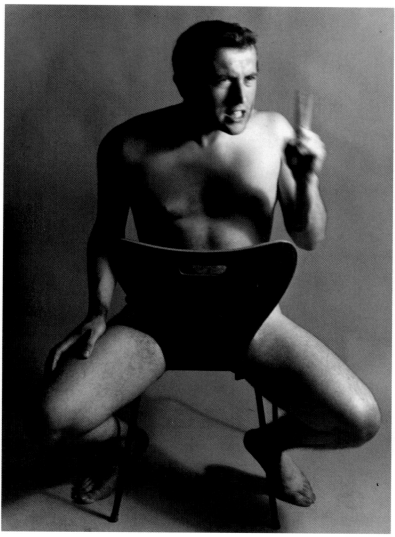

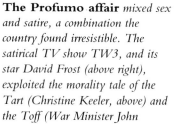

**The Profumo affair** *mixed sex and satire, a combination the country found irresistible. The satirical TV show TW3, and its star David Frost (above right), exploited the morality tale of the Tart (Christine Keeler, above) and the Toff (War Minister John*

*Profumo) to the full. Thirty years later, David Frost, worth several million, was married to a daughter of the Duke of Norfolk, and Christine Keeler lived alone in a council flat. Perhaps there is a Sixties morality tale in that, too.*

[Photos: Lewis Morley]

reading: 'Please whip me if the service fails to please.' Coincidentally, divorce proceedings between the Duke and Duchess of Argyll were taking place in Edinburgh, behind doors not closed enough to conceal the fact that a pornographic photograph of a man, explicit in all details but his face, was important evidence in the case. 'Come ye and stare at ye breasts of a duchesse', ran the pastiche of a scurrilous eighteenth-century print in *Private Eye*, 'Come buy my sweete pornographie, pictures of ye famous lovinge me.'

Headless men, men in masks... 'Sex has exploded into the national consciousness,' the American *Time* magazine reported. 'Britain is being bombarded with a barrage of frankness about sex...' Not just sex; spying too. In April, marchers on the Easter Aldermaston demonstration were handed details of the sites of the secret underground bunkers, or 'regional seats of government', into which the government would retreat in case of nuclear war. The self-styled 'spies for peace' who distributed these Official Secrets had found them when they stumbled across a bunker whose door had been left unlocked. Early in May, a British businessman named Greville Wynne was gaoled in Moscow for spying for British intelligence; in a reversal of normal roles, the traitor in the case was a Soviet colonel, who was shot. The Keeler case rumbled on. Plans were announced to make a film of her life.

were withheld from Britain for fear of prosecution; Profumo was awarded £50 damages against one, *Tempo Illustrato*, that got through. He gave the money to charity.

The satirists had a field day. A new version of 'She was Poor but She was Honest' was sung on TW3:

*See him in the House of Commons*
*Making laws to put the blame*
*While the object of his passion*
*Walks the streets to hide her shame.*

New stories circulated. A cabinet minister, in the most persistent of these, waited on dinner parties dressed in nothing but a black mask and lace apron, with a sign round his neck

**The aristocracy was down**
*but not out. Lord Home (far right,
seen on left) became Prime Minister
when Macmillan resigned in the
aftermath of the Profumo scandal.
He relinquished his peerage in order
to do so. Harold Wilson (left), artful*
*dodger and Labour leader, mocked
him as an 'elegant anachronism…
a fourteenth earl'. Home retorted
that his opponent was 'the
fourteenth Mr Wilson'.*
[PHOTO, LEFT: PAUL HILL]
[PHOTO, RIGHT: BURT GLINN]

At the end of the month, the new cathedral at Coventry was inaugurated next to the ruins of its bombed predecessor. A huge tapestry by Graham Sutherland of Christ Enthroned hung behind the altar and a great window by John Piper lit it richly. Benjamin Britten's War Requiem was given its first performance, the words of the mass alternating with Wilfred Owen's poems from the trenches. It was a memento of prouder days; Jacob Epstein's statue by the entrance jarred with the present, for it showed St Michael triumphant over the Devil.

Stephen Ward issued a statement to newspapers on 21 May. It said that he had given the Home Secretary 'certain facts of the relationship between Miss Keeler and Mr Profumo.' He had done so, he wrote, because his efforts to conceal the facts in the interests of the minister and the government made it appear that he had something to hide – 'which I do not.' The newspapers did not publish the statement for fear of libel, but leaked it to Labour MPs. Ward saw the prime minister's private secretary, who then summoned Profumo. The minister again denied the allegations.

Two days later, a Labour MP submitted a question to the Home Secretary, asking what conclusions he had reached over the Ward statement and what was being done 'to prevent the increase of expensive call-girl organisations.' The question was withdrawn and then resubmitted. Parliament broke up for Whitsun. The Profumos went to Venice, returning to London on Whit Monday. On 4 June, he admitted that he had 'misled' the House. The Conservative minister Lord Hailsham used the word 'liar' seven times during a short television interview, pronouncing it with such venom that, in the fevered state of

national make-believe, the audience thought him drunk. 'A great party,' he said, 'is not to be brought down because of a scandal by a woman of easy virtue and a proved liar.'

Four days after Profumo passed into honourable obscurity, devoting himself to social work in the slums, Stephen Ward was charged with living on immoral earnings. Christine Keeler began her story in the *News of the World*, and the 'Darling' letter was published. The government had no breathing space; the mood was so volatile that Labour climbed from a deficit in the opinion polls to a twenty per cent lead, the biggest swing recorded since the polls had been introduced eighteen years before. The Chancellor of the Exchequer, Ian Macleod, found the Prime Minister in 'a terrible state' when he met him, muttering about a rumour involving eight High Court judges and an orgy. 'One,' Macmillan said, 'perhaps two, conceivably. But eight – I just can't believe it.' When Macmillan posed at a garden party for a picture with the small daughter of a constituent, an onlooker hissed: 'Take your hands off that little girl. Don't you wish it was Christine Keeler?'

The *Daily Mirror* used an old trick in June to smear the royal family. 'Prince Philip and the Profumo Scandal' ran the headline, above a very small story saying that any rumours of this were 'utterly unfounded'. At the end of the month, a rush of immigrants clogged ports and airports in their eagerness to get to Britain before new regulations restricted entry to those with work permits or special skills. In July, the King and Queen of Greece paid a State Visit to London; they were too right-wing for some, and crowds of demonstrators booed them, and Queen Elizabeth herself. Mass arrests followed clashes with the police. A police sergeant was found to have planted a brick on a demonstrator; in Sheffield, two detectives were said to have beaten confessions out of suspects with a rhino whip. To the list of the year's fallen idols was added the British bobby.

The speculative bubble in office blocks and shopping centres was bursting; one of the leading developers, Walter Flack, committed suicide in financial ruin, and another, the flamboyant Jack Cotton, was thrown off his own company board. It was officially confirmed that Kim Philby, the former counter-intelligence officer who had disappeared from his job as a foreign correspondent in Beirut in January, was the Third Man who had tipped off the spies Burgess and Maclean. They were easily seen as upper-class traitors who had been allowed to escape by their complacent and amateurish fellows. A search now began for a Fourth Man. A young Labour peer, Viscount Stansgate, won his battle to allow hereditary peers to renounce their titles so that they could sit as MPs in the House of Commons. He duly reappeared there as Anthony Wedgwood

Benn. The world had turned upside down – not long before, men had squandered fortunes to buy titles.

The Ward trial opened in late July. The prosecuting counsel was Mervyn Griffith-Jones, the man who had lost the Lady Chatterley case. Prostitutes paraded through court, with twilight tales of two-way mirrors – such devices had also recently featured in the racy life story of the actress Diana Dors – and procurers and drug addicts. Griffith-Jones described Ward as a 'thoroughly filthy man', which the defendant accepted, and as a pimp, which he strenuously denied. Two of the prostitutes were later to admit that they lied when giving evidence against Ward; Christine Keeler was herself to be found guilty of perjury in the parallel trial of an ex-boyfriend, 'Lucky' Gordon. Had judicial calm been preserved, Ward's case would most likely have been thrown out before it got near a jury. He was adrift in a dangerous current of lies, and took an overdose of Nembutal. He was in a coma when he was found guilty; on 3 August he died.

Five days later, a gang with impeccable Sixties credentials – no 'squares' these, but a racing driver, a hairdresser, a silversmith, an antique dealer – provided the panting public with a fresh sensation. On the night of 8 August, a Royal Mail train was halted by a Stop signal in the Buckinghamshire countryside. The driver was coshed – he later died – and the engine and two coaches were driven to a bridge. Here the robbers transferred 120 mailbags to waiting Land Rovers and took them to a farmhouse. It took the robbers five hours to open all the bags and count the banknotes. 'When the count reached £1 million,' one of them, Ronnie Biggs, recalled, 'we were invited to take a look at it, just so that we could have the pleasure of knowing what a million looked like.' It was a pop age crime; Biggs remembered a gang member dancing the twist in excitement whilst another 'was singing the Gerry and the Pacemakers song "I Like It".'

A senior law lord, the Master of the Rolls – more grist for the satire mills here, rolls in the hay, nudge, nudge – was commissioned to inquire into the Profumo affair. Lord Denning's Report was awaited so eagerly that bookshops opened at midnight on the day it went on sale. Denning left no rumour unturned, but what he found beneath them was less sensational. He gave 'The Man in the Mask' his own sub-head, and interviewed him, but revealed that he was not, after all, a cabinet minister. As to 'The Man Without A Head' in the Argyll divorce case, a cabinet minister had submitted to medical examination and thereby proved that he was not the man in the photograph.

The report was calming; as if ashamed of its frenzy, the public turned its back on TW3 when the satire show resumed after its summer break, and sales of *Private Eye* fell sharply. Viewers switched to a stylish new secret agent series, *The Avengers*, with particular interest shown in the black leather boots and outfits worn by its heroine, Honor Blackman; the hero, Patrick McNee, a bowler-wearing Old Etonian, was a reassuring link to an Old England that had not, after all, entirely disappeared.

The summer had left its mark on Macmillan, now in his seventieth year. It was announced that he needed prostate

surgery; it was hinted that this – minor – operation might involve his resignation. The Conservative party's autumn conference was held at Blackpool, during which, from his sickbed, he confirmed that his store of political spite was still intact. His natural successor was Rab Butler, the deputy prime minister, a figure of experience and quality. Butler had, however, run Macmillan a close second in the leadership race when Eden had gone. It was not forgotten. Rival names were tossed about in the gales that blew off the Irish Sea; one not mentioned was that of Lord Home, a man thought too old and tweedy to survive in an age of shiny PVC and black leather. Nevertheless, it was his name that Macmillan, like some magician, muttering about the 'soundings' he had made deep within the party, plucked from the air to the astonishment of all.

**Superstars.** *The actor Peter O'Toole, carried in triumph by his wife Sian Phillips after the opening night of* Hamlet, *made a worldwide reputation portraying the troubled soldier, Arabist and writer T. E. Lawrence in the epic film* Lawrence of Arabia. *Film and TV drama makers found that nostalgia for the imperial past was a saleable item –* Zulu, *which made the reputation of Michael Caine, is another example. They peddled it with the same gusto that the rock groups of the new Britain, like The Who (right), smashed their instruments on stage. The face behind is the model Jean Shrimpton's.*
[PHOTO, LEFT: EVE ARNOLD]
[PHOTO, RIGHT: DAVID WEDGEBURY]

The means of removing the obstacle that would have prevented him from becoming premier a few months before, his ancient peerage, had been provided by the unwitting Benn. The Earl of Home renounced his title and, having won a by-election, entered the Commons as Sir Alec Douglas-Home. He was engagingly modest; he confessed that he found it difficult to follow the arithmetic of economic policy without the help of a box of matches. Harold Wilson mocked him as an 'elegant anachronism', a throwback. In his own 'message for the Sixties', the Labour leader projected himself as a sort of human nuclear reactor, promising 'a Socialist-inspired scientific and technological revolution releasing energy on an enormous scale…' It was the purest mumbo-jumbo; it caught the spirit of the age.

The closing weeks belonged to the Beatles. 'I Want To Hold Your Hand' sold ten million copies. The *Sunday Times* said that they were 'the greatest composers since Beethoven'. The music critic of *The Times*, not to be outdone, wrote of their 'autocratic but not by any means ungrammatical attitude to tonality… exhilarating and often quasi-instrumental vocal duetting… melismas with altered vowels.' They were the stars of the Royal Variety Show in November; their Christmas season in Finsbury Park was a 100,000-ticket sell-out. 'Beatlemania' followed hard on the heels of the Profumo madness.

It had been a year of overblown follies. In itself, the Profumo affair proved nothing beyond the obvious fact that men in public life often keep skeletons in private cupboards. The war minister was hardly, in the jargon of the time, a 'kinky trendsetter'; Gladstone had recalled that eight of the eleven Victorian prime ministers he had known were adulterers. But the cumulative effect of 1963 – the corrosion of old pillars, Church, Tory party, police, the law itself – was more serious. Cynicism and an unappealing prurience embedded themselves in the national psyche. 'I'm All Right Jack' was the mantra; idleness, 'bunking off', 'skiving', was admirable, virtue was a mug's game. Between them, Bernard Levin wrote, the two leading politicians,

Macmillan and Wilson, had combined to 'empty the decade of political principle and scour the vessel clean…'

The small civilities of life were eroding, and it was the fashionable who put the boot in first. Socialites made a living by betraying the confidences of their friends to gossip columnists for £30 or £40 a week. Peddling half-truths was no longer shameful; it was a bright new industry. 'Some dress manufacturer comes up to you, say,' explained one public relations practitioner. 'You spread a report about a fantastic party he's giving, pass on a tip that he's bidding against Niarchos for a Renoir, and he's in.' The *Observer* and the *Guardian*, not the gutter press, were the first to print 'fuck' in their columns; as the Oxford-educated Kenneth Tynan was to say it on television. 'But I love vulgarity,' enthused the designer Mary Quant. 'Good taste is death, vulgarity is life… Only ugliness is obscene.'

The British had always sworn, of course, and mocked their elders, and robbed; but never with such apparent self-satisfaction. It was a sea change and some had already had their fill. The 250 islanders of Tristan da Cunha, a remote British possession in the South Atlantic, had been evacuated to Britain in 1961 after a volcano threatened their homes. In 1963, all but five of them voted to return home. 'We was like brothers and sisters,' one explained. 'We never done any crimes. Each mother bring her children up at her knee in the way they must go. They is taught right from wrong and true God.'

The Beatles arrived in New York on 7 February 1964, 'B-Day'. The writer Tom Wolfe observed the arrival of the 'short, slight kids… who wear four-button coats, stovepipe pants, ankle-high black boots with Cuban heels.' He estimated that 4,000 'skipping and screaming kids' were at Kennedy Airport to greet them. They played Carnegie Hall and the Ed Sullivan Show to a frenzy of applause; Beatlemania was transplanted. For most of the century, Hollywood and its music and dance had given the Americans a near-stranglehold on the world's mass culture. The British were the first, and would remain the only people seriously to challenge it.

After the Beatles came the Rolling Stones; Britain had an inexhaustible supply of bands with the required driving sound and drug-taking lifestyle. 'They don't wash too much,' said the Stones' manager. 'And they don't play nice mannered music, it's raw and masculine.' There was more to the phenomenon than pop music. It spilled over into couture and graphic design, the paintings of David Hockney and Peter Blake, the boutique revolution in retailing, the cinema and theatre. London shows

transferred to Broadway, reversing the normal flow; playwrights of astonishing variety were at work, Joe Orton with the black humour of *Entertaining Mr Sloane*, Robert Bolt with his noble study of conscience *A Man for All Seasons*, Peter Shaffer and the questioning of faith in *The Royal Hunt of the Sun*, the ex-Rugby League player David Storey with *The Changing Room*. Dead heroes were successfully repackaged; *Lawrence of Arabia* won six Oscars. The actor Peter O'Toole, brought up in unromantic Leeds, became an international star; Laurence Olivier had directed him in *Hamlet*, the first play performed by the new National Theatre company.

French fashion buyers made unaccustomed cross-Channel trips from Paris, which Mary Quant declared to be out of date. The 'face of the Sixties' belonged to an English girl, the model Twiggy. London was its city; even Americans allowed that, and sent their reporters to cover it. *Time* ran a cover story on 'London – the Swinging City'; *Esquire* said that it was 'the only truly modern city' and *Life* Magazine hailed the 'Swinging Revolution' in which 'Even the Peers Go Mod.' There was, however, a seedy side to those 'Mods', sharp-suited pill-

**Beatlemania**. *In early 1963 (above),
The Beatles — here Paul McCartney, George
Harrison and John Lennon — were a semi-
obscure pop group playing at the Cavern in
their native Liverpool. Within eighteen
months, their fame was enough for even the
older generation (top right) to recognise
McCartney aboard a train. The following
year the Queen honoured the 'Fab Four' as
Members of the British Empire. John Lennon
was photographed by Bryan Wharton shortly
after he had received his award at
Buckingham Palace (bottom right).
Beatlemania swept to Munich (near right)
and stormed America. 'We're more popular
than Jesus now,' Lennon told an interviewer.
'I don't know which will go first — rock and
roll or Christianity.'*

[PHOTO, ABOVE: MICHAEL WARD]

[PHOTO, RIGHT: BILL ORCHARD]

[PHOTO, TOP RIGHT: DAVID HURN]

[PHOTO, BOTTOM RIGHT: BRYAN WHARTON]

**Twiggy, elfin, big-eyed** and less vulnerable than she looks (left), was one of the faces of the Sixties. Her manager Justin de Villeneuve, with her as she drives out to dinner (top right) in the days before animal rights activists attacked ladies wearing fur, projected her career from modelling into show business. De Villeneuve was a true Sixties figure. A bricklayer's son, he worked as a fairground boxer, a blue-movie salesman... 'I was at eleven hairdressers in one year'. He was a bouncer in the slum racketeer Peter Rachman's Soho strip club before running an antique stall when he met 'this lovely little girl, so tiny and so beautiful'.

The model Jean Shrimpton, 'Shrimp', had one of the decade's best-known bodies. Here (above), she is photographed by David Bailey modelling a Paris collection, as the fashion for things British knocked French mannequins off their perch. The photographer was himself an icon. 'David Bailey', the rhyme went, 'makes love daily'.

[PHOTO, LEFT: BURT GLINN]  [PHOTO, ABOVE: DAVID HURN]
[PHOTO, RIGHT: DAVID STEEN]

German and French competition. A pay and dividend freeze split the cabinet; Frank Cousins, a trade union leader who feared and despised innovation, the 'nation's leading luddite', resigned from the post of Technology Minister which Wilson had bizarrely created for him. The Soviet spy George Blake escaped from prison; slurry from a coal tip above the Welsh mining village of Aberfan cascaded down the slope and buried 116 children and twenty-eight adults.

Crimes of violence were growing steadily by more than ten per cent a year. In 1955, there had been fewer than 6,000; by 1960 that had almost doubled. In 1964, the first year in which more than one million indictable crimes were recorded, the number of violent crimes reached 16,000. Cocaine and heroin addiction rose tenfold in the first half of the decade, whilst the use of soft drugs was becoming commonplace. Almost half the telephone kiosks in the country were vandalised each year; car thefts jumped by forty-five per cent in 1965 alone. The Great Train Robbers were not the only criminals to become fashionable. The photographer David Bailey's 'Box of Pin-Ups', a series of photographs of glamorous figures, included Ronnie and Reggie Kray, protection racketeers. 'I shot him in the forehead,' Ronnie Kray recollected of his murder of a rival gangster in a London pub. 'There was some blood on the counter… I felt fucking marvellous. I have never felt so good, so bloody alive, before or since.' Was a psychopath such an unlikely hero, for an age which spawned the Theatre of Cruelty, and the ghastly and hugely reported Moors Murders, in which a young couple tortured children to death? Depravity seemed to produce a vicarious pride.

In 1967, parliament caught up with the new morality. Women's rights were more fully recognised, whilst the state accepted some financial responsibility both for unplanned conception and for contraception. Legal abortion had effectively been subject to a means-test; the existing Victorian law was a legal minefield through which a woman needed the help of private specialists and psychologists to be steered to an expensive clinic. Back-street abortionists remained the standby

poppers on motor scooters who clashed violently in seaside resorts with leather-jacketed Rockers, whose drug was alcohol and mode of transport the motorbike. 'Little sawdust Caesars', a Margate magistrate said, jailing four of them for stabbings; they laughed. In business, the hero of the moment was John Bloom, a young washing machine tycoon. He flaunted his wealth; cinema-equipped yacht, flat in Park Lane with butler and cook, gold cufflinks shaped like washing machines. An admiring interviewer asked him if he would like a knighthood. 'Not at the moment,' he said. 'But I might when I'm forty.' This was fantasy-land; three months later, his empire collapsed.

Harold Wilson's white-hot world of technology transpired to be fantasy, too. Labour won a narrow victory in the 1964 election, improving on it handsomely two years later. The economy deteriorated; Japanese competition forced motorcycle manufacturers and shipbuilders closer to the wall. Merchant seamen went on strike; Wilson declared a state of emergency and muttered about Communist conspiracy. Car workers came out, further weakening an industry already hurt by better-built

**Heroes.** *England captain Bobby Moore (far left), carried by Geoff Hurst and Ray Wilson, holds the football World Cup as the nation that gave the world its most popular game celebrates victory in the final at Wembley in 1966. The librettist Tim Rice and composer Andrew Lloyd Webber (above) are seen outside St Paul's Cathedral after the* first public performance *of Joseph and the Amazing Technicolour Dreamcoat. Less endearing, but equally fashionable for some, the Kray brothers, Ronnie and Reggie, pose (left) with their mother Violet. The gangster twins were lionised by smart society in mid-decade, but given life sentences for murder in 1969.*

[PHOTO, ABOVE: BRYAN WHARTON]

for the poor. Under a bill introduced by the Liberal MP David Steele, abortion was legalised provided that two doctors agreed that it was necessary on medical or psychological grounds. Private clinics multiplied and their charges dropped; it also became possible to get a free abortion on the National Health Service. A Family Planning Act allowed local authorities to provide contraceptives and planning advice. Again as the result of the private initiative of an individual MP, Leo Abse, homosexual acts between two consenting adults in private ceased to be a criminal offence. Divorce was made easier; an 'irretrievable breakdown of marriage' became sufficient grounds. Capital punishment was abolished.

Wilson had the air of an action man; but it was mere bustle. 'A lot of politics is presentation,' he had once said, 'and what isn't presentation is timing.' It was, Bernard Levin pointed out, a 'masterly analysis of his own character.' When he was forced in 1967 to devalue the pound by almost fifteen per cent, from \$2.80 to \$2.40, he assured the public that it did not mean that 'the pound in your pocket or purse or in your bank has been devalued.' Devaluation was a clear sign of national decline; Wilson sketched it as an opportunity for exporters. He fashioned an industrial relations act to deal with the wildcat strikes that were playing havoc with industry. When he ran into cabinet and trade union opposition, he gave way. Instead, he agreed to a formula by which the trades unions themselves would monitor disputes under an agreement which they had little intention and no ability to enforce.

**Heroines.** *Sandie Shaw (far left) combined two dream careers; she was a pop singer and she had her own boutique. Her trademark was to appear barefoot. The fashion designer Mary Quant (centre left) reigned as uncrowned queen of the King's Road, Chelsea, in her boutique, Bazaar. She thought the 'young today are less materialistic and more intelligent than they've ever been. And they've got sex in perspective… they take it or leave it alone.' Other boutiques like Granny Takes a Trip, or I Was Lord Kitchener's Valet, or Biba (bottom left) added to the fashion flood, fuelled by teenage and young adult spending power, and Annie Trehearne, the fashion editor of the rejuvenated* Queen *magazine (top left), adjudicated it. Bridget Riley (right) was the leading Op artist, using repeated shapes and lines to create illusions of movement. The results were said to dazzle the beholder. She was the first English painter to win the major painting prize at the Venice Biennale in 1969.*

[PHOTOS, CENTRE LEFT AND RIGHT: JORGE LEWINSKI]

[PHOTO, BOTTOM LEFT: F. J. MORTIMER]

In matters imperial and nautical, the Prime Minister's actions were a risible apeing of the past. In 1967, the year that the last great British liner, the *Queen Elizabeth II*, was launched, the tanker *Torrey Canyon* ran onto the Seven Stones reef between Cornwall and the Scilly Isles. Wilson took personal charge, flying over the tanker in a helicopter. He ordered Royal Navy Buccaneer aircraft to bomb the wreck. This increased the flow of oil into the sea; Wilson sent in RAF Hunters to drop inflammable aviation spirit on the oil slicks. Much of the tanker's crude washed onto the beaches, where Wilson called on the army to clear it.

As to empire, British troops withdrew from Aden after 128 years of occupation, while the 220,000 whites in Southern Rhodesia unilaterally declared their independence. The population at home was growing restive at continued coloured immigration; the Tory MP Enoch Powell found himself filled with foreboding – 'like the Romans, I seem to see the River Tiber foaming with blood'. He said that Britain must be 'mad, literally mad as a nation' to allow 50,000 dependants of immigrants to enter the country each year. Powell was sacked as shadow defence minister for his pains, but a public opinion poll giving him seventy-four per cent support was not lost on Wilson. He had no intention of sending troops to Rhodesia and merely slapped the rebels on the wrist with sanctions. Instead, he put the Parachute Regiment on alert to invade Anguilla. The tiny island had been bundled into associated statehood with the neighbouring islands of St Kitts and Nevis as part of Caribbean decolonisation. The islanders felt themselves dominated by the St Kitts federal administration and declared themselves a republic. Wilson despatched two

**The Dreamtime.** *By 1968, the 'children of the Sixties' had become so self-obsessed that they believed that kicking London bobbies outside the American Embassy (right) would solve the Vietnam problem. Many also carried the 'Little Red Book' of Chairman Mao, apparently oblivious to the millions of Chinese being humiliated and killed in the Cultural Revolution. The Tory MP Enoch Powell (left) dreamed too, of 'rivers of blood' if coloured immigration continued.* [PHOTO, ABOVE: PAUL HILL] [PHOTO, RIGHT: DAVID HURN]

companies of paratroops and some London policemen to restore order; they landed amid puzzled islanders, delighted press photographers and general hilarity.

Such posturing seemed to have engulfed the country. Youths fought the police at huge demonstrations in Grosvenor Square outside the American Embassy, apparently convinced that a battle among non-combatants in London would bring peace to Vietnam. A pop festival on the Isle of Wight attracted 150,000 pot-smoking, flower-painted hippies, a larger crowd than could be crammed into Wembley for the World Cup Final, when the England football team beat Germany 4-2. Mick Jagger, the Rolling Stones singer, though recently arraigned on a drugs charge, was flown by helicopter to a secret rendezvous to discuss the state of the nation with the editor of *The Times* and

the Bishop of Woolwich. 'We're more popular than Jesus now,' John Lennon told an interviewer. 'I don't know which will go first – rock and roll or Christianity.' The Beatle allowed that 'Jesus was all right, but his disciples were thick and ordinary.' So much for St Paul; Lennon transferred his own spiritual allegiance to an Indian guru, the Maharishi, whose proximity to the Beatles' fortune enabled him, as *Private Eye* pointed out, to become Veririshi. The television star David Frost, a household face on both sides of the Atlantic, a chameleon who had turned himself from satirist to champion of the new Establishment, held a champagne and caviar breakfast at the Connaught hotel for the decade's other celebrities; Paul McCartney was too busy to attend, but the Prime Minister found time.

It was a decade that was, as John Osborne later wrote of his own part in it, 'pitifully naive'. His 'duped perceptions', he said, 'exactly matched the sentimental orthodoxy that has since shifted its bleeding heart from atomic destruction to even dreamier preoccupations like rain forests.' A real world still existed, however, and closer at hand than Anguilla. In August 1969, the army was sent into Northern Ireland to prevent Protestants from burning the Catholics out of Belfast. 'We went down in box formation, as though we were putting down a riot in some banana republic,' an infantry lieutenant said. 'A burning garage and a shirt factory on fire, all six or seven storeys absolutely alight. The streets were strewn with stones and pebbles and cars on fire. The whole place was a nightmare…' The decade was ending in a bad trip.

**All smiles.** *Dame Margot Fonteyn's career (right) reached a new peak after she first danced with Rudolf Nureyev at Covent Garden in 1962, following his defection from Russia. The actress Julie Christie (left), the star of 'swinging London', won an Academy Award for her part in* Darling.
[PHOTO, LEFT: DAVID HURN]
[PHOTO, RIGHT: JANE BOWN]

## CHAPTER NINE

# 'THE WINTER OF OUR DISCONTENT...'

**A load of old rubbish.** *The new decade started with piles of garbage like these left uncollected by striking dustmen in 1970, on a bleak Sixties housing estate that is already turning into a high-rise slum. It ended with even the dead left unburied when gravediggers came out on strike in 1979. In between, it passed a startling milestone. In 1977, the British imported more foreign cars than they built themselves, having been the world's largest car exporter after the war. The collapse was self-inflicted, and unique; other countries were vying to enter the car market, whilst the British argued over who was to blame for their leaving it.*

[PHOTO: ALDEN]

AUDEN WAS PREMATURE. HIS 'LOW DISHONEST decade' arrived in the Seventies, tarnishing most of what it touched. The champions of the working man, the union leaders and their pickets, became bully boys; they helped chase two Prime Ministers from office. The defenders of the rights of Ulster Catholics turned to the bomb and mass murder. Proud companies went to the wall, or, cap in hand, to the State for bail-outs. The young sensed what was afoot. Skinheads shaved the foppish locks of the Sixties to the skull, while Punks spared some, but tortured them into stiff cockscombs dyed inky black, or orange or green. They had been tricked: Love wasn't all you needed. So they tried Hate instead.

The violence in Northern Ireland had not crept up overnight. The province was called 'John Bull's political slum'. Since its birth half a century before, it had been ruled by a Protestant ascendancy, looking after its own in housing and jobs. It supplied 97.5 per cent of Corporation workers in Belfast, though a quarter of the city's citizens were Catholics. The supremacy was jealously guarded. When Captain Terence O'Neill, the patrician Ulster Premier, had a historic first meeting with his Dublin counterpart, he was branded 'Arch Traitor' for his pains. No truck was tolerated with the South, or with the Civil Rights movement in the North.

At the beginning of 1969, members of People's Democracy set off to march from Belfast to Derry – not Londonderry: Catholics dropped the prefix – to demand equal opportunity in jobs and housing. A Protestant mob was waiting for them at the Burntollet Bridge, a pretty spot a few miles from Derry, overlooked by a bank from which the marchers were attacked with abuse, stones and cudgels. The Royal Ulster Constabulary, overwhelmingly Protestant, made eighty arrests. All were marchers. Rioting in April escalated into full-scale violence in August; houses were set ablaze, the RUC's B-special reservists, mingling with Protestant mobs, using tear gas and live rounds on Catholic petrol bombers. British troops were sent onto the streets of Derry on 14 August and Belfast two days later to restore order.

A republican tricolour flew over the Catholic Bogside district of Derry; southerners talked of gun-running to the north, but the Irish Republican Army, perpetual campaigners against British rule, seemed ghosts. Their tradition was the gun, not the demo and the sit-in. 'IRA – I Ran Away', the graffiti read. Over the winter, they argued over how best to exploit a situation they had done little to create. A split developed between Officials, of a Marxist bent, and Provisionals. The latter named themselves for the provisional government proclaimed in the Dublin GPO by the martyred Patrick Pearse in the Easter Rising of 1916; the Orangemen were not alone in their obsessions with the past.

Union power was the other theme of the coming decade whose outline was visible early. Strikes and demarcation disputes, official and unofficial, were undermining industry. Eighteen distinct trades were involved in the building of a ship; a humble porthole needed men from five separate unions for its installation. One metalworkers' union represented every worker in the German car industry. British managers, now ruefully wondering who had won the war, had to deal with a score. In the same month as Burntollet Bridge, Barbara Castle, Wilson's employment minister, produced a government White Paper called 'In Place of Strife'. This sought a twenty-eight-day 'conciliation pause' to allow tempers to cool in disputes, strike ballots, and imposed settlements in inter-union disputes, with penal powers.

The unions reacted furiously and the cabinet itself split, with the Home Secretary, James Callaghan, rejecting any statutory controls. Scores of stoppages greeted the Castle bill on May Day. The TUC 'voted' by 7.9 million to 846,000 to oppose it; in the bizarre world of the 'block vote', union leaders claimed the support of all their members without bothering to consult them. Union members were fodder; in calling a strike, an intimidatory show of hands under the malicious eye of a 'shop steward', a local union official with a nose for scabs and blacklegs, served in place of a secret ballot.

The strikes were a clear affront to an elected government.

Wilson recognised it as such – 'get your tanks off my lawn' he told a union leader – and then gave way. The TUC offered him a patronising face-saver; it would itself monitor strikes and disputes and offer 'considered opinion and advice'. This was akin to letting the inmates run the asylum. Wilson declared it a 'solemn and binding' agreement; satirists responded with a weak-kneed character known as 'Solomon Binding'. The *Economist* noted sourly that In Place of Strife had led to In Place of Government. Within a month, Welsh blast-furnacemen were out on strike. Six million days were lost to strikes in the first six months of 1970. Wilson withdrew into a 'kitchen cabinet', leaning on cronies and his private secretary, Marcia Williams, for advice, his fears of plots and scheming in the outside world fed by George Wigg. His credit was used up; the Conservatives won the June election.

The new premier, Edward Heath, was reserved and remote, kindly but with a brittle charm that slid easily into tetchiness. The son of a Kent builder, he was a scholarship boy who, like Wilson, had made his way to Oxford. He was a bachelor, a rarish breed in politics. He had grown up in a man's world – wartime army officers' mess, civil service, the Whips' Room in the House of Commons – but he was not a man's man; he had been an efficient disciplinarian as Chief Whip, but as leader he lacked the backslapping and bar-propping that often oiled Tory politics. His sentiments and passions were poured into music, sailing and work; he was labelled a technocrat.

He was a 'one nation' Tory in the Butler mould, promising

**The last laugh.** *It took little time for the smile to die on the face of the new Tory Prime Minister, Edward Heath (left). He found the unions implacably hostile to any attempt at reform. Despite his U-turn on labour legislation, the miners came out on strike in 1972. A state of emergency was imposed, factories worked a three-day week, customers in the capital's main post office in Trafalgar Square (right) were served by lamplight as electricity supplies were severed, and families were urged to heat only one room. A further humiliation at the hands of the miners saw Heath lose office in 1974; it was becoming unclear who ruled the country, the unions or the government.*

[Photo, left: Jean Gaumy]

lower taxes, less government intervention in prices and incomes, entry into Europe, a modicum of privatisation and new laws to curb union power. He achieved none of them, except Europe; his modest ambitions foundered amid flying pickets and power cuts, and this moderate man was obliged to call more states of emergency than any premier in history.

Luck ran against him from the start. Ian Macleod, the one recognised heavyweight in a fresh-faced cabinet, died as he moved into the Treasury. His replacement, Tony Barber, lacked gravitas and fuelled an unsustainable boom with tax cuts and cheap credit. The growth rate touched 7.4 per cent, sucking in imports and letting inflation rip. Savers were mugs, their capital steadily dwindling as the cost of living rose more swiftly than interest payments. Anyone borrowing to buy a house made money; inflation reduced the value of the loan whilst escalating wages made it easy to service the debt. The British, always keen gamblers, had no difficulty in scenting a one-way bet. House prices exploded as they scrambled to buy; the government encouraged the addiction with generous tax credits on mortgages. The old, on fixed incomes, suffered.

As both inflation and unemployment rose, a word was coined for this British phenomenon, 'stagflation'. With Heath pledged to a hands-off policy on pay, wage increases rapidly reached fifteen per cent a year, with few gains in productivity to finance them. An industrial relations act was passed in 1971. It established an Industrial Relations Commission and a National Industrial Relations Court with penal sanctions to order pre-strike ballots and cooling-off periods. It suffered the same fate as the Castle effort. The TUC simply threatened to expel any union that registered under the act. The only targets were thus shop stewards and ordinary members who went on unofficial strike. When some such dockers were imprisoned, the 'Pentonville Five', the embarrassed government found itself with martyrs on its hands. The Official Solicitor had to apply for the famous five to be released on the grounds that action should not be taken against individual union members. The act

was effectively suspended. Strikes official, unofficial and wildcat, overtime bans, non-cooperation, pickets flying and static, work to rule, work-ins – a whole armoury was available to men who quixotically described the idleness that resulted as 'industrial action'.

Far from privatising, Heath was next obliged to nationalise. Wage demands were at crippling levels; the postmen came out in 1971 for a 19.5 cent increase, the first strike since the introduction of the universal penny post in 1840. Add weak management, low productivity, disputes, and casualties were inevitable. Rolls-Royce was among them. Its aero-engines had powered the Spitfire and its limousines carried the Queen; the government could not lightly abandon it. The State took it over.

In severe January weather in 1972, the miners came out. By mid-February, fourteen power stations were completely shut down. A state of emergency had been declared; industry worked a three-day week, a million workers were laid off, offices were reduced to candlelight and families were urged to heat only one room in a house. A young Yorkshire Miners' official called Arthur Scargill used 'flying pickets' of men carried in vans to block access to coal and coke depots and prevent supplies moving to the power stations. Some 15,000 pickets were massed at the Saltley coke depot in the Midlands. A committee of inquiry was set up; the miners rejected the large award it recommended. After six weeks, they returned to work with rises of up to twenty-four per cent, with longer holidays and bonuses included in normal pay. The defeats of Black Friday and 1926 were avenged; Scargill was elected President of the Yorkshire Miners.

The Ulster crisis deepened. The civil rights movement had passed beyond peaceful idealism; its heroine, young Bernadette Devlin, had been jailed for inciting a riot, despite her lawyer's plea that she was 'Joan of Arc and Florence Nightingale'. There were no more cups of tea for the army in the Lower Falls and the other Catholic ghettoes of Belfast. The walls of the mean streets were whitewashed to head height, not through any sense

**Divided loyalty.** *Violent hatreds between poor Catholics and Protestants in Ulster produced waves of bombings, sectarian murders and army intervention in cityscapes of torched houses, burned-out cars and barricades. Thirteen civilians were killed by the army in Londonderry in January 1972, and later that year, Catholic boys there were still goading the security forces, running (left) as the CS gas canisters came in.*

*Reacting to IRA 'provocation', the Protestant loyalists formed their own Ulster Defence Force, which engaged in grisly tit-for-tat killings across the province. Here (above, on right) its commander, 'Gusty' Spence, poses for his picture in prison after his arrest on terrorist charges.*

[PHOTO, LEFT: DON McCULLIN]

of civic pride, but the better to silhouette patrolling soldiers for a sniper. Women drummed on dustbin lids as they passed, and flashed torches, to spoil their night vision and their hearing; girls tempted three off-duty soldiers into a bar, a honey trap, where a gunman murdered them. House to house searches uncovered firearms, explosives, home-made bombs and 21,000 rounds of ammunition; the IRA Provos were set on making the province ungovernable.

The internment without trial of 324 IRA suspects provoked even the moderate Catholics of the new Social Democratic and Labour Party. Brian Faulkner, the Ulster premier, claimed it would 'flush out the gunmen'; many of the internees were middle-aged men who had done little more than sing IRA songs and carry tricolour handkerchiefs. As the miners' strike unfolded on the mainland, an anti-internment march was planned in Derry for 30 January 1972, a Sunday. The police banned it; 15,000 marchers went ahead anyway. The Bogside area of the city had become effectively a no-go area for the infantry units normally deployed around the city. A battalion of paratroopers was in Derry that day, however; its experience was drawn from Belfast, where both sides knew that rioting was a dangerous business, in which soldiers were shot by gunmen using mobs for cover, and soldiers fired back. The IRA bombed intensely in Belfast; a counter-atrocity by Protestants

had recently killed fifteen in a Catholic pub. Derry was a more innocent place.

'I thought it was going to be an ordinary riot,' a Catholic who watched the march as a boy recalled, 'and the police'd try to contain it as they usually did, by shooting off some rubber bullets and perhaps sending in some gas... Then somebody on the balcony said... "Jesus, that's rifle fire, they're using real bullets they are!" And we saw the marching column start to break up, people beginning to run away from it as hard as they could...' Thirteen civilians were killed and twenty-nine wounded; the army claimed it had been fired on, and that rioters had nail bombs, but no weapons were found on the dead.

In Dublin, crowds burned down the British embassy in protest at 'Bloody Sunday'. The IRA held their own 'Bloody Friday' in Belfast when eleven were killed in twenty-one separate bombings. Across the province, 321 civilians and 146 soldiers and policemen were killed that year. Heath suspended the Stormont parliament, and direct rule was imposed from Westminster. Protestant shipyard workers marched in protest against the end of self-government; Catholics marched in anger at the bulldozing of their barricades in Derry and the creation of 'Diplock courts', secret trials for terrorist offences in which a judge sat alone to prevent the intimidation of witnesses. The 'blanket men', convicted IRA terrorists, lay naked in their cells and smeared themselves with their own excrement in strange protest against a refusal to grant them the status of political prisoners. At a referendum, ninety per cent voted for Ulster to retain the union with the UK; most Catholics boycotted it.

The British – and the Irish – joined the EEC on the first day of 1973, the link to the Continent a historic moment celebrated by few. Enthusiasm for Europe was barely skin deep and the European Community Bill had a majority of a mere eight votes on its second reading in the Commons. Its institutions – a non-elected Commission, a feeble European Parliament, and a bureaucracy free of electoral constraints – ran counter to British tradition, but enough persuaded themselves, or were misled into thinking this did not matter, since what they were joining was nothing more than a free-trade area with no real political dimension or ambition to it.

The EEC meant an end, too, to a policy of cheap food that had survived since the repeal of the Corn Laws more than a century before. Naturally enough, the nation's farmers were delighted. Helped by comprehensive production subsidies since 1947, they had made themselves the most efficient in Europe. They now benefited from EEC protection with both markets and vastly increased prices guaranteed under the Common Agricultural Policy. The price of British wheat went up two and a half times in as many years; farmers ripped out hedgerows to grow more, creating windswept, bleak prairies in East Anglia.

Increasing food prices exacerbated inflation and a further U-turn was forced on Heath; the non-interventionist was driven into a statutory prices-and-incomes policy. A period of pay freeze was to be followed by maximum increases of £350 a year. The miners wanted almost double that; Joe Gormley their leader warned the Prime Minister that his 'lads' chests were a mile wide and they thought they were the kings of the castle'. They had tasted blood recently enough, and the Yom Kippur war in October 1973 gave them favourable terrain. A combination of oil embargo and a quadrupling in the price of crude led to an energy crisis and long queues at petrol pumps. The miners put in their demand, and imposed an overtime ban to show they were in earnest.

A state of emergency was declared on 13 November. A month later, industry moved to a three-day work week. Heath was exhausted by oil, coal and inflation crises, a threatened rail strike, the worst trade deficit on record, a painstakingly constructed agreement for power-sharing in Ulster already running into a loyalist boycott. Television was blacked out after 10.30 pm to get people to bed early. A 50 mph speed limit was imposed. Petrol ration books were issued. Appeals were made to the wartime spirit, but it was now a country at war with itself.

The strike proper – the overtime ban was merely an appetiser – was due to start on 9 February 1974. Heath was urged to hold a snap election before it began; he dithered, thus blunting the stark question of whether the country wished itself to be ruled by the unions or the government, and settled on 28 February. His early lead in opinion polls dwindled. Labour won 301 seats to the Tories' 296, with the balance of power held by Liberals and Welsh and Scottish nationalists. Wilson, much to his surprise, was back. Two days later, the miners settled for thirty-five per cent.

It was a surly time. The women's liberation movement – a phrase redolent of guerrilla war – had a strident tone. Its seminal work, if so masculine a word could be used, was Germaine Greer's *The Female Eunuch*. In it, she explained that the first feminist wave, of genteel suffragettes clamouring for reform, had given way to a second, of 'ungenteel middle-class ladies calling for revolution'. The male psyche was dominated by loathing for womankind. She asked why a woman should struggle daily for superhuman beauty when this would be

**A startled housewife** *recoils in shock (left) as an army patrol reacts to stone-throwers in Ulster. They are wearing flak jackets against IRA snipers, and knee boots to protect their legs against petrol bombs. Some of them have special guns to fire rubber bullets.*

[PHOTO, LEFT: DON McCULLIN]

**The Female Eunuch.** *In her book of that name, Germaine Greer (right) described marriage as the legal enslavement of women. In practice, growing numbers were co-habiting rather than marrying, but the women's liberation movement added its strident voice to the other pressure groups – anti-nuclear, anti-racist, ecological, Animal Lib, Gay Lib, Lesbian Lib – battering at the nation's confused psyche.*

[PHOTO: ANITA HOFFMAN]

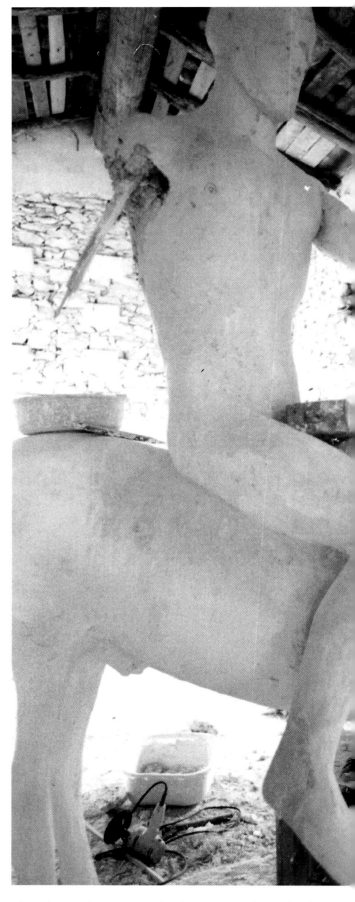

**Artists' portraits.** *Frank Auerbach (bottom left) worked over his subjects for months and years, building up thick layers of paint. Francis Bacon (top left) painted slashed, screaming and gory figures, a spill-over from his sado-masochistic private life. Elisabeth Frink's rugged and naturalistic bronzes (centre) played variations on human heads and horses, in particular. David Hockney (top right), a master of line*

and of portraiture, was seduced by the blue pools and other bright colours of California. Lucian Freud (bottom right), Sigmund's grandson, developed from a Neo-Romantic style to an, often nude, realism of profound intensity.

[PHOTOS, TOP LEFT, BOTTOM LEFT AND TOP RIGHT: JORGE LEWINSKI]

[PHOTO, CENTRE: IAN BERRY]
[PHOTO, BOTTOM RIGHT: BRUCE BERNARD]

offered 'to the caresses of a subhumanly ugly mate', a male with 'pot-belly, wattles, bar breath, farting, stubble, baldness…' The feminist magazine *Spare Rib* extended the assault to marriage and motherhood.

The flower children gave way to thugs. Skinheads uglified themselves with crop heads, tattoos daubed like graffiti on pale necks, strutting with thumbs in braces and combat boots. Punks shaved their hair like Mohicans, and wore torn sweaters and clown make-up; they draped themselves with bondage gear, chains and leashes, and pierced themselves with safety pins. In Stanley Kubrick's film *A Clockwork Orange*, based on the Anthony Burgess novel, the young swung through acts of violence like ballet dancers. Malcolm McDowell's spider-webbed eye smiled from beneath a bowler hat in the film's cult poster, his hand on a razor knife and a gouged-out eyeball on his cuff.

Life imitated art. The Sex Pistols were the first punk rock group, gobbing at their audience and swearing on the BBC, dressing up these displays of petulant bad manners as 'anarchy'. 'I'll never forget it,' the rock star Adam Ant said breathlessly of their first gig. 'John had baggy pinstripe trousers with braces and a ripped-up T-shirt saying "Pink Floyd" with "I Hate" over it… Matlock had paint-spattered trousers and a woman's pink leather top… They did "Substitute" and "Whatcha Gonna Do About It" with the lyrics changed: "I want you to know that I *hate* you baby".' Above all, 'they looked like they couldn't give a fuck about anybody.' It was hardly an original sentiment − large sections of the population were taking the same attitude to their workplace each morning − but it was

dangerous if pushed to the extreme. The group's leader called himself Johnny Rotten; the bassist flaunted himself as Sid Vicious. On a drug-fuelled trip to New York, Vicious killed his girlfriend, dying himself later of an overdose.

Crimes of violence had risen to almost 100,000 a year by the mid-Seventies. Sir Keith Joseph, a Tory thinker of quality and influence, complained that British cities were becoming unsafe for the first time since Sir Robert Peel had reorganised the London 'Bobbies' in 1830. Murder attached itself to the high-born. The Earl of Lucan murdered his children's nanny, mistaking her for his wife, whom he also attacked. The earl disappeared; there were unproven allegations that rich friends had smuggled him out of the country. Another disappearance involved a former Labour minister of technology in the Wilson government, John Stonehouse. His clothes were found on a beach in Miami following a banking collapse, and he was presumed drowned until he was found living under an assumed name in Australia. He was gaoled for fraud on his return to Britain.

Scandal among the Liberals reached higher, to the leader, Jeremy Thorpe, when it was alleged that he had paid £5,000 to have a troublesome male lover killed. His acquittal did not prevent his ruin. The Conservatives had their problems; a pair of junior ministers had resigned over their involvement with London prostitutes, the fact that both were peers adding to the salacity; Reginald Maudling, the Home Secretary, had also gone, victim of an association with a corrupt architect.

These were no more than individual falls from grace. A

**The Killers.** *Pop music became a dangerous pastiche of itself. The Sex Pistols were largely the creation of 'hype' and a publicity machine that glorified them as foul-mouthed punk radicals. Sid Vicious, the bass guitarist, is seen here (left) partying in 1977 with his girlfriend Nancy Spungen. Vicious acted up to his name. Arrested for the murder of Nancy Spungen in a New York hotel, he died of a drug overdose whilst awaiting trial. Lord Lucan was the decadent aristocrat writ equally large. He is seen here (right, far right) in a nightclub; a hard-drinking and unsuccessful gambler, he frittered away his life and fortune in clubs, before allegedly murdering his children's nanny – apparently mistaking her for his wife – and disappearing in 1974; he has not been traced since.*

[Photo left: Jill Furmanovsky]

people with a selective folk memory of a straitlaced Victorian past, however, allowed itself to be disturbed by them. Forgetting about the sexually voracious Palmerston, it was taken as evidence of the degeneration of politicians that Thorpe should be an heir to a man of Gladstone's moral standing; few reflected that the great Victorian liberal, who had a charitable concern for the fallen women of the London streets and yet flagellated himself for his interest, might well have been driven from office himself in the unfolding prurience of the new Britain. 'They're all at it,' people sniggered of the high and mighty.

Other falsehoods debilitated the land. The mainland Celts were thought to be drifting out of the union with England, which had embraced the Welsh since 1536 and the Scots since 1707. The growth in nationalist parties across the English borders was heralded as the wave of the future; yet, when put to a referendum, only thirty-two per cent of the Scots eligible to vote, and twelve per cent of the Welsh, opted for devolution.

A Race Relations Act was passed to stamp on the 'racism' with which the British were said to be infected. IRA terrorists crossed to the mainland; bombs planted in Birmingham pubs killed seventeen young people, but there was little backlash against the large Irish community. The British supposedly despised Continentals; they voted in a referendum by 17 million to 8 million to remain in the EEC. Much was made of the revival of the neo-fascist National Front; it, and the crop-haired youths in White Unity T-shirts and bovver boots who supported it, made no visible impact on the electorate. The arrival of a new

wave of immigrants, Asians driven from East Africa by naked black racism, did spark new resentment. But the British discriminated against immigrants to a much lesser extent than the immigrants discriminated between each other, Pakistanis, Indians and West Indians keeping warily apart; their community leaders had little in common other than in attaching the catchall racist epithet to their hosts.

The most damaging untruth was the notion that the country was sliding into poverty. It might deserve to; in 1977, more cars were imported than were built at home, an almost incredible collapse in an industry that had been the world's largest exporter not long before, and which had pioneered the mini-car and the transverse engine. Yet the standard of living continued to rise. Nine million took foreign holidays each year. More than half the country's homes had a telephone and a car; central heating was becoming standard. It was, nevertheless, an embitteredness and a scramble for more than the country could afford that slowly destroyed the new Labour government. The Militant Tendency and other Marxist groups infiltrated local party organisations. At Labour conferences, they declared their support for CND, black power, gay rights, lesbianism, mass nationalisation and Sinn Fein, the political wing of the IRA. Oxford twinned itself with a town in Nicaragua, a gesture intended more to irritate the Americans than to give solace to the Sandinistas.

The wound was partly self-inflicted; Tony Benn remained in the cabinet, though he was the patron saint of Trotskyites, dissidents, streetfighters and the other foot soldiers of extra-

**Kingdom of churls.** *The Queen's subjects were out of sorts with themselves; their country was the 'sick man of Europe', their youth prided itself as punks (left) and hooligans.*

[PHOTO: FERI LUKAS]

parliamentary activism. It stemmed more, however, from an economy driven close to collapse by the oil shock. Shoes, steel, textiles, shipbuilding, heavy engineering, the old staples, were bleeding. State money poured into British Leyland to keep the car maker afloat. Inflation reached twenty-eight per cent. In 1976, Wilson resigned. His timing was adept. James Callaghan, his replacement, inherited a sterling crisis so acute that Denis Healey, the Chancellor of the Exchequer, had to turn back from Heathrow airport to deal with the run on reserves.

Keeping the 'sick man of Europe' alive was expensive. Healey announced a $3 billion loan from the IMF; the strings attached to it were big cuts in public spending and the sale of £500 million worth of government stock in British Petroleum. The pound, and 'Sunny Jim' Callaghan's government, appeared to stabilise. Lunacy, however, was escalating. Workers, including union members, were sacked by the owner of an obscure photo-processing plant in London, Grunwicks. The plant was picketed for a year, sometimes by as many as 18,000 people; Labour cabinet ministers joined the pickets to show 'solidarity', a Seventies buzzword, and there were daily confrontations with the police.

Two million were unemployed by mid-1978; this was a level unknown since the Thirties, and with the added sting that it was far from shared by the big European economies. Callaghan announced in July that pay rises would be restricted to five per cent for twelve months. He thus exposed himself to the organised labour movement, an arcane world of banners embroidered with battle honours like regimental standards, of shop stewards and fathers of chapels, and strange acronyms, COHSE, NUPE, SOGAT, NATSOPA and scores more.

Car workers set out to smash the five per cent limit with no

**Waving the flag.** *A touching loyalty to the Queen remains as this woman (right) prepares to celebrate the Silver Jubilee of her reign, on an improvised stage made ready for a street party.*

[PHOTO: IAN BERRY]

further ado. By the end of September, all twenty-three Ford plants were idle. After two months, the employers granted seventeen per cent. The dam crumbled; firemen followed with twenty-two per cent, bakers with fourteen per cent, heating and ventilation engineers trumping them with thirty per cent. In January 1979, a nationwide truck drivers' strike began. Callaghan returned to Heathrow from a meeting on Guadeloupe with a suntan and a smile. 'I don't think other people in the world would share the view that there is mounting chaos,' he said. That was not what the newspapers said he had said. 'Crisis – What crisis?' they quoted him. The truck drivers were soon back at work with rises of up to twenty-two per cent. The public-sector workers now piled into the percentage game; the 'winter of discontent' grew colder. A twenty-four-hour national strike was followed by selective stoppages. Schools closed as caretakers, cooks and cleaners walked out. Rubbish rotted uncollected in the streets. In Liverpool, bodies went unburied. The gravediggers were on strike. In February, Callaghan gave way. He agreed to rises of nine per cent; to give him a figleaf, the unions said they would draw up guidelines on picketing and the closed shops where union membership was compulsory.

In March, the government lost a vote of confidence on its handling of the crisis. It fell, the first to lose office through a Commons motion since 1924. The unions had done for Callaghan as they had for Heath. Their membership now exceeded 13 million. It was a moment of triumph and they did well to savour it. The electorate took stock of the wreckage from a wasted decade. It, and the woman who now led the Tory party, had a very different future in mind.

## CHAPTER TEN

# IRON LADY

'THE lips of Marilyn Monroe, the eyes of Caligula'; thus the French president, François Mitterrand, described the new premier. The British liked to call her 'Mrs T', the grocer's daughter from Grantham. It seemed intimate, even affectionate, but it was sometimes tinged with loathing and always with a certain fear; the minister who dared to refer to her as 'the blessed Margaret' or 'the Leaderene' on TV chat shows did not last long. The Russians dubbed her 'the Iron Lady'.

Beneath her freezing resolve she was tempestuous and variable, like the decade she so marked. 'There's blood there, you know,' the Tory MP Julian Amery said of her, 'no doubt about it, there's blood.' Margaret Thatcher was the most powerful Englishwoman ever to emerge through her own efforts; dynastic whims had produced Elizabeth I and Victoria. Luck was involved, of course - she was lucky in her friends, most strikingly with Ronald Reagan, and in her enemies, foreign and domestic: Argentinian generals, a weak and divided Labour leadership, a miners' leader who badly mistimed the key strike of the decade. But she rode her luck with dash, and the aura of power that she wore, and her enjoyment of it, were tangible; she was a carnivorous orchid, perfumed and hungry.

At first, she was cautious and wary. She had every reason so to be. The country was beset by fears and mood swings; wracked by strange currents, it was incapable of maintaining station. A few weeks before her election victory in May 1979, Irish terrorists killed Mrs Thatcher's close friend and adviser Airey Neave in the House of Commons car park; in the summer they murdered Earl Mountbatten, the Queen's cousin, on his boat off the Irish coast. Gunmen seized the Iranian embassy in London in 1980; a world television audience watched hooded members of the Special Air Service smash through the windows of the stuccoed terrace house and heard the explosions of stun grenades and automatic fire as the SAS freed the hostages and killed four of the five terrorists. Ten IRA prisoners starved themselves to death in protest at the withdrawal of special status for terrorists; the death of the first, Bobby Sands, again attracted world attention.

Inflation reached 21.8 per cent, where in Germany and France it was less than four per cent; with unemployment doubling to three million, Britain seemed to be parting company with the industrialised world. The non-appearance of British newspapers through strikes was so regular that the *Sunday Times* readers renamed it the Sunday Sometimes. English football fans, once a template of good manners, ran amok in Turin; in a generation, the English had passed from liberators of Europe to become its hooligans. The 'Yorkshire Ripper' claimed his thirteenth victim. Only America had serial killers on this scale, it had been thought; only in New York would John Lennon have been murdered – but then the race riots, arson and looting that swept through Liverpool, London, Hull, Wolverhampton, Birmingham and Chester in July 1981,

**Loadsamoney.** *Margaret Thatcher supervises a fund-raising drive at the Tory Party conference at Blackpool in 1983 after her second election victory. The moderate Tory 'wets' have been dumped from her cabinet; the long tradition of political consensus and compromise is under assault, and she is getting up steam for a radical programme of privatisation that eventually will be copied by much of Europe, and beyond.*

*As well as her firsts – first woman prime minister and first to win three successive elections – she was the most dominating peacetime prime minister of the century. Her virtues included constancy in objectives – 'the lady's not for turning' she said of herself – and personal and political courage. She was a permanent target for assassination by the IRA. In time, her forthrightness lapsed into a triumphalism that offended many in her own party, and eventually dulled her sense of danger; she prolonged the national ambivalence to Europe; and she was accused of promoting an amoral private affluence at the cost of public squalor. Nevertheless, her great campaigns – the sale of State-owned companies and council-owned housing, the reform of trade unions, the concept of affordable welfare – survived her fall.*

[PHOTO: MIKE ABRAHAMS]

with black and white youths attacking police, also had been thought to be an American phenomenon.

From the urban ghettoes, the cameras moved seamlessly to St Paul's Cathedral at the end of the month to record the wedding of Prince Charles to Lady Diana Spencer, a young aristocrat of striking freshness and beauty. The worldwide audience was put at 1.2 billion. The British were becoming used to being looked at, as the decline and fall of their empire and aristocracy was portrayed with brilliant nostalgia in a succession of films or TV serials: *Gandhi*, *A Passage to India*, *The Jewel in the Crown*, *Brideshead Revisited*.

Mrs Thatcher believed in self-help, private morality, lower direct taxation, the free market, the entrepreneur and the individual; there was, she said, 'no such thing as society'. Her dislikes were as clear: the middle ground, social engineering, State-owned industries, welfare dependency, trade union power and, particularly, 'wets', the Tories who believed in the

consensus politics and compromise of the Heath days. 'You turn if you like,' she famously told the Tory conference in 1980. 'The lady's not for turning.'

She applied an intuitive litmus test to people; any trace of dampness in their resolve led to the fatal label, 'not one of us'. Wets were in a majority in her first cabinet; she was pragmatic enough to work with them whilst she must. They brokered an honourable settlement to the long-running Rhodesian crisis; Robert Mugabe – a Marxist, decidedly 'not one of us' – became the first president of Zimbabwe as the rebel whites in Rhodesia lost their supremacy and their country its old imperial name. A few years before, Ian Smith, their leader, had blustered at the British adviser, Lord Goodman, demanding one good reason why they should give way to the blacks. Goodman raised his immensely shaggy eyebrows and said 'Arithmetic'. Early trade union legislation was moderate; public money was provided for union members to be balloted on strikes and leadership elections, and secondary picketing made illegal. She avoided early confrontations with steelworkers and miners; the lame ducks – Rolls-Royce, British Leyland, British Rail (British Everything, it seemed) – hobbled on with government money.

She brooked no compromise, however, in her assault on the economy. The 1981 budget slashed public spending and squeezed out demand with savage increases in indirect taxes. Industrial output fell by ten per cent that year; inflation ran back over twenty per cent, and unemployment reached 13.3 per cent, the worst in western Europe. 'The great she-elephant', as a Tory backbencher called her, was wounded. A mass of economists – 364 of them – signed a letter to *The Times* denouncing government policy as ruinous. Industrialists should have been natural allies; instead, the head of their confederation spoke openly of the need for a 'bare-knuckle' fight with her. Opinion polls showed her personal standing to be the lowest of any premier since Neville Chamberlain. The cabinet wets demanded public spending increases to cut the dole queues; she sacked three of them, one victim, Ian Gilmour, accusing her of steering the ship of state 'straight onto the rocks'.

Survival that year was ensured because the opposition was busily destroying itself. Labour adopted a new constitution in which all parliamentary candidates, including sitting MPs, would have to undergo compulsory reselection. This was an open invitation for meddling by Trotskyites, Gay Libbers, Bomb-Banners and the rest of a lunatic fringe mocked with gusto by the pro-Thatcher press, notably the *Sun*, a tabloid

whose flair and scurrility matched that of the decade. The party failed to elect as its leader Denis Healey, a heavyweight bruiser; instead it chose Michael Foot, a nuclear disarmer, ageing, endearingly shabby and literary, but whose rambling prophecies and wild white hair cast him as the Jeremiah of the 'loony left'. Unlike Healey, he had no eye for the jugular; an idealist, he had little sense of party unity either.

Surveying the wreckage, the 'Gang of Four' – one-time Labour ministers Roy Jenkins, David Owen, Shirley Williams and William Rodgers – quit to found the Social Democrat Party. They were joined by twenty-nine Labour MPs; the party they had left put up a young, gay, Marxist Australian to fight a by-election in Bermondsey, a solid dockers' seat in London, and seemed surprised when he was thrashed by a Liberal. The SDP set out to 'break the mould' of British politics. It seemed for a time that it might succeed; the creation of a strong centre party was attractive to voters tired of stop-go, left-right lurches. In March 1982, Roy Jenkins won an outstanding by-election victory. It seemed deeply ominous; Mrs Thatcher was at the nadir of her unpopularity.

Salvation came from the South Atlantic. Argentine troops overran the Falkland Islands in a few hours on 2 April, Good Friday; the next day the House of Commons had its first Saturday sitting since the war. Most Britons needed a map before they could place the islands – forty minutes' flying time from Argentina, 8,000 miles from Britain – but the shame of

**Who dares wins:** *members of the Special Air Service (left) live up to their motto as, wearing black uniforms and balaclavas, they storm the Iranian embassy in London in May 1980. Four of the hostage-takers inside the building were shot dead as the SAS men smashed through the windows with stun grenades and sub-machineguns; a fifth was captured alive.*

**Peacepaint.** *Hostile to such military machismo, a demonstrator outside the base at Greenham Common (right), where American Cruise missiles were to be sited, wears her feminist credentials on her face. A tented 'peace camp' sprang up round the base, which was ringed by 20,000 women at one stage. Other women, however, successfully insisted on their right to serve aboard Royal Navy warships.*

[PHOTO: JUDAH PASSOW]

**'A crowded marriage'** *was what Princess Diana ruefully called it shortly before her divorce. As Lady Diana Spencer, she arrives (left) at the steps of St Paul's Cathedral for her wedding to the Prince of Wales. The royal romance was a global fairy tale; a television audience of 1.2 billion watched the royal couple exchange their soon-to-be-broken vows.*

*Prince Charles took up again a long-standing liaison with a married woman, Camilla Parker-Bowles; he is seen with her (above) on Valentine's Day in 1975, after visiting the theatre in company with her husband, an Army major. The prince was godfather to the Parker-Bowles's eldest child. Lady Diana*

*met her future rival at the races (above top) in 1980. Arranged dynastic marriages had survived such behaviour in more deferential times. 'Lady Di' was no long-suffering Continental import, however; she was the spirited descendant of Whig aristocrats. By the 1980s the pursuit of scandal had become a blood sport.*

*The marriage foundered in a flotsam of eavesdropped telephone calls, snatched photographs and television interviews. The princess was stripped of her title of Royal Highness; in a counter-attack of which her great soldier-ancestor the Duke of Marlborough might have been proud, she responded to this ambush by declaring herself the 'Queen of Hearts'.*

**The Empire strikes back.** *The Royal Navy, operating an ocean away from home with scant air cover, was highly vulnerable in the Falklands campaign that followed the Argentine invasion of the South Atlantic colony. HMS* Antelope *took a bomb in her engine-room whilst lying in San Carlos Water on 25 May 1982. A fire broke out and the ship exploded (above) three hours later. Once ashore, the endurance and professionalism of British troops made up for their numerical inferiority against Argentine conscripts, two of whom are seen (right) a few moments after their surrender.*
[PHOTO, ABOVE: MARTIN CLEAVER]
[PHOTO, RIGHT: TOM SMITH]

defeat was instantly clear from the first pictures of Royal Marines lying in surrender on the turf. It was compounded by the government incompetence that had caused it; the Argentines had long claimed sovereignty over the crown colony, and the announced withdrawal of the only Royal Navy presence in the region, the ice patrol ship *Endurance*, had convinced the excitable General Galtieri and his military junta in Buenos Aires that the British would not fight to retain such a fag-end of empire.

The foreign secretary, Lord Carrington, acknowledged the miscalculation by resigning. Mrs Thatcher was left exposed, and utterly vulnerable. Any military effort to dislodge the invaders at such a distance was manifestly risky. The Royal Navy would have to operate beyond the limits of the tolerable. Only two aircraft carriers remained to it, one destined for the breaker's yard; it was so short of support ships that the cruise liner *Canberra* had to be turned into a bizarre luxury troopship, and container ships were stripped from the merchant fleet as makeshift helicopter and Harrier jump-jet transporters. There was no air cover beyond the limited range of the Harriers; lose a carrier, and the game was up, even should it be thought worth playing. The Falklands had 2,000 souls, sheep farmers for the most part, and a Governor of such little significance that his official car was an old London taxi.

No Falklander or Marine had been killed in the invasion. Little was involved beyond pride, and diplomacy could salve that; so the junta, reasonably and fatally, lulled itself. In fact, it blundered into a minefield in which the historic instincts and unforced patriotism of the British were buried. The Falklanders might be derided as mere 'sheep shaggers', but they were kith and kin. Few believed that the junta had any intention of respecting their rights; it was confirmed by a petty-minded order that the Falklanders must no longer drive where all freeborn Britons had always driven, on the left-hand side of the road. If that was *casus belli* enough for Tory backwoodsmen, the hard left at the other extreme had no time for military dictators. Since 1947, the British had withdrawn from every territory in which a majority no longer wanted their rule; it was a measure of the dignity with which this was accomplished that forty-eight countries remained voluntary members of the Commonwealth that had succeeded the Empire. Where a majority wished to remain British subjects, it was not to be dissuaded by the gun. It was true of Ulster, and the country expected no less for these remote possessions, an opinion poll showing more than four in five supporting military action to free them. It was expected, too, that the hastily assembled Task Force would deal with the matter, though in truth it was more a lash-up than an armada. Great expectations, indeed, that would have toppled Mrs Thatcher had they not been met.

The British should have drawn no comfort from the failure of King Philip of Spain, Napoleon and Hitler to invade them, for it underlined the prodigious difficulties of the amphibious

assault they were themselves contemplating; but they did, mocking Galtieri for his pretensions to join such company. However deep they judged the rot in their own standards to have penetrated – civilian society had long lost its self-confidence – they thought, rightly, that the services were isolated from permissiveness. The military was all-volunteer, professional and disciplined, its loyalty unquestioned.

The Task Force sailed on 10 April; 'The Empire Strikes Back' ran an American headline as the world, having barely absorbed the riots and royal romance, settled down to a new British theatrical. On 25 April, the outlying island of South Georgia was taken; 'Rejoice!' Mrs Thatcher snapped at reporters in Downing Street. A diplomatic solution was unlikely. The wound to pride was too deep for Mrs Thatcher to accept a face-saving formula, and the junta would not budge; with sarcastic reference to Prince Andrew, a serving helicopter pilot, a Buenos Aires newspaper mocked: 'Send Us Your Little Prince!' On 2 May, the nuclear-powered submarine HMS *Conqueror* sank the battleship *General Belgrano*, with the loss of 360 Argentine sailors; 'GOTCHA!' responded the *Sun*.

Two days later, the hazards of a seaborne enterprise so far from land-based air support became clearer. An Argentine fighter pilot fired an Exocet missile; it travelled at 700 mph below the radar screen, the captain of the destroyer HMS *Sheffield* having time only to shout 'take cover' before it hit. The 'Shiny Sheff' turned black as her aluminium superstructure caught fire; she was the first major British warship to be lost for thirty-seven years. Others followed her to the bottom, *Coventry*, *Ardent*, *Antelope*, the merchantman *Atlantic Conveyor*, packed with scarce supplies; there would have been more if the old 'iron bombs' carried by the Argentines had been reliable, and if the Americans had not provided the fleet with satellite and other intelligence data. Nevertheless, on 22 May, after six weeks at sea, the British landed at San Carlos on East Falkland Island.

They were outnumbered – in the manual, an attacking force needs comfortable superiority against an entrenched defence, and the Argentines had 18,000 men against a British force little more than half that – but quality and endurance told against poorly led conscripts. At Goose Green, a parachute battalion took 1,200 prisoners, and lost Col. H. Jones, its commander. There was hand-to-hand fighting as, at the end of a long march, the British broke through the defences on Mount Tumbledown above Port Stanley on 14 June. They saw Argentines fleeing in all directions. A British journalist, Max Hastings, was first into the tiny capital. He found thousands of soldiers milling around,

**Victory at a price.** *Colonel H. Jones was awarded a posthumous Victoria Cross after he was killed leading his paratroops in an assault on dug-in Argentinians at the farming settlement of Goose Green. This (left) is the last photograph of him, taken a* *short time before his death; it was on a roll of film found later in his camera. The crew of HMS* Exeter *were welcomed home with a quayside forest of banners (right); history does not relate why Trevor was met with the stark warning 'No Buts…'*

'looking completely like an army in defeat with blankets wrapped around themselves.' He walked to the local pub, the Upland Goose. 'It wasn't in the least like being abroad,' he wrote. 'One talks about the Falklanders and yet it was as if one had liberated a hotel in the middle of Surrey or Kent or somewhere…' The Union Jack was raised, the Argentine commander surrendered. 'The Falkland Islands are once more under the government desired by their inhabitants,' the message to London read. 'God save the Queen.' A week later, the Queen had a new grandson, Prince William, son of the Prince and Princess of Wales, and a future heir to the throne.

It cost 255 British lives, and almost a thousand Argentinian; but it was a 'good war' to the degree that it rid Argentina of its junta, and gave the British a sense of renewed honour. It was certainly good for the Prime Minister, for it promoted a 'feel-good factor' at odds with economic reality. In April 1983, for the first time in its industrial history, Britain, the old 'workshop of the world', became a net importer of manufactured goods. It was a staggering decline; steelmills, car plants, shipyards,

engineering works in other European countries faced foreign competition, but in none was the collapse so complete. Blame was variously allotted, to the unions, to weak managers, to the paramountcy of the accountant and the lawyer and the low status of the engineer, to the class system, to the snobbery that turned the best educated away from trade and manufacturing and into financial services and the professions, and, of course, to successive governments; none could adequately explain the derelict swathes of country that were losing contact with employment.

Labour was in no condition to exploit the situation. It entered the election in June 1983 with a manifesto described as 'the longest suicide note in history'. It pledged support to gays, lesbians, Greens and, a year after a famous victory, unilateral disarmament; in case traditionalists failed to get the message, it also committed itself to the abolition of foxhunting and the House of Lords. 'Mrs T' was swept back with a majority of 142; the uneasy SDP-Liberal Alliance trailed Labour close in terms of votes, if not seats. The Tories did miserably enough in Scotland and the North, where the 3.2 million unemployed

were concentrated; they all but swept the board in the recovering Midlands and South.

The last wets were dumped from the cabinet; in their place, she elevated men as unsentimentally dry as Norman Tebbit, whose famously brusque advice to those without work was to 'get on yer bike' and start looking for it. Francis Pym, the outgoing Foreign Secretary, had the classical profile of the old Tory grandee, educated at Eton and Cambridge, and a moderate middle-grounder who now tried to recruit an anti-Thatcher 'Centre Forward' group from the back benches. He failed, and accepted a peerage; the wets were not natural rebels. Tebbit, by contrast, was the son of a shop manager who had left school at sixteen and learned to fly in the RAF. He later headed the British airline pilots' association; his gruff invective against unions was based on experience. The new Chancellor of the Exchequer, Nigel Lawson, was a former financial journalist; like several of Mrs Thatcher's closest colleagues – her mentor Sir Keith Joseph, the Home Secretary Leon Brittan –

he was Jewish. The old Tory grandee Harold Macmillan quipped that the cabinet had more Estonians (code for Baltic Jews) than Etonians in it. Little was deferential in Thatcher Toryism and its appeal to the working class broadened. The sale of council homes to tenants accelerated; by 1984, there were 800,000 new owner-occupiers. The policy was highly popular, and so was the effort to prevent workers from becoming strike-fodder. Measures against illegal strikes and secondary picketing were toughened; a printing union, the NGA, was heavily fined when it tried to force a freesheet newspaper publisher, Eddie Shah, to sack non-union labour.

New shareholders joined the new property-owners, and were often one-and-the-same. Millions were created when the old State telephone monopoly was privatised as British Telecom in 1984, the sale raising £4 billion. It was privatisation that confirmed Mrs Thatcher as a radical of true significance; others had pioneered supply-side economics and deregulation, but she was the first to mount a consistent sales programme of major

**Big Bang.** *For generations of the fortunate few, London's financial markets had been controlled by an old boys' network of brokerage houses and partnerships. This cosy cartel was exploded by the wholesale deregulation of markets, including the London Stock Exchange (left). The process was named Big Bang after the hypothetical explosion that gave birth to the expanding universe; immodest, no doubt, though the accompanying influx of international banks and brokers multiplied London's global importance, and laymen found the new products pioneered by the City's financial engineers to be quite as arcane as the theory of the cosmos.*
[Photo: Ian Berry]

**The homeless,** *too, exploded. Those who made their way to the capital from the decaying industrial heartlands (right) found no golden paving stones on which to lay their cardboard boxes and sleeping bags. In 1983, for the first time since the Industrial Revolution, Britain imported more manufactured goods than it exported.*
[Photo: Gideon Mendel]

State assets, in an era when Mitterrand's France had been nationalising. In time, the sceptics – French, Germans, even Argentines – followed. British Aerospace, Britoil, Rolls-Royce, British Airways and the airports authority went on the block; British Gas was to fetch £5.4 billion and help finance the tax cuts and boom that created two new social stereotypes: the yuppy, the young upwardly mobile City professional with a line in champagne and Porsches, and 'Essex Man', the lager-drinking wage-earner celebrating the acquisition of 'loadsamoney' with sprees on the Spanish Costas and a Ford Escort XR3i with go-faster stripes. The no less formidable 'Essex Girl', glowing with blonde highlights and pina coladas in the karaoke nights, was also very much part of the scene.

Harold Macmillan might complain that Mrs Thatcher was selling off 'the family silver'; but then Macmillan had said that no Conservative government should ever take on the Catholic Church, the Brigade of Guards or the miners. She had backed down when Joe Gormley had threatened to ballot members of

the NUM for a strike against pit closures in 1981. Gormley had gone, replaced by Arthur Scargill, tyro of the flying picket and spoiling for a fight. The miners had done for Heath; now, as part of the class war against capitalism, they would do for his successor. Fear of the dole had made union members leery of strikes; car workers now shunned 'Red Robbo' and other agitators, and Scargill had himself been defeated in a national strike ballot in 1982. Unlikely to win the fifty-five per cent majority needed in any new ballot, he fastened instead on the NUM's Rule 41. This allowed different mining areas to call out their men on strike with or without a ballot.

The government was set on making the coal industry self-supporting; the French subsidised their coal by £19 a tonne, and the Germans by £12, but Mrs Thatcher wanted Britain's £4 to be phased out. In March 1984, the Coal Board announced the closure of the Corton Wood colliery in Scargill's South Yorkshire territory. He named another twenty pits he said were on the Board's 'hit list'. Scottish miners joined

**The flying squad.** *Massed police charge pickets (right) outside the Orgreave coking plant near Sheffield at the height of the miners' strike in May 1984. Arthur Scargill, the miners' leader, harangued the police behind their riot shields (above) for turning South Yorkshire into a 'police state'; but he had himself denied his members a strike ballot and he badly overestimated his ability to disrupt an economy in which 'King Coal' had been usurped by oil and natural gas.*

[PHOTO, RIGHT: JOHN STURROCK]

the Yorkshiremen as a 'rolling' national strike got underway. No ballot was held. Scargill recklessly thought it would be won in a few weeks, but coal had been stockpiled at power stations, warm weather was starting and he underestimated the clout of the new legislation. Secondary picketing – of places not directly involved in a strike – was now against the law. Yorkshire pickets were bussed to the Nottinghamshire coalfield, where a majority was hostile to striking; other pickets were deployed in Scotland, South Wales and Durham.

Barricades went up outside working pits; 8,000 pickets arrived at Harworth colliery, but a new coordination centre improved police intelligence and made it easier to intercept them. The Nottingham men were bitter at the lack of a ballot; 30,000 of them worked on despite the intimidation and formed their own Union of Democratic Mineworkers. The major battles were at the Orgreave coking plant, on the outskirts of Sheffield, which supplied the Scunthorpe steelworks. Truck drivers continued to shift coke, their cab windows protected by wire mesh. Policemen fought pickets on foot; they pursued them across the fields on horseback. 'What you have now in South Yorkshire is an actual police state tantamount to something you are used to seeing in Chile or Bolivia,' Scargill said when he visited Orgreave on 29 May. 'Come here in your thousands to make everybody aware that we are not prepared to see this kind of brutality inflicted on working men and women.' The police, 1,700 of them drawn

from thirteen forces, had a different tale to tell, of spikes, ball-bearings, wire stretched across roads to bring down horses, potatoes with nails sticking out of them. 'The pickets began throwing stones, half house-bricks, wood torn from fences,' a senior officer said, 'and our officers were being injured.'

In October, the IRA bombed the Grand Hotel in Brighton, where the failing strike had the Tory party conference in high spirits. The explosives had been planted months before; Mrs Thatcher and much of the cabinet was staying in the elegant seafront building. Four were killed; Norman Tebbit's wife was left permanently paralysed. The IRA had got close enough to destroy Mrs Thatcher's bathroom, which she had used two minutes before. 'Today we were unlucky,' the IRA said. 'But remember we only have to be lucky once.' Salman Rushdie, the author who had displeased Islamic fundamentalists with his book *The Satanic Verses*, was an anti-Thatcherite; though 'not one of us', he and she were to become the most endangered duo in Europe.

The winter was mild; King Coal was already losing its title to natural gas, oil and nuclear energy, and coal imports continued. Truck drivers broke an attempted blockade by pickets at Dover. The NUM was fined £200,000 for contempt of court and its funds were frozen. It was announced that there would be no power cuts throughout 1985 regardless of what the miners did. In debt, depressed, men drifted back to work in Scotland and Lancashire; by early January 1985, 71,000 out of 187,000 were back in the pits. The cars of working miners at Markham Main colliery in Yorkshire were set alight; it had no effect. In March, after twelve months, a special delegate

**The century's worst riots**
*disfigured the cities of the Eighties. Here (above) children watch as the Toxteth area of Liverpool burns. Churchmen, seen paddling for charity at Hastings (right), blamed unemployment and government indifference to the poor, but their own lack of moral influence was also a factor. Britain had the lowest Church membership in Western Europe.*
[PHOTO, ABOVE: JOHN POWELL]
[PHOTO, RIGHT: JANE BOWN]

conference agreed a return to work by all, 'heads held high'. The defeat was utter; Thatcher triumphant had no place for magnanimity. Five years later, 5,000 men were working Welsh pits that had once employed a quarter of a million; barely 3,000 miners survived in Scotland and Lancashire, and the militant Kent coalfield was an abandoned memory.

Strike violence was at least explicable; old industries were still haemorrhaging jobs and the unions were to lose three million members over the decade. Rupert Murdoch's new publishing plant at Wapping became the next battle zone. Symbolically, the site itself was in the vanished London docks; each night for a year up to 7,000 pickets, most but not all sacked printers, tried to block trucks with copies of *The Times* and the *Sun* aboard. They failed; 'Fortress Wapping', surrounded by razor wire to prevent former employees from breaking in, became known as the 'Lost City of the Inkies'.

Urban deprivation, and drugs, were blamed for the sporadic riots that blotched the inner cities – Tottenham and Brixton in London, Handsworth in Birmingham, St Paul's in Bristol – and the 'sink' housing estates, vandalised and scribbled with graffiti, where youths amused themselves by ramming stolen cars into shop fronts. The excuse had a hollow ring; the unemployed of the 1980s were incomparably better off than any predecessors, and deterioration was moral, not economic.

No social fig leaf could cover the all-white football hooligans, who resembled the 'droogs' of *A Clockwork Orange* in their love of a 'bit of the old ultraviolence'. The Italian club Juventus had the misfortune to draw Liverpool in a European Cup match in Brussels in 1985. The rival fans taunted each other; then the Liverpudlians attacked the Italians with bottles, iron bars and flagpoles. A wall and safety fence collapsed as a panic started, and forty-one Italian and Belgian spectators were

killed. English clubs were banned from playing on the Continent and Mrs Thatcher spoke of the 'shame and dishonour' it brought the nation; but it was chillier than that. It was evidence of a brutal depravity. Recorded crime in England and Wales doubled during the Thatcher era; respect for the legal system itself was undermined by a series of wrongful convictions – most notably of alleged IRA pub bombers, the Guildford Four and the Birmingham Six – that took a decade and more to be righted.

Britain had the lowest Church membership in Western Europe; though seventy per cent of the population still claimed a religious affiliation, only one in ten went so far as to attend any service other than a wedding or funeral. It had, by contrast, the highest number of single-parent families in Europe and an illegitimacy rate exceeded only by Denmark. At the time of the First World War, three per cent of Britons were born

illegitimate. At the end of the Second, the figure had crept up to five per cent; by the end of the 1990s, it was more than twenty-eight per cent. In the current generation, almost twenty per cent of girls had had sex below sixteen, the age of consent; in their grandmothers' generation, the figure was one per cent. The acceleration in divorce was more rapid still. One marriage in a hundred had foundered before 1939; by 1989, one had become fifty.

Those who held that such figures were a shocking indictment of the nation's morality met with shouts of 'fascist' – or the still worse insult, 'Thatcherite' – from pressure groups and, remarkably, from some churchmen themselves. Pressure groups were a growing phenomenon; every issue, it seemed, had one, well organised, strumming the national guilt complex like a guitar. At their best, they were magnificent. The 'Live Aid' concert, organised by Bob Geldof at Wembley and the JFK stadium in Philadelphia, attracted the cream of British rock – Mick Jagger, David Bowie, Queen – and a television audience of 1.5 billion to provide money for the starving in Ethiopia. At their frequent worst, however, they had an excuse – generally government action or inaction – for every individual failing, and a strident extremism. It was indeed shameful that bastardy had been a stigma; they turned it into a battle honour, and then refused to entertain the notion that a child's upbringing might suffer from the absence of its father.

Income tax was reduced to its lowest level for fifty years. Those without work festered in large parts of Scotland and the North, but the South boomed. London's huge financial markets were deregulated; old boy networks and cartels dating back for two centuries disappeared in a process named 'Big Bang'.

**Tycoons.** *The rise – and fall – of the individual entrepreneur was writ large in the Eighties. The Australian Rupert Murdoch (far left) bought* The Times *and* Sunday Times *for a pittance at the start of the decade; after the power of the print unions was broken, the profits from the latter helped to underpin an expanding global media empire. Robert Maxwell (right), owner of the* Daily Mirror, *ran up debts of £2.6 billion and looted his employees' pension funds in a vain attempt to rival Murdoch before his naked body was found floating in the sea in 1991. Anita Roddick (above) – despite her fear that 'wealth corrodes, it separates you from the human condition' – created her 'Bodyshop' cosmetic empire valued at over £400 million. Richard Branson, taking a bath (far right) on his houseboat, built a fortune from his Virgin record label and airline.*

[PHOTO, FAR LEFT: JUDAH PASSOW]
[PHOTO, ABOVE: CHARLES HOPKINSON]
[PHOTOS, RIGHT AND FAR RIGHT: MICHAEL WARD]

International banks and brokerage houses arrived; they bought venerable native banks and stockbrokers, only to find some of them worthless once their key players had left for richer pastures. There was little, indeed, that the British would not sell; even County Hall, the fine Thames-side building from which the Greater London Council had administered the world's largest local authority until Mrs Thatcher abolished it, went to the Japanese. To the east of the City, where the bankers and brokers were concentrated in a golden square mile, new apartment blocks and Europe's largest office building, Canary Wharf, were built on old docklands sites. A plasterer could earn £800 a week; in City trading rooms, amid the products of financial 'rocket science', swaps, derivatives, a young man could make that in a day; and spend it in a day, too, on good living. The price of an average house in London rose by more than a quarter in 1987.

A bandwagon of affluence swept Mrs Thatcher to a fresh election victory in 1987; it was her third in a row, a feat no other prime minister had achieved in the century. She seemed secure. Her rapport with Mikhail Gorbachev – 'a man I can do business with' she said on meeting him – combined with the Reagan friendship to make the Iron Lady a world figure. If her relations with the Queen were frosty, the younger royals, particularly 'Fergie', who had married Prince Andrew to become Duchess of York, shared the freespending ethos of supply-side economics. The house the newlyweds had built was so reminiscent of South Fork, the sprawling mansion in which the Texas soap opera *Dallas* was set, that it was dubbed 'South York'.

New jobs were being created, and not only in the South. Scotland, long depressed, was rising on the back of oil, financial services and high-tech development, its 'Silicon Glen' a centre of European electronics manufacturing. Glasgow, a place known for its gloomy tenements and drunkenness, had so revived that it was to become European Cultural City of the Year. It was true that public squalor was on the increase. The British spent a sixth as much on their railways as the French, a fifth as much as the Germans; hospitals were grossly underfunded by Continental standards, while mental asylums were emptied and their patients left to the tender mercies of 'care in the community'. The danger to Mrs Thatcher, however, came from her own imperious nature.

She feasted on work, from early morning to a nightcap of Scotch in the late evening. Her mastery of briefs unnerved her civil servants; the backbenches beckoned any minister who displeased her. Impregnably armoured in so many areas, there were two where she turned out to be vulnerable. The first,

European federalism, had its champions and sworn enemies; most were merely uneasy and in this, if little else, Mrs Thatcher was also without conviction. It cost her the Chancellor, Nigel Lawson, who wished to have sterling shadow the Deutschmark as a preliminary to monetary union; he resigned on the issue, thus avoiding the bust that was preparing to replace his boom. One of Lawson's legacies was a return of the inflation the Tories had tackled with such pain; to combat it, Mrs Thatcher was reluctantly persuaded to permit Britain to join the European Exchange Rate Mechanism, thus tying the pound to the Deutschmark at an unsustainable rate of 2.95 Deutschmarks. Ultimately, the European issue lost her the Foreign Secretary, Sir Geoffrey Howe. To compound it, she determined to replace the local property tax, based on the value of a house, with a flat per capita 'poll tax'. The British did not like poll taxes. In 1381, one had caused the Peasants' Revolt; now the new tax sparked off riots and a revolt by the peasants on her own back benches.

The diarist, philanderer and Tory minister Alan Clark was 'one of us'. 'Her hand did not shake *at all*,' he wrote of her reaction to one crisis in the Commons. 'It was almost as if the House, half horrified, half dumb with admiration, was cowed. A few rats came out of the woodwork… Serene and haughty, at its end she swept from the Chamber.' Such hauteur might be magnificent, but it also dulled her sense of danger. Many rats were out for her; one of them, Howe, she had carelessly underestimated. His resignation speech came in November 1990. 'The Party is virtually out of control,' Clark noted. 'Dissidents get bolder and bolder…' Denis Healey had described Howe as a 'dead sheep'; 'who gives a toss for the old dormouse?' Clark wrote. Howe was far from a dumb animal, however. His speech was barbed and fatal. 'I have done what I believe to be right for my Party and for my Country,' he said. 'The time has come to consider my own response to the tragic conflict of loyalties with which I myself have wrestled for perhaps too long.'

Michael Heseltine, who had resigned as Defence Minister in 1986, 'a great basket of bitterness, thwarted personal ambition and vindictive glee', stood against the Prime Minister as party leader. Mrs Thatcher was in Paris; 'lovely and haughty', she declined to return for the ballot and her loyalists at home ran a listless campaign. Her victory was not convincing enough to prevent a humiliating second ballot, and she resigned.

Her successor was John Major, the son of a trapeze performer and maker of garden gnomes, born in London's insalubrious Brixton, a one-time minor banker who had risen from near oblivion in the Tory ranks to Downing Street in two years. Despite this exotic background, cartoonists launched him as 'the Man in Grey'; a former Tory party chairman described him as 'a pair of curtains'. It was to be business as usual, without the panache.

The Gulf War, to which Mrs Thatcher had committed British troops, was won. The economy lurched back into the longest recession since the Second World War. House prices slumped; those who had bought at the top of the Lawson boom found themselves caught with 'negative equity', the new phrase for debt; house repossessions peaked in 1991. Nevertheless, two-thirds of all homes in Britain were owned by their occupiers, one of the highest rates in Europe, and twenty per cent of adults were shareholders, five times more than in pre-Thatcher days. An electorate with such vested interests opted, to the surprise of most observers and possibly itself, to return the Tories in the 1992 election. Major's majority was small, however; it was eroded by by-election defeats, and it persuaded him to allow a corrosive ambivalence to the European Union to infect his party. Sterling was chased out of the Exchange Rate Mechanism in September 1992; in a day, a panicking government raised interest rates from ten per cent to twelve per cent at 11 am, and to fifteen per cent at 2.15 pm, before accepting the inevitable and reducing the rate to twelve per cent and leaving the ERM at 7.30 pm. The British were often accused of bloodymindedness over Europe – 'Up Yours Delors' the *Sun* had memorably suggested to the President of the European Commission – but it was, perhaps, because they had examined Brussels and federalism more closely than Continentals, and had found much to distrust.

A reason for Britain to stay in Europe, and for Continentals to mutter about an offshore 'Trojan horse', was its success in attracting foreign industry which wished to locate within the EU. Though more than half the cars sold in Britain were imports, exports were boosted by Japanese plants in Sunderland and elsewhere. The natives themselves were brilliant automotive engineers – British-built and designed cars, Williams, Maclaren, utterly dominated Formula One racing, while the entrepreneur Bernie Ecclestone held a billion-pound stake in its administration – but they no longer owned any volume car maker. Proud Jaguar went to Ford; Rover, its

**'New Labour' and 'New Britain',** *an American observed memorably of Tony Blair's 1997 electioneering slogans, sounded like 'small towns in Connecticut'. Blair nevertheless won in a landslide. The Tories retired, not to lick their wounds but to re-open them. Blair paid some lip service to old Labour in pledges (right) to reduce class sizes and hospital waiting lists. The central theme, however, was that his party's spendthrift days were over: 'Income tax rates will not rise.' The voters were reassured; inheriting an economy in excellent fettle, Blair swept on to enjoy the longest political honeymoon of the century.* [PHOTO: SEAN SMITH]

Range Rover as British as tweed and afternoon tea, sold out to BMW. An early lead in home computers, Sinclair, Acorn, Apricot, Amstrad, flickered and died. The British no longer built things, it seemed; though they were skilful enough at providing services, and consultancy and advertising, and designers and architects of the calibre of James Stirling, Norman Foster and Richard Rogers, for those who did. With this ran a flair for other arts, entertainment and leisure. Their package tourism was a wonder of the travel industry; their musicals, *Cats*, *Phantom of the Opera*, their painters, Bacon and Lucian Freud, their films, from *Four Weddings and a Funeral* to *Trainspotting*, their humour – cerebral, *Monty Python* and John Cleese, smutty, Benny Hill – found eager buyers.

A start was made on tackling the awful misdirection of education, where teachers, administrators and academics had run rings round the government and common sense with 'child-centred' ideas adopted from the 1960s onwards. The result was innumeracy, illiteracy and an abysmal ignorance of the country's past or the world about it. League tables of school exam results, greater powers for headmasters and more choice for parents at last began to halt the rot. Major's efforts to restore moral equilibrium through a 'Back to Basics' campaign misfired, however. A Tory minister, David Mellor, was exposed by the eager tabloids for dallying with a resting actress; he

vowed to remain with his wife, then left her. Tory MPs were discovered to be taking money in return for asking parliamentary questions; this was not in itself illegal, but their lack of candour led to cries of 'sleaze'. The directors of privatised utilities rewarded themselves with huge pay and pension increases, whilst simultaneously laying off workers; one water chairman's salary increased from £41,000 to £136,000 in four years.

The increases were legal enough, but there was much in the business world that was not. The publisher Robert Maxwell had set a new benchmark in fraud and avarice by looting £500 million from his own Mirror Group pensioners. His body was found floating near his yacht; none of his associates or relations was successfully prosecuted for implication in this fraud. The promoter Asil Nadir absconded to Turkish Cyprus rather than face trial when his Polly Peck empire collapsed under huge debts. An obscure young British dealer in his twenties ran up losses of £800 million in Singapore, breaking Barings, a 200-year-old bank, in the process. Insurance underwriters at a yet older institution, Lloyds, lost billions of pounds for outside amateur investors, 'names' who were liable 'to their cufflinks' for losses; most insurance market professionals themselves avoided ruin. The buck, it seemed, had been passed.

The 'loony right' had arrived. Even The *Sun*, once stridently dry and Thatcherite, a prime beneficiary of her war against the print unions, declared itself for the Labour leader, Tony Blair. Blair spoke of 'New Labour', but its essentials – more help for the health service but no renationalisation, no going back on union reform, moderation in all things – were familiar. The man chasing the Tories from office was the very clone of a Tory wet.

After 18 years of power, the Conservative party imploded in the worst defeat since 1832. On May 2 1997, a generation of the young woke for the first time in a non-Tory Britain. 'We are not the masters,' Blair told his MPs after his landslide, 'The people are the masters.' The oldfangled man in the street had gone, from what Blair called the 'new modern Britain.' The use of twin adjectives was telling; they cranked up the soundbites which were now substituted for parliamentary debate. It wasn't just in its politics that New Labour seemed to be repackaged Old Tory: Blair was a public school and Oxford educated Scot with an English accent (in the tradition of Harold Macmillan and Lord Home); undeclared home loans and strange happenings on Clapham Common took their toll of government ministers, as Mohammed Fayed's largesse – free nights at the Paris Ritz, cash in brown envelopes – had with their Tory predecessors.

people, however, created a new force previously associated with foreigners of unstable political temperament. 'The will of the people can and must prevail,' a hunting abolitionist insisted. But it could justify interference in almost anything – the coach of the national football team, genetically modified soya beans, the former president of Chile – where emotion could masquerade as moral force.

Its first target was the one British institution which had still seemed touched by a unique moral grace, the monarchy. The Queen's children had married out of the royal fold, to the equestrian Mark Philips, to Fergie and Lady Di; the majesty of the Windsors seemed the greater for settling closer to the common man. It came at a price. Earlier princes had married for duty; liaisons were a natural by-product and the press was then discreet. The new royals had married for love, or so they declared. The illusion was broken, cheaply, in eavesdropped telephone calls, snatched photographs, books that were not denied, and by television interviews in which the royal protagonists confirmed their infidelities to the prurient world. Tell-tales of trouble mounted through the summer of 1997. In July, Prince Charles gave a 50th birthday party for his mistress Camilla Parker Bowles. The *Sun* warned him that Queen Camilla would not be tolerated, adding the blunt reminder that the last king to lose his head was also called Charles. The coverage of his ex-wife became frenetic; Diana was seen among minefields on visits to Angola and Bosnia, powerboating with her new boyfriend Dodi Fayed in St Tropez, visiting a medium. At the end of August, after a car crash in a Paris underpass, she was dead.

The grief that followed was personal, for the television and tabloid age had created a vivid and intimate sense of her presence; but it was debased by a whiff of malice – the demand that the Queen speak to the people and fly a flag at half-mast over the Palace, the applause that met Earl Spencer's damning funeral address at Westminster Abbey – and it came at a price.

Kipling had sensed the end of empire, even at its apogee during the Diamond Jubilee celebrations of 1897:

*Far-called, our navies melt away;*
  *On dune and headland sinks the fire:*
*Lo, all our pomp of yesterday*
  *Is one with Nineveh and Tyre!*

A hundred years later, in June, in a ceremony of rain and bagpipes and the last voyage of the royal yacht *Britannia*, Hong Kong was returned to China. It was the last colony of real significance to go, and the first to be handed over to a pre-existing dictatorship. Now, only the odd governor of an obscure island gave living flesh to the ghostly rollcall of viceroys and the officers of colonial regiments, rubber planters and taipans, counter-jumpers and remittance men. Other species of people were threatened or extinguished: coal miners, BBC commentary teams at important sporting events and native-born footballers in the Premier League, hereditary peers sitting in the House of Lords. Deerhunters, as old or older than the Norman Conquest, had gone; foxhunters almost went too.

The prime minister's addition of the definite article to

**Summer of 1997** *saw the passing of the last major colony as the flag came down in Hong Kong (left), lowered by a Scottish soldier about to be replaced by the People's Liberation Army.* [PHOTO, LEFT: JOHN STILLWELL]

**'Lady Di' and 'Princess Di'** *became the wooden and formal 'Diana, Princess of Wales' in death – at odds with all that she had displayed in life. Millions had felt themselves involved with her, and the tonnage of flowers strewn outside Kensington Palace (right) reflected their grief. The men in her life – Prince Charles, her sons William and Harry, her brother Earl Spencer – bowed their heads (bottom left) as her coffin was carried into Westminster Abbey. Her brother had his say; Prince Charles maintained a quiet dignity, and the public anger ebbed.*

[PHOTO, BELOW LEFT: FIONA HANSON]

[PHOTO, RIGHT: MARTIN ARGLES]

At Churchill's funeral, the cranes on the Thames dipped their jibs as the launch carrying his body sailed past, a quiet tribute from dockers who were not his political friends; at Diana's, the flowers were measured in the hundreds of tons, the tabloids wrote of a river of tears that 'few events our world has seen have produced', The Prime Minister dubbed her 'the people's princess', and the people themselves feasted on rumours of a drunken driver, dying last words, an engagement ring. 'So much for the stiff upper lip,' an American diplomat commented. Grief was no longer private; it was flaunted.

Britain's unforced and restrained sense of national identity was also giving way. The issue of a federal Europe remained unresolved, but Wales and Scotland were granted their own assemblies. Devolution, Blair said, was 'about giving power back to the people'; but only half of the Welsh bothered to vote in the referendum about it, with a majority of less than 1 per cent in favour among those who did – and the implications appeared not to have been thought through. Blair claimed confidently that sovereignty 'will remain with me' in Scotland. That is not how many Scotish Nationalists see it; for them, it is a stepping stone to separation. Other questions were begged. Why should England not have its own assembly? London has a population half as big again as Scotland's. Why should its devolution be restricted to a future mayor whose powers, like the composition of the non-hereditary House of Lords, were still undefined? What, indeed, is it to be English? It was clear once. 'You wish to kill me because I am a Frenchman,' Voltaire had told an 18th-century London mob. 'Am I not punished enough in not being born an Englishman?' The Englishman is no longer the confident product of divine providence; he has become a muddled creature, sensitive to the slurs of others, a keeper of guilty secrets.

History, in the proudly proclaimed 'cool Britannia', became bunk. At the handover of Hong Kong, Blair pointed out that it was useless to pretend that the empire was still there. 'My generation has moved on beyond that,' he said. 'My generation has come to terms with its history.' It was a strange boast. Even in trivial matters, tradition proved hard to shift: the synthetic fur used in experimental bearskins for guardsmen stuck up in spikes when marched under power lines, and the Lord Chancellor, though wishing to scrap his full-bottomed wig and silk tights, still spent £100,000 on dressing up his official apartments in 19th-century wallpaper and light fittings. Elsewhere, the meddling was a graver matter. Countries evolve; begin to devolve them in ignorance of old fractures, and the process may go further than assemblies and window-dressing. Certainly, Ulster was still subject to its historic feud; despite the peace process, Omagh was bombed and paramilitaries on both sides refused to surrender their weapons.

Blair's response to that Omagh bombing was particularly revealing: it was of his own feelings that he first spoke as, with furrowed brow and stammer, he declared 'I am very full of emotion'. Such self-indulgent parading of one's own responses was very much of a piece with the pursuit of the 'more compassionate nation' that Blair suggested 'the people want to be a part of.' It was felt that the Diana tears had washed away the last traces of Victorian coldness and repression. A more caring society had been born; 'nurse', redolent of Dettol and discipline, became ranked lower than 'carer', as 'husband' and 'wife' became the more comradely 'partner.' In truth, the Victorians had been pioneers of charitable causes, and they might see little that was warm or caring in their descendants' achievement of the highest illiteracy, innumeracy and illegitimacy rates among the major European countries.

The new value awarded to emoting was revealed in another area of life – and death – with the bombing of Serbia that began in March 1999. This was not the product of national interest – no Kuwaiti oilfields, no Falklands kith and kin, no Kaiser or Hitler rampaging across borders – but of moral outrage. Formerly, the British had been wary of outrage, though this did not imply that they were morally blind – they fed the defeated Germans in 1947 at the cost of rationing their own bread for the first time, they freed the empire with better grace than other imperialists. But it did involve giving priority to wisdom when dealing with the wickedness of the world. Outrage 'degraded' – the soft new word for 'destroyed' – more than the Serbian capability for ethnic violence. A sense of proportion was an early casualty; the prime minister referred to the dark hours he spent waiting for the return of aircraft, as if he were Churchill and the aircrew numbered 8,000 instead of a thousandth of that number. Common sense was another; ethnic cleansers cleanse, but no advance strategy was mapped for the resulting refugees, and Nato's attempt to bomb the Serbs back to the negotiating table was not backed at first by any threat to use ground troops. 'It used to be "I think therefore I am"', said a military man, catching an end-of-century essence. 'Now it's "I feel therefore I am."' In the end, the aerial dismemberment of Serbia's infrastructure broke Belgrade's nerve, and Blair deserved much credit for maintaining the shaky resolve of other Nato members. The price paid by Kosovan refugees and Serb civilians was high.

Yet the British had left indelible marks on the century. For half of it, from 1939 to 1989, they were engaged in checking Nazi and Soviet expansion, whilst, for much of that time, disengaging themselves from their own empire. In the dominions, the descendants of the century's British emigrants, the Canadian steerage fodder and Australia's 'ten pound Poms', numbered in the millions. Their music, fashion, snobberies and scandals added greatly to the gaiety of nations. The century started at such a height that descent was certain; the British were skilful at the painful business of retreat from power.

Their retreat from their own values is perhaps another matter. Dr Johnson's morality, the American writer Nathaniel Hawthorne had observed, was 'as English an article as beefsteak.' It survived long after the good doctor, robust and uncomplicated, but, at the 20th century's last gasp, it seemed as threatened as the beefsteak itself.

**The century's dramas** *were many and intense; world wars, the end of empire, old habits and hierarchies abandoned. For all that, these women gazing at a portrait of Queen and corgi in Birmingham show that, in its essentials, the country was ending the century as it had begun – as a democratic, dog-loving democracy.*
[PHOTO: ELLIOT ERWITT]

# BIBLIOGRAPHY

Biographies of individuals, obscure and renowned, are to be found in the volumes of the *Dictionary of National Biography* that cover the date of their death. Many, of course, with varying degrees of accuracy, wrote auto-biographies; the indefatigable Churchill wrote histories, too. Among the many books on the British Empire, the trilogy by James (Jan) Morris - *Pax Britannica* (1968), *Heaven's Command* (1973) and *Farewell the Trumpets* (1978) - remains one of the most readable. *The Rise and Fall of the British Empire* (1994), by Lawrence James, provides an excellent one-volume account from 1600 to the present. Imperial women are covered in *Britannia's Daughters* by Joanna Trollope (1983); *The Settlers' Guide, New Houses under the Old Flag* (1914) gives an intriguing list of the land bargains available to British emigrants, whilst *The Kenya Pioneers* by Errol Trzebinski (1985) provides an insight into an individual colony.

The excellent Penguin Social History of Britain covers the century in three volumes. *Private Lives, Public Spirit* by José Harris covers the period from 1870 to 1914, followed by John Stevenson's *British Society 1914–45* and completed by Arthur Marwick's *British Society since 1945*. The Edwardian period is detailed in James Bishop's *The Edwardians*, whilst *Round About A Pound A Week* (1913), by Maud Pember Reeves, offers a chilling contemporary picture of the poor. Literature on both World Wars is exhaustive. Nevertheless, Peter H. Liddle's *The Soldier's War* and *Voices of War* (1988), together with the Somme section of John Keegan's *The Face of Battle* (1976), capture the horrors of the trenches, whilst *Working for Victory?* by Diana Condell and Jean Liddiard (1987) shows the role played by women in the First World War. Angus Calder's *The People's War* (1969) is the classic account of the Home Front in the Second World War, whilst Philip Ziegler's *London at War* (1995) details life in the capital and David Reynolds examines the 'American Occupation' of Britain between 1942 and 1945 in *Rich Relations* (1995). The telling diary kept by George Beardmore between 1938 and 1946 is published as *Civilians at War* (1984).

Robert Graves and Alan Hodge chronicle the interwar years with wit and detail in *The Long Weekend* (1940), whilst *Children of the Sun* by Martin Green (1976) deals with the dandies. The voices of industrial Britain, that vulnerable and bleeding colossus, are caught in *All Our Working Lives* (1984) by Peter Pagnamenta and Richard Overy. Two excellent histories – Peter Hennessy's *Never Again*, on the austere period from 1945 to 1951, and Kenneth O. Morgan's *The People's Peace*, from 1945 to 1990 – cover the post-war period. Anthony Sampson's *Anatomy of Britain* (1962) analysed the Establishment shortly before it came under prolonged fire. *In the Sixties* (1995), edited by Ray Connolly, catches the fizz of that decade, whilst Christopher Booker's *The Neophiliacs* (1969) and Bernard Levin's *The Pendulum Years* (1970) offer darker insights into the Sixties. Booker continued with *The Seventies* (1980). Mrs Thatcher is the subject of biography (notably by Hugo Young) and autobiography; the raciest read of the Thatcher years is Alan Clark's *Diaries* (1993).

# ACKNOWLEDGEMENTS

The following have kindly granted us permission to use the photographs on the pages listed below:

Kathryn Abbe, New York, 168
AlFayed Archive 160L, 160R, 161L
Barnardos, London, 23T, 23B
Cecil Beaton, courtesy Sotheby's, London, 137, 146C, 150-151C, 161R
Bruce Bernard 273B
Jane Bown 261, 291
By kind permission of the British Library, London, 17, 24T, 25T, 28, 32, 33, 35, 44, 45
By kind permission of the Trustees of the Broadlands Archive 144-145 (all photos), 223
Camera Press 214L, 219B, 253R, 272, 288
John Chillingworth 241
Corbis-Bettmann/UPI 220-221
Canadian Centre for Architecture, Montreal, 12, 13
E.P. Trust, London, 91
The Guardian, London, 295, 297
Philip & Adrian Goodman Collection, London, 112, 118B, 149, 150T, 151T, 151L, 151R
Harland & Wolff Collection, Ulster Folk & Transport Museum, Co. Down, 73
Edith Tudor Hart/Wolf Suschitzky Collection 141, 157, 165
Nick Hedges 240T, 240B
Paul Hill 246, 258
Charles Hopkinson 292R
Hulton Getty Collection, London, title page, contents page, 19, 20, 21T, 21B, 22, 27, 29L, 43, 52, 56-57 (all photos), 64, 66R, 70, 74, 75T, 75B, 76, 77, 79, 80, 81, 82T, 82B, 83T, 83B, 84, 85, 86, 87, 97, 110, 111, 115, 126-127, 128, 131, 133, 134, 135, 136, 140, 143, 146, 147, 150B, 153, 154TR, 154B, 155, 156, 158, 163, 167, 168, 169, 170-171

(all photos), 172, 174-175 (all photos), 176, 181, 186, 189, 190T, 190B, 191, 194, 197, 204, 208L, 208R, 209, 210, 211, 215, 216L, 216-217, 218-219, 219T, 222, 224, 225, 227, 228, 229, 230, 231, 232, 233, 242, 243, 254T, 254B, 256, 256BR, 258, 258B, 262, 265, 267, 280-281
Imperial War Museum, London, 89 (Q2041), 99(Q5970),100(EAUS.577), 101 (Q7872), 102(Q4602), 102-103(Q1332), 105(Q105931),106T(Q30134), 106B(Q8470), 107(Q30035), 109(Q13603), 113(Q5794), 114(Q2216), 116(Q23584), 117(E.AUS4945), 118T(Q161783), 120-121(Q9535), 122-123(Q59576), 124(C.O.3302), 125(Q108161), 179(D1511), 182(HU59067), 183(PL10644), 192TL(HU47238), 192-193(HU1891), 198(B5103), 199(B5218), 200, 200-201, 203(S.E.399)
Mrs H. Jones 284
Michael Joseph 234-235, 238
Yevgeny Khaldei 195
Jorge Lewinski 256CR, 257, 270T, 270B, 271T
Magnum Photos, London, 170, 177, 178, 180, 184, 196, 206-207, 221, 226, 231, 239, 247, 248, 251T, 252, 253L, 259, 260, 264, 269, 270-271, 275, 286, 299
Lee Miller Archive 188, 231BR
Lewis Morley/Akehurst Bureau 236, 237, 244-245 (all photos)
Alastair Morrison 104
Don McCullin 266-267, 268
Network Photographers 277, 279, 287, 289, 292L, 301
By courtesy of the National Portrait Gallery, London 11, 29T, 92, 119, 154TL
National Trust 148T
Michael L. Nash 18T, 18B
News International Syndication, London, 278, 281T, 281B

Overseas Missionary Fellowship 34
PA photos, London, 296T, 296B
John Powell 290
Popperfoto, Northampton 40, 50 (all photos), 51
Press Association, London, 282, 285
Grace Robertson, half-title page
Royal Commonwealth Society Collections, by permission of the Syndics of Cambridge University Library, 26, 31, 38-39, 46, 47, 48, 49
Rex Features, London, 250B, 274
Royal Photographic Society Collection, Bath, 37, 58, 59, 62, 63, 68, 69, 71, 90, 95, 148B, 162
Royal Archives, Windsor, © 1997 Her Majesty The Queen, 36, 96
Radley College Archives, Abingdon, 94
Royal Geographical Society, London, 24-25, 152
Tom Smith 283
Annie Trehearne 256TR
Gusty Spence 217
Humphrey Spender 138, 139
Wolf Suschitzky 185, 204-205, 212-213
Sutcliffe Gallery, Whitby, 15, 65, 72
Mr & Mrs Richard Traill 67
U.S. Army 202
Courtesy of the Board of Trustees of the Victoria & Albert Museum, London, 54, 55, 60T&B, 61, 93
Michael Ward 250T, 293L, 293R
Bryan Wharton 251B, 257
David Wedgbury 249

**The Dome at Greenwich** *(right)* its £750 million price tag paid by the nation's gamblers through the National Lottery.

[PHOTO: MARK POWER]

# INDEX